Frederic George Stephens

A History of Gibraltar and Its Sieges

With photographic illustrations

Frederic George Stephens

A History of Gibraltar and Its Sieges
With photographic illustrations

ISBN/EAN: 9783337316440

Printed in Europe, USA, Canada, Australia, Japan

Cover: Foto ©ninafisch / pixelio.de

More available books at **www.hansebooks.com**

A

HISTORY OF GIBRALTAR

AND

ITS SIEGES.

With Photographic Illustrations,

By J. H. MANN.

Library Edition.

LONDON:
PROVOST & CO., 5, BISHOPSGATE WITHOUT, E.C.
1870.

Contents.

CHAPTER		PAGE
I.	Introduction .	1
II.	Calpe and Abyla . . .	9
III.	First Inhabitants of the Rock	21
IV.	Under the Carthaginians .	23
V.	In Roman hands	31
VI.	In Visigothic hands .	37
VII.	The Visigothic Kings . . .	45
VIII.	Differing Histories of the Invasion	54
IX.	Legends of King Roderic . .	72
X.	Sketch of the History of the Conquest	90
XI.	The Fortress. Cadiz	93
XII.	Muza Ibn Nosseyr . .	99
XIII.	The Splendour of Andalus	105
XIV.	Early state of Gibraltar . .	110
XV.	The First Engineer of Gibraltar	123
XVI.	Transitions .	128
XVII.	The First Siege . . .	135
XVIII.	Relations of the Nasserite Dynasty with Gibraltar. The Second Siege .	141
XIX.	Gibraltar offered as a Ransom	149
XX.	The Third Siege, 1333	154
XXI.	The Fourth Siege, 1334 .	158
XXII.	The Siege of Tarifa .	162

CONTENTS.

CHAPTER		PAGE
XXIII.	The Siege of Algeciras, 1342-4. The Fifth Siege of Gibraltar	165
XXIV.	The King of Gibraltar. The Sixth and Seventh Sieges	170
XXV.	The Eighth Siege, 1462	175
XXVI.	Termination of the Arabian Realm of Spain	182
XXVII.	The Ninth Siege, 1466	195
XXVIII.	History of Gibraltar under Ferdinand and Isabella. The Tenth Siege	204
XXIX.	The Attack by the Corsairs, 1540	213
XXX.	The Last Moorish Hopes. Dutch Victory in the Port	216
XXXI.	Oliver the Protector's Estimate of the Rock	221
XXXII.	War of the Succession — Capture of Gibraltar by the English	224
XXXIII.	The Twelfth Siege	236
XXXIV.	The Thirteenth Siege	240
XXXV.	Further Negotiations	248
XXXVI.	The Fourteenth Siege—The Great Siege, 1779-1783	251

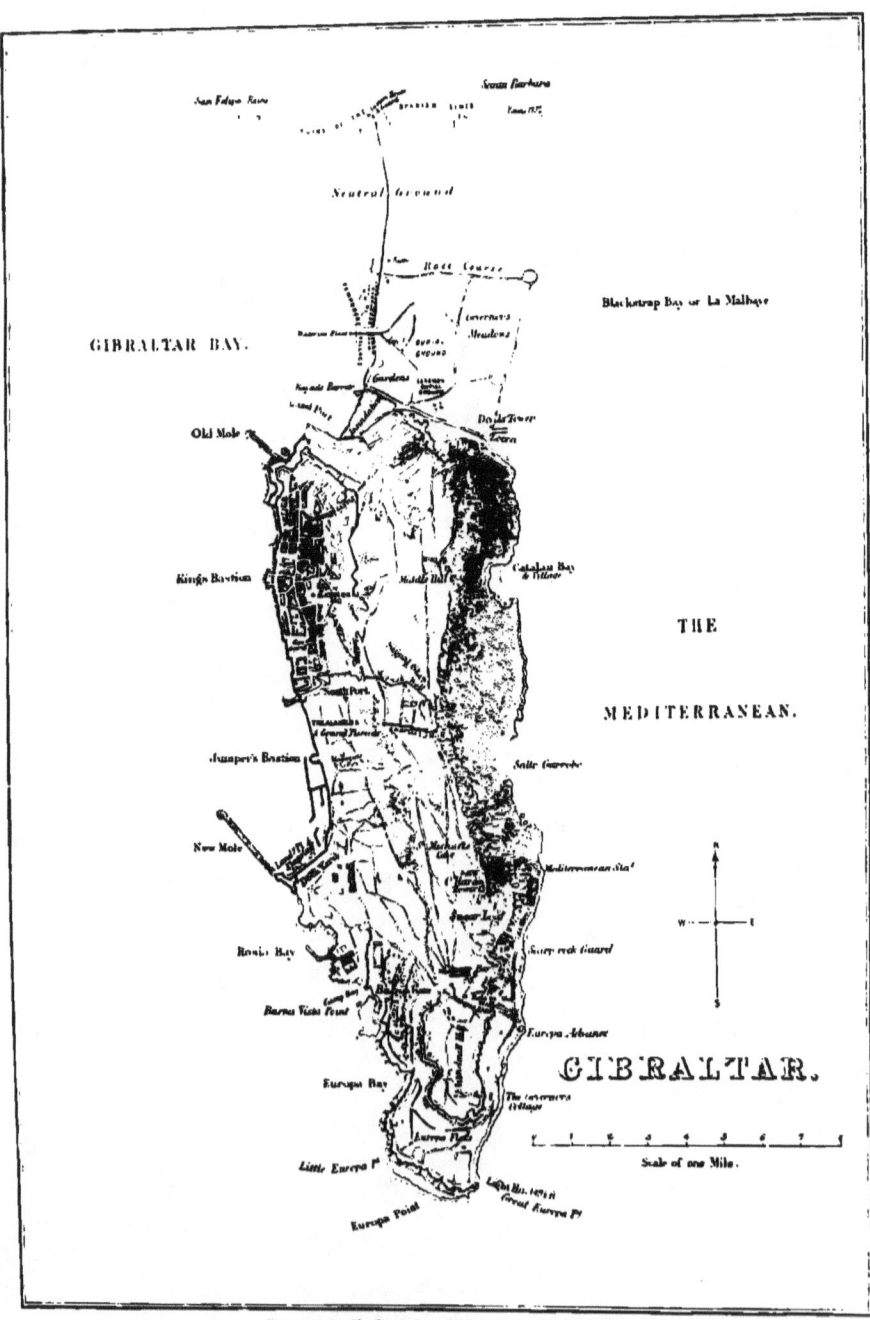

A HISTORY OF GIBRALTAR AND ITS SIEGES.

CHAPTER I.

INTRODUCTION.

WE propose to recite the history of Gibraltar, describe the sieges it has undergone, and, in doing so, to take the famous Rock itself as a centre round which may be ranged the figures of the chieftains who have been concerned in its attack and defence; also to travel with these champions into their own countries, and trace the sources of their actions. It will be by no means desirable to omit the second section of our purpose, and leave the champions to themselves before or after they have quitted the place of battle, because it is undoubtedly true that if Gibraltar has conferred fame upon them, they, in turn, have, by deeds done elsewhere, reflected light upon the noble Rock itself. As to this effect of glory sent back from rock to warrior and from warrior unto rock, the matter has an image in the place itself, as, ages ago, when the first Phœnician voyagers were creeping out of the resplendent Mediterranean, or Great Sea, so they called it, into the *Mare Tenebrosum*, or "Dark Sea," which their imaginations filled with shadows, they, as the sun went down, saw his glory shine backwards from the pillar of ancient fame. In like manner, craft, drifting through those Straits, which have taken many names from that mount which we call Gibraltar, still see dawn shine from its sides long before the sea mists are broken up. Thus, Al-makkari, the Arabian writer, says : " The water surrounds Gibraltar on almost every side, so as to make it look like a watch-tower erected in the midst of the sea, and facing Algeciras." " The mountain of Taric " (Gibraltar), says a Granadian poet, quoted by him, " is like a beacon spreading its rays over the sea, and rising far above the neighbouring mountains. One might fancy that its face almost reaches the sky, and that its eyes are watching the stars in the celestial track." "I sailed once," says another Moorish writer, " with my father, from Ceuta to Gibraltar, and had an opportunity of verifying the truth of this assertion. When we came near the coast, my father told me to look in the direction of Gibraltar; I did so, and saw the whole mountain shining as if it were on fire." Thus it was a beacon to many a store-ship or swift-running craft going to the relief of the garrisons which were beleaguered there. Thus the Moors described it when the Spaniards besieged it; thus the Spaniards said, in turn; and thus, with reversed reference to the last, the English sea-captains spoke, when they were " running in," as the term was, with stores from Britain or from Lisbon, on the one hand, and from Mahon on the other.

The fame of the Great Siege, or last attack, with which the military history of Gibraltar for the present ceases, has so much outshone that of what was done and suffered before, that not a few readers will learn for the first time that this victory was the fourteenth of its order. By these Gibraltar is mostly made lustrous; but to English eyes, at least, its lustre should be increased by recollections of many naval victories which have been obtained by Englishmen, and almost within sight of the Rock. Thus, there is the never-to-be-forgotten Trafalgar, the greatest of these external combats. The fights off Cape St. Vincent are many. Thus, Sir George Rooke was beaten by Tourville, of France, in 1693; Rodney's victory over the Spaniards, under Langara, happened there in 1780; that of Sir John Jervis (Earl St. Vincent) took place seventeen years later; and the capture of Don Miguel's fleet was effected by Admiral Napier in 1833. We shall show that the Romans of old fought Carthaginian galleys in the bay, and that the very Northmen, when going to the Crusades early in the twelfth century, obtained naval victory in sight of the Rock of rocks.

In 1607 was conducted, under the batteries of the Rock, which were then in Spanish hands, that naval combat which Sully describes as "the most furious battle which was ever fought in the memory of man." This happened between the Dutch Vice-Admiral, Jacob Heemskerk, with ten or twelve vessels, and the Spanish Admiral, Don Juan Alvares d'Avila, with a force which was four times as strong as that of his enemy. In spite of this disproportion the Hollander utterly ruined the Spaniard, "and filled all Spain with horror." Heemskerk was as audacious as Blake at Santa Cruz, and as valiantly resolute as Nelson in the fight off the neighbouring Cape Trafalgar, which occurred almost two centuries after this glorious Dutch sailor sealed with his blood the freedom of his country, made Henri the Fourth of France rub his hands, and dashed the schemes of Spinola to pieces. Of this memorable combat, so important in its results, few Englishmen know anything. Probably not one in ten of the garrison of Gibraltar ever heard of it. By and by we shall tell more about it.

The Bay of Cadiz seems yet to ring with the names of Drake, Howard of Effingham, Blake, Collingwood, and Nelson. These combats took place to the north and east of the place; from the south, off Cape Spartel, Howe's and Cordova's guns were heard in Gibraltar on the 20th of October, 1782, as those of Rooke and Thoulouse had been audible, so they say, when in combat at sea, off Malaga, and far to the eastward, on the 13th of August, 1704. This last was a tremendous fight, which is, however, hardly named in what are called "Histories of England"; yet more than fifty ships on each side were engaged, and nearly six thousand men disabled or killed. On our side, besides lesser men, were Rooke, Byng (Lord Torrington), Sir Cloudesley Shovel, and Sir John Leake. These are but a few of the famous Englishmen; these are a few of the acts they have performed, external to, but in direct relationship with, the fortress of which we write. It was in the mood caused by memories of these deeds that Browning wrote "Home Thoughts from the Sea"; and, in words that sound like the voice of some enormous organ, thus expressed the feelings of many, when sailing into the Straits:

> "Nobly, nobly Cape St. Vincent to the north-west died away;
> Sunset ran, one glorious blood-red, reeking into Cadiz Bay;
> Bluish, mid the burning water, full in face Trafalgar lay;
> In the dimmest north-east distance dawned Gibraltar, grand and gray;
> 'Here and here did England help me,—how can I help England?'—say,
> Whoso turns as I, this evening, turn to God to praise and pray,
> While Jove's planet rises yonder, silent over Africa."

These triumphs or defeats deeply concern us, the English, although our holding of the Rock is but of little more than a century and a half's duration; yet what must be the thoughts of a Spaniard with regard to this piece of his own territory, which was held by his countrymen in uninterrupted possession for two centuries and a half before it fell into our hands; the very armorial bearings of which we have adopted from those given by Henry of Castile and Leon, armorials which are at once suggestions of the position and the value of the place. They are a castle with a key pendant at the gate. These insignia express that the place is the key of the Mediterranean and of Spain, and seem to signify that it belongs, and has belonged, to the greatest maritime power. Such were the Moors who first fortified the Rock; such the Spaniards until its capture notified their loss of that position; so, it is hoped, are the English. Again, as to the first military holders, the Moors can hardly be so sunk from memories of old fame as to be indifferent to this place. From the fortifying by Taric-ebn-Zeyad, in 711,* until 1309, a period of five hundred and ninety-eight years, or, to measure by our own history, as long as the space of time which has elapsed since the last of the Crusades, this place remained in Moorish hands: they made it what it was. Ferdinand the Fourth then besieged and took it; the Spaniards had but short tenancy this time, for twenty-five years later, the Mahommedans again captured it. They held it until 1462, when the Duke of Medina-Sidonia took it for his people, or rather for himself. Thus it remained until the daring of an English admiral in 1704 placed it in the present ownership. Thus altogether the Moors held the place about seven centuries and a quarter (seven hundred and twenty-six years), which, to measure back in our own history an equal space, brings our thoughts to the year 1142, or nine years after the birth of Henry the Second, *i.e.* to the eighth year of King Stephen.

Such was the holding of the Moors, in all about seven centuries and a quarter from the making a castle on the Rock, to

---

* Gibbon dates the first landing of the conquering Moors in 710 A.D.

the last sorrowful departure of the remnants of the nation. It has been said, with more of poetical than absolute truth, that Gibraltar was the landing-place of the vigorous Moorish race, and that it was the point of departure on which their footsteps lingered last. In short, it was the European *tête de pont* of which Ceuta stands as the African fellow. By these means myriads of Moslems passed into Spain, and with them much for which the Spaniards are wrongfully unthankful. It is said that when the Moors left their houses in Granada, which they did with, so to say, everything standing, many families took with them the great wooden keys of their mansions, so confident were they of returning home again, when the keys should open the locks, and the houses be joyful anew. It was not to be as thus longed for, but many families in Barbary still keep the keys of these long ago deserted and destroyed mansions, retain keys of houses which have crumbled into dust centuries since.

As to the Spaniards who reside in San Roque, a town which was founded in 1704 for the reception of those who were pitilessly expelled from Gibraltar by the English under Rooke, they still look upon themselves as citizens of the Rock, and by no means despair of returning to their former possessions. The King of Spain still includes Calpe in his dominions, and natives thereof are entitled, says Ford, to the rights and privileges of Spanish birth.

The feelings of the French on the subject of the Rock are thus humorously described by Ford, the writer to whom we have just referred, in his "Handbook for Spain," part I. page 270: "Gibraltar, *l'ombrageuse puissance*, is excessively displeasing to all French tourists; sometimes there is too great a *luxe de canons* in this fortress *ornée*, then the gardens destroy 'wild nature,' in short, they abuse the red jackets, guns, nursery-maids, and even *the monkeys;* ever perfidious, say they, is the ambitious aggression of England. The truth simply is, that this key of *their* lake is too strong, and can't be taken by their fleets and armies."

We have referred mainly to great naval battles which were fought in the neighbourhood of the Rock, to the exclusion of the military achievements of the nations here in question. Of recent or modern combats on land, it is not needful to recall to the memory of the reader those which took place at Tarifa, almost within sight of Gibraltar, and Barrosa. Napier's "History of the Peninsular War" has fully accounted for these in the memories of Englishmen. Finally, as to its broad significance, the Rock is, as Burke said, when debating in order to the retention of Gibraltar in our hands, "a post of power, a post of superiority, of connections, of commerce; one which makes us invaluable to our friends, and dreadful to our enemies."

Out of the antagonistic feelings of the Moors and Spaniards, wrath and hatred, which have been cherished for centuries—that is, for more than one thousand years, and may, as representing opposed lands, date even before the Carthaginians and the Romans went to war—a source of comfort and security for our possession of Gibraltar has been established. *We* do not interfere with the folks on the south side of the Strait; *they* supply us with provisions, which, during the Great Siege were of enormous value to the garrison. It is noteworthy that the Gothic tribes of Spain were by the Moors called Rüm, or Romans. These Moors—a comprehensive name we give to the tribes that rose or were pushed forward under the influence of Mahommedan fanaticism and desire for territory, which means plundering of other folks' goods—were successors of the Carthaginians whom the Romans had ravaged many a year before. Frequent attempts had been made to capture the southern provinces of Spain before the successful landing of Taric; these attempts failed because the Goths were strong: they succeeded when they were weak. The Goth, or Visigoth, was the conqueror and inheritor of the Roman, and " came in " for his responsibilities of hate. Thus it has been even from the time when the Phœnician people kept the Straits by fraud or force, to the last Morocco war of the Spaniards; thus the hate is illustrated when the Moors shoot the Spanish convicts who straggle or try to escape from Ceuta, that little hell upon earth, the other Pillar of Hercules, which Spain holds by way of attempt at a bridle to Gibraltar, as, before the Moorish conquest, she held it as a companion to the Rock of Taric—a fatal companionship as it turned out, if the legend be true which makes Count Julian the traitor to King Roderic the Goth, and Lord of Ceuta. There seems no end to this inheritance of wrath, the beginning of which is lost in the night of ages.

Thus much of the feelings of men with regard to this Rock —" THE ROCK " *par excellence,* as all men who are familiar with the spot style Gibraltar—the Mountain or Rock of Taric.

CHAPTER II.

CALPE AND ABYLA.

O save the trouble of referring to a map, a few words may be given here in describing the topography, or rather geography of the spot in question. The Phœnician name of the Rock signifies an earthen vessel, or hollow mountain resembling a vessel, for on the west side, and facing the setting sun, it is open like an urn or pitcher. Pomponius Mela wrote, "The narrow sea then opens, and the mountains Abyla and Calpe make the coasts of Europe and Africa appear nearer than they really are. Both these mountains indeed, but that of Calpe in particular, stretch themselves towards the sea; beyond this is a bay where, as some think, Cartcia was placed, formerly called Tartessus, which the Phœnicians who came from Africa inhabited." Several points should be fixed in the reader's memory as better for service than a map. As the most ancient account has it, the truth of which is still obvious, the Rock of Gibraltar, or, anciently, *Calpe*, stands at the extremity of a tongue of sandy land, is of an elongated form, with its greater axis running nearly north and south. On the west side of this rock and its point of sand is the so-called Bay of Gibraltar, a very deep inlet to the land, on the western side of which is Algeciras; the opposing horn faces the Rock, and is called Cabreta Point. On the west side of the Rock the Mediterranean rolls, at the edge of lofty cliffs. It is not the most southern part of Spain, for the spot to the westward of

the bay whereon Tarifa stands owns that distinction. From the latter point the coast trends to the north-west and is marked by many bays or notches, and forms part of the Bay of Cadiz. On the east side of the Rock the land runs to the north-east towards Malaga. Gibraltar stands within the Straits on the east in a position which corresponds to that of Tarifa on the west. Between these points is the Strait or Gut of Gibraltar, the *Fretum Gaditanum* or *Herculeum*. The south coast of the Strait is composed of the other Pillar of Hercules, or *Abyla* as they called it of old, as now it is named Ceuta, and the adjacent land. This is the most northerly point of that part of Africa, and the land slopes to the south-west or towards the Atlantic, including Old and New Tangier, as the sites of these towns are respectively called, on each side of a bay. Cape Spartel is at the western extremity of this, the south side of the Strait, and Cape Trafalgar, erst the Cape of Juno, forms the opposing point of the north or Spanish land. The whole coast is, at intervals, strewn with remains of Phœnician works, with Roman wrecks of towns and temples. We have the *Luciferi Templum*, or Temple of Venus, at Gades, the modern Cadiz, said to be the most ancient town in Europe; Tarifa, which is reputed to be the ancient Julia Traducta. On the other hand, so to write, of Gibraltar, are Carteia and Ximena, where Crassus was hidden. In the very name of Medina-Sidonia we recall the Phœnician Asidon, the City of Sidon itself. The name of Pillars of Hercules refers to classical and most antique belief, for such columns were reputed to exist wherever the utmost extent of land was known. Thus Tacitus, writing of the Frisii, who inhabited the extremities of Friesland, as we now style it, states, "Their settlements stretch along the border of the Rhine to the ocean, and include, besides, vast

lakes which have been navigated by the Roman fleets. We
(the Romans) have even explored the ocean itself on that side;
and fame reports that the Columns of Hercules are still
remaining on that coast; whether it be that Hercules was
ever there in reality, or that whatever great and magnificent is
met with, is, by common consent, ascribed to his renowned
name. The attempt of Drusus Germanicus to make dis-
coveries in these parts was sufficiently daring; but the ocean
opposed any further inquiry into itself and Hercules. After
a while no one renewed the attempt, and it was thought more
pious and reverential to believe the actions of the gods than to
investigate them." So, with fine irony, wrote Tacitus, in a
time when Drusus Germanicus was to be flattered, but in a
spirit very different from that which animated the Romans
centuries before the day of the historian. The setting up of
pillars as landmarks not only appears in the Roman traditions
as concerning Hercules in Frisia, and the Greeks, from whom
the Romans borrowed the notion of his labours, in Spain, but
was the practice of the Assyrians in their conquests in the far
east, of the Egyptians, and, lastly, of the Hebrews, as their
Scriptures tell us in more than one case. There were Pillars
of Hercules in Southern India itself. Among the early names
of *Calpe* (Gibraltar) and *Abyla* (Ceuta) were variously the Pillars
of Briareus, Ægæon, and Cronos. These termini—for such
they were believed—were described as standing on the western
margin of the earth, on the road to Elysium and the Hesperides,
where "the primeval waters of the circling Oceanus were
first seen, in which the source of all rivers was then sought."
"At Phasis," wrote Humboldt, whose words picture antique
ideas of the Gaditan Straits better than any others which we
know, "the navigators of the Euxine again found themselves
on a coast beyond which a *sun lake* was supposed to be situated,

and south of Gadeira (Cadiz) and Tartessus (supposed to be Carteia) their eyes, for the first time, ranged over a boundless waste of waters! It was this circumstance which, for fifteen hundred years, gave to the gate of the Inner Sea a peculiar character of importance. Ever striving to pass onwards, Phœnicians, Greeks, Arabs, Catalans, Majorcans, Frenchmen from Dieppe and La Rochelle, Genoese, Venetians, Portuguese and Spaniards, in turn attempted to advance across the Atlantic Ocean, held long to be a miry, shallow, dark and misty sea, or sea of shadows, until, proceeding from station to station, as it were, these southern nations, after gaining the Canaries and the Azores, finally came to the new continent, which had, however, already been reached by the Northmen at an earlier period and from a different direction.

It is not less as a grand modern fortress and "coign of vantage" to England in these ages, than as one of the gate-pillars of all knowledge, to the west of the Mediterranean, of commerce illimitable and splendid energies, that we must look with eyes of intensest interest upon the SHINING ROCK. There can be very little doubt but that the Phœnicians were the first to pass the Straits, of which Calpe and Abyla are now the landmarks, and, as of old, the guardians. Whatever may be thought of the ancientness of Medina-Sidonia, an inland place, there can be no doubt that the people of Phœnicia founded their Gadir, the Roman Gades, as an entrepôt for silver, and a commercial port on the very borders of the Shadowy Sea, or that Tartessus, where was a temple to the son of Baal, Malcarthus, the Tyrian Hercules, was a station of theirs two hundred years before the settlement at Carthage. Doubtless, also, is it that the real fears of these early navigators of the Inner Sea, or their cunning commercial jealousy of other races, invested the ocean beyond it with prodigious terrors. By such means these voyagers long kept the secret of trade to themselves; and whether they stole along the coasts of Spain and France to Britain, where were the Cassiterides or Isles of Tin, or struck boldly, *very* boldly, straight to the Cornish shores, the secret of the sea was kept for at least an age before the foundation of Carthage, the rival of youthful Rome. Tin was the chief inducement of this secrecy and these voyages. To realise the value of this trade, one must think how important was that metal to the needs and civilising of a world without iron, and which could not make a tool or a weapon of bronze without its aid. Thus, the Phœnicians held, as we said, the secret of the sea; and they were a people whose governors were not likely to be negligent of means for maintaining the mystery, or merciful towards those who might endeavour to unravel it. What chance would the crew of a Greek galley have with a more powerful Phœnician craft, if they met outside the Pillars? It was not until long after the time of Homer that a Grecian ship passed the Rock of Calpe into the Outer Sea. The voyage of Ulysses' old age, when he is said to have vanished in the western seas, hardly extended so far, although the declaration of Proteus to Menelaus points to that Elysion of the Greeks which was placed in the Outer Sea, beyond the darkness; for the god said to Menelaus, after referring to Ulysses:

> "He is Laertes' son, whom I beheld
> In nymph Calypso's palace, who compell'd
> His stay with her; and, since he could not see
> His country earth, he mourn'd incessantly.
> For he had neither ship instruct with oars,
> Nor men to fetch him from those stranger shores.
> Where leave we him, and to thyself descend,
> Whom not in Argos Fate nor Death shall end,
> But the immortal ends of all the earth,
> So ruled by them that order death by birth,

> The fields Elysian, Fate to thee will give;
> Where Rhadamanthus rules, and where men live
> A never-troubled life, where snow, nor showers,
> Nor irksome Winter spends his fruitless powers;
> But from the ocean Zephyr still resumes
> A constant breath, that all the fields perfumes.
> Which, since thou marriedst Helen, are thy hire,
> And Jove himself is, by her side, thy sire."
>
> *Chapman's Homer's Odysseys.**

The stories of a Blessed Land out in the Atlantic, Elysium, Hesperides, and what not; the alleged, and by no means improbable, discovery of America itself by the Phœnicians; the dark rumours that antique poetry hinted at, all referred to the Straits of Hercules, Briareus, or Cronos, where Calpe and Abyla stood and stand like shining pillars, no less geographical than historical in their infinite relationships and connections of ideas.

"On the north-west coast of Africa," says Strabo, "there were seven hundred cities of Tyrian origin; and the explorations of that people had reached farther than the limits of Cape Bojador, and a long way to the south of the Canaries, which islands were known to them." From Cadiz (Gades) Columbus himself sailed, on his second voyage to the discovery "of that great antiquity, America," as Sir Thomas Browne wrote of it. From Palos, which is on the Tinto, a river of the Bay of Cadiz, his first setting out took place. "Starting from the

---

* Readers of the Laureate's verse will be reminded by this fragment of "Chapman's mighty line" in reproducing Homer, of the noble description of that northern or British Elysium, Avilion, to which King Arthur was bound.

> "The island valley of Avilion;
> Where falls not hail, or rain, or any snow,
> Nor ever wind blows loudly; but it lies
> Deep-meadow'd, happy, fair with orchard-lawns
> And bowery hollows crown'd with summer sea."
>
> *Morte D'Arthur.*

Pillars" is the expression of Strabo at the very opening of his "Geography," in describing the circumnavigation of the Mediterranean.

The circumnavigation of Africa, thus described by Herodotus, refers to the Pillars of Hercules in a very interesting manner, if we consider the joy with which the travellers must have hailed the well-known landmarks as they shone upon them in the sea. "Libya" (Africa), writes the father of history and first recorder of science, "shows itself to be surrounded by water, except so much of it as borders on Asia. Necho, King of Egypt, was the first whom we know of that first proved this; he, when he ceased digging the canal leading from the Nile to the Arabian Gulf, sent certain Phœnicians in ships, with orders to sail back through the Pillars of Hercules into the Mediterranean (Northern Sea of Egypt), and so return to Egypt. The Phœnicians accordingly, setting out from the Red Sea, navigated the Southern Sea; when autumn came they went on shore, and sowed the land by whatever part of Libya they happened to be sailing, and waited for harvest; then, having reaped the corn, they put to sea again. When two years were thus passed, in the third, having doubled the Pillars of Hercules, they arrived in Egypt, and related, what to me does not seem credible, but may to others, that, as they sailed round Libya, they had the sun on their right hand. Thus was Libya first known.

"Subsequently the Carthaginians say that Libya is surrounded by water. For Sataspes, son of Teaspes, one of the Achæmenidæ, did not sail round Libya, though sent for that very purpose; but, dreading the length of the voyage and the desolation, returned home, and did not accomplish the task which his mother imposed on him; for he had violated a virgin, daughter of Zophyrus, son of Megabyzus; whereupon, when he was about to be impaled for this offence by King Xerxes, the mother of Sataspes, who was sister to Darius, begged him off, promising that she would inflict a greater punishment upon him than he would, for she would constrain him to sail round Libya until, sailing round, he would reach the Arabian Gulf. Xerxes having agreed to these terms, Sataspes went into Egypt, and, having taken a ship and men from thence, sailed through the Pillars of Hercules; and, having sailed through and doubled the Cape of Libya, whose name is Soloeis (Cantin), he steered to the southward; but, after traversing a vast extent of sea for many months, when he found he had still more to pass, he turned back, and sailed away for Egypt. From thence, going to King Xerxes, he told him that in the most distant part of the world he sailed past a nation of little men, who wore garments made of palm leaves, who, whenever they drew near the shore, left their cities and flew to the mountains; that his men, when they entered their country, did them no injury, but only took some cattle from them. Of his not sailing completely round Libya, this he said was the cause: that his ship could not proceed any farther, but was stopped. Xerxes, however, being persuaded that he did not speak the truth, as he had not accomplished the task imposed upon him, impaled him, inflicting the original sentence."

This happened in Herodotus's own district, for he says, going on in his delightful way to give local colour to the matter in question, "A eunuch of this Sataspes, as soon as he heard of his master's death, ran away to Samos with great wealth, *which a Samian detained;* though I know his name, I purposely conceal it. The inuendo of the last sentence is delicious. As to the difficulty of getting any farther than where indicated by the outward route of Gibraltar, readers will note what Strabo states in his " Introduction ": " All those who have sailed along the shores of Libya, whether starting from the Arabian Gulf or the Pillars, after proceeding a certain distance, have been obliged to turn back again on account of a variety of accidents." " Ephorus," adds Strabo, "tells us it is reported by the Tartessians, that some of the Ethiopians, on their arrival in Libya, penetrated into the extreme west and settled there, while the rest occupied the sea coast."

What had, at the time of Christ, which is that of Strabo, become of the civilisation established by the Phœnician people in Spain, we may learn from what the geographer tells us of the people who then inhabited the western part of modern Andalusia, *i.e.* the Turdetani, that they "were esteemed the most intelligent of all the Iberians, they had an alphabet, and possessed ancient writings, poems, and metrical laws which are six thousand years old, *as they say*. The other Iberians are likewise furnished with an alphabet, although not of the same form, nor do they speak the same language. The country of the Turdetani, which is on this side of the Guadiana, extends eastward as far as the country about the sources of the Guadalquivir (Oretania), and southward along the sea coast to the Pillars. But it is necessary that I should enter into particulars concerning this and the neighbouring places, in order to illustrate their industry and fertility. Between this coast, where the Guadalquivir and Guadiana discharge themselves, and the extremities of Maurusia, the Atlantic ocean forms the strait at the Pillars, by which it is connected with the Mediterranean. Here is situated *Calpe*, the mountain of the Iberians, who are denominated Bastitani, by others Bastuli. Its circumference is not large, but it is so steep and high as to resemble an island in the distance. Sailing from the Mediterranean into the Atlantic, it is on the right hand. At the distance of forty stadia from this Rock, is the considerable and ancient city of Carteia, formerly a marine arsenal of the Iberians. Some assert that it was founded by Hercules: of this number is Timosthenes (the admiral of Ptolemy the Second, one of Strabo's frequent informants), who tells us it was anciently called Heraclea, and that vast walls and ship-sheds are still seen. Next to these is Mellaria *(Val de Vacca)*, where they make salted provisions. After this the city and river of Belo (Barbete). Here the merchandise and salted provisions for Tingis (Tangiers), in Maurusia (Morocco), are principally shipped. There was a city named Zelis near to Tingis; but the Romans transferred it to the opposite coast (Spain), and having placed there, in addition, some of the inhabitants of Tingis, and sent over also some of their own people, they then gave to the city the name of *Julia Joza (Julia Transducta, Algeciras).*"

Further than this, our geographer gives an account of the district of the Turdetani, which would be worthy of a Government Commission of Inquiry in these days. He describes the nature of the coast, with its deep inlets, which the sea fills with extraordinary violence, and as suddenly leaves empty at the reflux of the tide; the Oracle of Menestheus, and the Lighthouse of Cœpio, " built upon a rock that is washed upon all sides by the sea;" the mouths of the Guadalquivir (Bætis); the Temple of Phosphorus—*Lux Dubia*; the Guadiana and the Sacrum Promontorium (Cape St. Vincent), Cordova, Cadiz, and Seville (Corduba, Gades, and Hispalis). The vastness of the population delighted Strabo no less than the richness of the banks of the Bætis, where the eye is delighted with groves and gardens in the highest state of cultivation. The fields are marvellously fertile; they are intersected with canals; the people trade with Italy and Rome; their ships at Ostia " are in number nearly equal to those of Libya," and are of the greatest size; corn, wine, oil, wax, honey, dyes, vermillion, "not inferior to that of Sinope," timber, salt, salted fish, wool, "finer than that of the Coraxi," and produced from sheep the breeding rams of which are worth a talent; woven stuffs of incomparable texture, cattle and game, oysters and other shell fish of prodigious size abound, says the evidently deeply-moved geographer, and he avers that the same is the case with all kinds of cetacea, narwhals, whales, and *physeteri*, which, when they blow up the waters from their snouts, appear to observers from a distance to make it resemble a cloud shaped like a column. The congers and the lampreys are monstrous, also the *kerukæ* and cuttle-fish of Carteia, which would contain as much as ten *cotylæ* (a gallon!); the polypes weigh about half a hundredweight, the squids are two cubits in length, and the tunnies abundant. Gold, silver, copper, and iron are better and more abundant in Turdetania than in any other part of the world; gold grains weighing half a pound have been found; the other metals are equal.

Strabo goes on to show that this province, which we now call Andalusia, was probably the "Fortunate Land" itself, that Homer might have founded the name of Tartarus upon that of Tartessus, that the air is pure as that of Heaven; the visits of Hercules had made the place glorious. He says, and doubtless truly, that the Phœnicians were the discoverers of this spot of heavenly earth before the time of Homer, and remained masters of it until the Romans conquered them; they continued, in his time, polished and urbane in their manners; finally, he adds, that their wealth was so great that Hamilcar found them using silver casks and goblets for wine; abundance and long-living were so proverbial of this district that Anacreon sung, "*Neither would I desire the horn of Amalthea, nor to reign over Tartessus one hundred and fifty years.*"

Pomponius Mela, who describes Gibraltar in terms which are still applicable, Pliny and Strabo, appear to have thought this glorious city of Tartessus was Carteia.

The legends of the journeyings of Ulysses, the voyage of the Argonauts, and the labours of Hercules in those regions, need no more than a brief reference here. After reading Strabo's description of Andalusia, rich as it is in frequent reference to *Calpe* (Gibraltar), the inspiration of the inventors of these legends is fully recognisable.

CHAPTER III.

FIRST INHABITANTS OF THE ROCK.

 S we have stated before, the first human inhabitants of the Shining Rock were the Moors, who fortified Gibraltar soon after their landing; but the aborigines were undoubtedly the monkeys, who still occupy the remoter portions of the place, and are very interesting to their military and civil British neighbours. These primitive creatures remained in possession during the Phœnician age, the Roman centuries, and those which followed, while the Visigoths and other tribes fought and cut each other's throats in the neighbourhood; they must have seen Taric land with his hungry Mauritanians and Berbers; they must have been disturbed when these new-comers built their fort, for, except some fishermen drying their nets on the sands below the haunts of the apes, or stray huntsman armed with the famous sling of Spain, no one had been there during the long ages while the Rock shone before Carteia. The Phœnician sails and the sounding oars of the Roman galleys were familiar enough to them; they saw the country rise again to full prosperity under the careful hands of the Moors; the shouts of Gothic and Oriental warriors were heard by them when king after king of Castile attacked the fortress; so the booming of the cannon of Spanish, Dutch, French, and English ships was heard as plainly as they hear the "gun-fire" of to-day. They saw Hanno pass the Straits with his Carthaginian galleys on a voyage of discovery, and

Strabo's friend, Timosthenes, admiral of Ptolemy, busy in his official work. Besides merchantmen of Tyre, Carthage, Tartessus, and Gades, the great ships of the last-named city were seen going to Ostia with corn; the Moor, the Algerian from within and the Salee rover from without the Straits, the galleys of the knights of Rhodes and Malta, the traders of Venice and Genoa, and those of Elizabeth, the Armada of Philip, the big Dutch craft bound for Smyrna or Aleppo, the Crusaders going to Jerusalem, and, among the first of these last, Sigurd, King of Norway, who, in 1109, fought a battle with certain Pagans in the very Straits of Gibraltar, or Norfa Sound, as the Northmen called it, after the first Viking who passed into the Inner Sea. All these were as well known to the countless generations of monkeys of the Rock, as the line-of-battle ships of Blake, Rooke, Rodney, Nelson, Byng, and Jervis, of Thoulouse, Langara, and Cordova of the last century, the "P. and O. boats" and iron-clads of to-day.

Except for a few more holes bored by the indefatigable English for their galleries of guns, there is very little change in the appearance of the Rock since the monkeys have held it. The first Phœnician merchant who passed the Pillars might almost have used the words of Childe Harold:

> "Through Calpe's Straits survey the steepy shore;
> Europe and Afric on each other gaze!
> Lands of the dark-eyed maid and dusky Moor
> Alike beheld beneath pale Hecate's blaze:
> How softly on the Spanish shore she plays,
> Disclosing rock, and slope, and forest brown,
> Distinct, though darkening with her waning phase;
> But Mauritania's giant shadows frown,
> From mountain cliff to coast descending sombre down."

CHAPTER IV.

UNDER THE CARTHAGINIANS.

WE have thus described the present aspect of the Rock of Gibraltar, so far as it is not an act of supererogation to do so, when our photographs efficiently represent the place, and give a far truer idea, on an inch or two of paper, than a million of words and the greatest literary craft could contrive. We have endeavoured to express the feelings of many nations in respect to the subject, and, in passing, referred to the early phases of its history. We left it, historically, in the hands of descendants of the great mother, Tyre. How the country passed into those of the Romans is next to be recounted. According to Mariana, the Spanish historian, whom it may be most convenient to consult here, the country we now call Andalusia, Strabo's commercial heaven upon earth, was, at about six hundred and twenty years before Christ, governed by Argantonius, King of the people of Tartessus. He went to war with, or otherwise came in opposition to, the Gaditans, subdued them, but gained for himself a troublesome course of "rebellions." Argantonius's reign was of long duration, and fame writes of the prosperity of his country. Either in course of rebellions or by the natural gravitating of weaker peoples towards a greater, the country hereabouts became Carthaginian; the people of this Tyrian colony captured Gades from the Phœnicians, which act offended the people of Carteia, who, being a mixture of Phœnicians and others, remained independent until Hannibal came to Spain.

The history of the efforts of the Carthaginians in Spain, which were mainly directed to obtain compensation for the loss of Sicily and Sardinia to the Romans at the close of the first Punic War, is known, and need be but briefly recapitulated here. Gades was, as we have seen, in alliance with Carthage at the time Hamilcar bent all the fierce and yet sullen resolves of his tremendous will to punishing the greed of the Romans with regard to the extorted cession of the first-named island, and a further demand of twelve hundred talents to the three thousand five hundred which were dictated by the treaty of peace, when the revolted mercenaries of Carthage in Sicily were accepted as allies of Rome. Hamilcar had dealt already with the mercenaries of the Inexpiable War, and this additional demand, which involved the cession of Corsica also, did but deepen his strenuous hate. Far-seeing as he was, Spain, where his people already had the seats and alliances which we have indicated, presented a field for the acquisition of power to replace the losses of the islands and of his people. He departed for that country, and the governing council of Carthage, that oligarchy of oligarchies, was glad to see his back turned towards them, inasmuch as this centralising leader was hardly less feared by them than the Romans. In the year 235 B.C., Hamilcar crossed the Straits of Gibraltar, taking with him Hasdrubal, and Hannibal, then nine years of age. The oath which Hamilcar accepted from Hannibal is thus described by Livy: " There is, besides, a story that Hannibal, when about nine years of age, while he boyishly coaxed his father Hamilcar that he might be taken to Spain, was conducted to the altar, and, having laid his hands upon the offerings, was bound by an oath to prove himself, as soon as he could, an enemy to the Roman people. Hannibal told the circumstances of this ceremony to Antiochus, when in his old age staying with that king." Hamilcar, says Dr. Liddell, set out, not as the servant of Carthage, but as the enemy of Rome, with feelings of personal hostility, not to be appeased save by the degradation of his antagonist. He so far succeeded that, although he left unaccomplished the work on which his heart was set, yet by a prudent course of policy he had won the hearts of the Spaniards, strengthened the power against Rome by their accession, and, after eight years of effort, died, leaving a new inheritance of force for the genius of Hannibal to employ for that end to which he was pledged, and into the prosecution of which he entered with unflinching and hearty zeal. Hasdrubal succeeded Hamilcar in power and policy, and was practically hereditary ruler of the south of Spain, the founder of Carthagena (New Carthage, as he called it), and entered into a nominal alliance with the Romans (227 B.C.), which fixed the Ebro as the boundary of the new empire in Spain. Hannibal succeeded Hasdrubal (221 B.C.). He so dealt with the tribes which remained unsubdued, that, except Saguntum, Spain within the boundary was in his power. Saguntum was an ally of Rome, but on the Carthaginian side of the Ebro by many hundred miles. The town was on the Palancia, where Murviedro stands now. The siege of Saguntum, which was undertaken by Hannibal in spite of Roman remonstrances, is recorded in "Livy," with all the picturesque power of that great literary artist, and is one of the most noteworthy events in the world's history. The place was taken 220 B.C. When ambassadors of Rome, after being repulsed by Hannibal, went to Carthage, Hanno, the great senator, thus addressed the Carthaginians in condemnation of the policy of Hannibal: "It is against Carthage that Hannibal is now moving his vineæ and towers; it is the wall of Carthage that he is shaking with his battering rams. The ruins of Saguntum—Oh! that I may be a false prophet—will fall on our heads, and the war commenced against the Saguntines must be continued against the Romans." So wrote Livy. It was in vain that he declaimed thus. The Carthaginians shared the feelings of Hamilcar and Hannibal too deeply to permit themselves to heed the warnings of the personal enemy and political opponent of those leaders. There was much to be said on both sides, and a great deal was said on that of Hannibal, while Hanno spoke alone. The place fell, and the Romans prepared for war; but first sent ambassadors to Carthage, demanding if the capture had the sanction of the home authorities. According to Livy, logic was on the side of the Carthaginian senate; but words rose high, and, at last, Q. Fabius Butes, chief of the envoys, folded a part of his robe, and said, " In this I offer you peace or war, choose which you will have." He might give which he chose, was the reply, so, letting fall the fold, Fabius gave them "*War!*" They answered that they accepted, and would maintain it in the same spirit with which they accepted it. We do but recall these anecdotes because of their connection with Gibraltar and its great neighbour Carteia. The latter city refusing, in common with others of the neighbourhood, to pay tribute, was attacked, stormed, and plundered by Hannibal, because it was the capital of the Olcades, who, with their allies, opposed him, in all one hundred thousand men. Livy states that Hannibal went to war by way of preliminary and pretence for his attack on Saguntum, which last act was expected and intended to provoke the Romans. There is no more of Carteia, the wealthy city, except a dim and incoherent rumour which is to the effect that out of its then long-desolate ruins the Arabs built Gibraltar, or the first fortress of the Rock.

After the taking of Saguntum, Hannibal marched to the

north of Spain, proceeded with his allies through Gaul, and crossed the Alps to Italy in that expedition which is probably the most wonderful military exploit on record. The second Punic War was begun practically, if not ostensibly, by the destruction of Carteia. Hasdrubal, who had been, in the absence of Hannibal, left to act as commander in Spain, furnished supplies to the Carthaginians during their straits in Calabria (211-207 B.C.). Publius Cornelius Scipio was sent on the Roman part into Spain, where the senate expected the great stress of the war would fall, and anywhere but at home, where Hannibal, nevertheless, caused it to fall. This commander, so tardy were his movements at first, found his enemy on the Rhone. His brother Cnæus came to Spain in his place. Hannibal had much of his wish for vengeance during all the early portion of this momentous struggle, and at Cannæ his unwearying hate must have been gleeful that he had bitten so very deeply into the hearts of the overweening Romans. Cnæus Scipio had enough to do with Hasdrubal, and, at last, was vanquished and slain, with Publius, his brother, who joined him on the passage of Hannibal-into Italy. Spain was thus lost, for the time, to Rome; Hasdrubal was expected in Italy to join his brother Hannibal, and the fate of Rome seemed sealed, when the fatal letters he had sent to the victor of Cannæ were intercepted, and the tide of fortune began to turn. The battle of the Metaurus brought death to Hasdrubal, and another lease of power to Rome.

The younger Scipio, son of one and nephew of the other of the slain consuls before named, had been sent to command in Spain (210 B.C.), where he was opposed by Mago and Hasdrubal, brothers of Hannibal, and the namesake of the second who was the son of Gisgo. He captured New Carthage (Carthagena), and by many was welcomed as the deliverer of their country from the Carthaginian power; they invited him to become their king, and all the country north of the Guadalquivir (Bætis) was in the hands of the Romans; meanwhile Hannibal's brother set out on the journey which was to end so fatally on the banks of the Metaurus. The Battle of Elinga, on the Guadalquivir, decided the fate of the Carthaginian power in Spain, as had that of the Metaurus the fate of the invasion of Italy. In 206 B.C. all Spain, except Gades, was in Roman hands, and Scipio prepared to attack Carthage in Africa itself. The slaughter which followed his brief visit to Africa, and the revolt of the towns of Andalusia, did not speak badly for the conduct of the Carthaginians towards their dependants in Spain. A report of Scipio's death awakened the old spirit against the Romans, although Carthage was not benefited by it, for the hopes of her people were narrowed. The Gaditans, long independent, and of Phœnician origin, shut out Mago, the last of the sons of Hannibal, so he seized their chief magistrates, crucified them, and retired by the Straits of Gibraltar to the Balearic Isles, intending to relieve Hamilcar, who was shut up in the Abruzzi. We read that ten thousand Celtiberians landed in Africa, and offered their services to the Carthaginians, or rather to their ally, Scyphax, and that they paid sorely for their act when Scipio defeated the army of Carthage in the Battle of the Great Plains. The war had thus been brought home to the city by a repetition of that system of Hannibal which was begun sixteen years before when he invaded Italy. At Zama (202 B.C.) the war was decided which begun at Carteia. It was to Tyre, the mother city of Carthage, that Hannibal fled after his brief command in the latter city, and when on his way to Antiochus at Ephesus.

It was towards the termination of the second Punic War that, under the command of Lælius, the Romans came with galleys and troops to the remains of Carteia in the Bay of Gibraltar. They had in view the capture of the city of Gades, having, as it seems, intelligence from traitors within the place of a mode by which that object could be effected. The scheme, however, was betrayed, and the conspirators were taken and put on board a heavy galliass, which was part of the naval force of Adherbal, the Carthaginian admiral on the station. This galliass was less swift in sailing than the regular " liners " or war-galleys of his fleet, so the commander, intending to follow with the rest, sent her on before. In passing the Strait she was discovered by the Romans, whose general, Lælius, got on board a galliass, and was carried by the current, which then, as now, set inwards, into the Strait. Adherbal, seeing this, and being discovered by the Romans, was doubtful which was best to be done, to fight or go after his own galliass. The Romans gave him little time to think, for they attacked the Carthaginians without delay. Livy describes how the ordinary rules of sea-fighting could not be observed in this rapid Strait; in fact, there seems to have been " a good deal of sea on " at the time. " The sea running high at that place (off Tarifa), they could not turn their galleys, but were tossed about against their friends as well as against their foes; and neither party could separate from his antagonist. Sometimes they might have seen a galley flying, turned suddenly against that which pursued her, by the whirling of the waves, and that which chased her seemed to fly away." At last one of the Roman galleys, a *quinquireme*, or five-banked ship, managed by her weight and the number of her oars, to deal better than her companions; she mastered the rough seas, and stemmed, *i.e.* rammed down, one of her antagonists bodily into the sea, as vigorously as the famous ram of the Confederates sent the Yankee ship to grief; and, by the practice of a manœuvre which was well understood in antique naval warfare, swept away the oars from one side of a second, as she swiftly passed her. This double loss was too much for the Carthaginian admiral, who fled for the African coast, whither Lælius did not follow, but returned to the Bay of Gibraltar, and from thence to New Carthage, where the head-quarters of Publius Scipio then were. So far as we know, this was the first of the long series of naval fights which have taken place in sight of Gibraltar. With the rest of Spain, the place fell into the Roman hands, by means of the treaty at the termination of the second Punic War, which may be said to have given all to the children of the Wolf. The Romans held their possession for six hundred and nineteen years. When Cæsar defeated the sons of Pompey, at Munda, Cneius Pompey took refuge at Carteia,* where his galleys were. Peace reigned, and thus the land grew to the state which we have before described in the words of Strabo.

* The ruins at Roccadillo seem to indicate the site of antique Carteia, and, it may be, that of Tartessus. These ruins are about forty stadia from Gibraltar; this was the distance from Calpe to Carteia, according to Strabo.

CHAPTER V.

IN ROMAN HANDS.

ANDALUSIA was included in the province of Farther Spain; this, which was the heritage of the Carthaginians, with Hither Spain on the eastern coast, was all Roman before about 198 B.C., when Cato the Elder was commander in the district. He controlled the whole peninsula, but left a series of threatened troubles as the result of his treatment of the people. The father of the Gracchi pacified the country, and it remained quiet for many years. Meanwhile, although all these victories seemed glorious, the vengeance of Hannibal would, had the man had prescience, have been sated to the very depths of its incorrigible hate by observing the growth of luxury among the Romans. The next generation of thirty years or thereabouts died in circumstances and with minds which were totally different from those of their fathers, and, as a free state, Rome was really far on the road to ruin. Spain, more probably than any other province, was open to the infamous extortions of the tax-gatherers; these reached such an extent that, in 149 B.C., public pleadings were made on behalf of the oppressed people, and the advocates named by the province of Farther Spain were Emil. Paulus and Sulp. Gallus; in the end the accused withdrew from Rome. Rebellions took place, and the country was by no means settled after this time. It was on the effort to enlist soldiers for a Celtiberian (Castilian) campaign that, for the first time in Rome, no volunteers were forthcoming, and that the Tribunes of the People resisted the attempt at forced enlistments. The tremendous significance of these facts needs no comment. New levies were, however, obtained, and the young Scipio, son of Paullus, had a command with success for the time, when the atrocity of Galba, blacker than Roman atrocity, worse than Italian treachery, marked no less plainly the brute nature of the man than the changed spirit of Roman war. Attacking the Lusitanians who had revolted, he wasted their country until they submitted, and he, with "apparent kindness," says Dr. Liddell, in condensing his ancient authority, "answered that he was grieved at the sight of the poverty of the people, and that, if they would meet him in three divisions, at places specified, he would assign lands and cities to each, as Gracchus had done. The simple people believed him. But Galba fell on each body separately with his whole force, and cut it to pieces. This infamous piece of treachery crushed the spirit of the Lusitanians; but retributive Justice awaited her time. Among those who escaped the sword of Galba was a young shepherd, Viriathus, of whom we shall hear another time." Meanwhile Rome was going on her course; she conquered her great enemy, and sowed, as they said, the site of the city with salt; if she did so, it was not until after she had bathed every inch of the ravaged soil with her own most precious blood. "*Assyria has fallen, and Persia and Macedon; Carthage is burning; Rome's day might come next.*" So said Scipio in presaging the fate of the merciless. The destruction of Carthage cost Rome more than the northern United States, with all their prodigality of blood, spent upon the subjugation of their former fellow-champions for freedom, their brethren of the South. *Delenda est Carthago* was a prophecy of Roman liberty.

Viriathus, the representative of Lusitanian freedom, having

gathered the people about him, maintained war for a long time against the Romans, and baffled their cunning as well as defeated their force in Numantia, a city which had a more glorious ending than even that of Carthage, and in that ending marked the terrible hate of all free peoples for the Romans. What Rome suffered, in turn, when the free peoples came upon her, and begun anew that civilisation which she had corrupted by ages of rapacity and tyranny, was not enough to expiate the crimes she had committed. Before Numantia fell, Viriathus, the fugitive from the atrocious Galba, although acknowledged as an ally of Rome, was betrayed and assassinated with an infamy of treachery that was worthy of the Romans. Like the Carthaginians, he had bitten deep into the hated heart of Rome. It was needful to employ Scipio again ere the freedom of Numantia could be drowned in blood, consumed in fire, and buried in ruins. The people of the city ate the bodies of their own dead, rather than submit to be civilised by the Roman process. The savage Scipio sold those who survived into the slavery they dreaded, and destroyed the city so that its ruins are not yet discovered. Another account in the dreadful reckoning against Rome was opened.

The Servile War did not wipe off a tithe of the reckoning of blood. The captives of many conquests had become more dangerous in the heart of Italy than at home, when in arms for their liberties. They took vengeance to the utmost of their power, and that was great. The city of Enna remembered their uprising. In Taurominium, of which the besieged slaves had taken possession, the revolters ate the children, the women, and even each other, rather than surrender to Roman greed. A nation which had provoked this frightful hate, deserved to have Nero and Elagabalus for its rulers—deserved to become, in turn, the slave of the Goths.

The peace which this treatment of the Spanish people brought about endured until the Marian party, under Sertorius, disturbed it, and produced in the country a sort of echo of the murderous wars and revolts of Italy, Rome itself, and Gaul. Sertorius was for a time overcome, and sought a refuge in those Fortunate Islands* which were held of old to represent Elysium, and are now known as the Azores. He returned at the invitation of the Lusitanians, and employed their valour so well that all the South of Spain, including Andalusia,† passed to the Marian party, and the Romans of the party of Sylla were compelled to send against him Metellus Pius, who, after an effort of Sertorius's to set up a national force in Spain, was successful, by means of the murder of Sertorius, and the aid of Pompey, who pacified the province anew, for a time. Sixty-one years before Christ, Cæsar came to Spain as proprætor; he plundered the country under the pretence of a revolt, and paid his creditors at home with the spoils. He returned to Rome to claim a triumph. He became one of the triumvirate, and that fate which had hung over Rome for so long a time came to pass at last. Spain fell to Pompey, who governed it by deputy, and in due time Cæsar came again, vanquished the adherents of Pompey, and, returning to Rome, conquered Pompey and was sole dictator. Again he returned to Spain, defeated the younger Pompey and his followers at Munda, which is not at a great distance from Malaga. From

---

* Among these Fortunate Islands was, according to the opinions of the Arabs, Britain, "which has no mountains or rivers, and where the inhabitants drink rain-water and cultivate the land."

† Al-makkari is inclined to ascribe the origin of the name Andalusia (which, in the form of Andalus, the Arabs gave to the whole of Spain) to Andalus, son of Tubal, son of Japheth, son of Noah. The name is corrupted from that of the Vandals, thinks Gayangos, who translated the work of Al-makkari on the "History of the Mohammedan Dynasties in Spain."

the triumph for this achievement to the death of Cæsar was not more than five months. After him came Octavius, and the Great Republic was at an end.

It is useless to follow the history of the Spanish provinces through the vicissitudes of the empire; suffice it here that, with intervals, the country shared fewer of the troubles of the Roman world than other provinces. Centuries of commercial prosperity followed the settlement of the Roman rule in Andalusia; year after year the ships of Cadiz and Carthago Nova sailed past the Rock, the sun shone there, and the light was reflected from it like a beacon. If any work was done there it must have been very little, for the monkeys remained in possession disturbed only by those who might dry nets in sight of their fortress; or who, with Balearic slings, came to knock them on the head. These creatures and their co-tenants, the rabbits, had it all to themselves. Readers will remember Strabo's account of the complaint of the Balearic Islanders to the Roman Senate, that the rabbits nearly burrowed them out of the islands, almost literally ate them out of house and home. From their Phœnician name, Saphan, the name of Spain itself is said to have come. The Franks (A.D. 255) seem to have been the first of the barbarians who penetrated far into the country, which they did in the reign of Gallienus, and destroyed Tarragona. Seizing ships in the Spanish ports, this people burst upon the Mauritanian province, and repeated there the havoc of Spain. From this expedition they returned, and the province relapsed into peace, that was unbroken until a second irruption took place, and effected an almost total change in the character of the inhabitants of the Peninsula, and inspired new military ardour into their hearts. This irruption happened as follows in the next chapter, in which we shall show how another human wave was to follow those of the

Iberians, or aborigines, and their Celtic followers, the Phœnicians and their kindred of Carthage, and the Romans; to say nothing of the Franks, Phocæans and Rhodians, all of whom, at times that were far apart, had influence in Spain. All these peoples were to leave traces of their occupations upon the history of Spain, nay, streams of their blood are yet recognisable in many parts of the country. Thus, the Basques are still Celts; the Iberian continues in the grave Castilian; a vast proportion of the names of things, or proper names, in the Spanish language, are to this day almost pure Arabic—a human influence of which we have yet to write; Greek and even more distinctly oriental characteristics yet appear in the people of Cadiz. Of the Visigoths, of whom we next write here, the traces are few and far between; the Romans left most numerous relics.

CHAPTER VI.

IN VISIGOTHIC HANDS.

AT the end of six centuries—it may be because nothing human can long endure—the Roman State became so thoroughly corrupt that, ten months before Alaric broke into Rome (A.D. 410), the Vandals, Suevi, and others, having traversed France, and gained the passes of the Pyrenees through the treachery of the Honorian Bands, poured upon Spain, and devastated it in their common fashion. The whole country was wrecked by them, even so far to the south, as we are led to believe, as the Pillars of Hercules. This, if a fact, gives one a most powerful idea of the effect of these incursions of savage tribes. That they should overrun a country, the physical aspect of which was so little obnoxious to the attempt as that of Spain, was almost as wonderful as that they should find the whole province so rotten as to make no effectual resistance. It makes us marvel that neither fear, hatred of the barbarians, nor the love of country, should supply force sufficient to resist the terrible scourging of those who, after all, must have been comparatively few, and almost without discipline. So it was, however. Gonderic, the Vandal, is recorded to have taken Seville, put the inhabitants to the sword, and destroyed all the towns of Andalusia. The name of Vandalusia was then given*

---

* So says Col. James, *History of the Herculean Strait*, to which laborious but not luminous work we here refer. Col. James wrote his history " for the satisfaction and to the district which, until that time, was called Bætica; and it received this title on account of the majority of its new owners being Vandals of the branch called Lilingi. From this questionable fact it is said the name Andalusia was supplied.

Ataulphus, or Adolphus, King of the Visigoths, left Italy for the south of Gaul, overcame Jovinus and Sebastian—who had revolted at Metz—and assumed the purple, slew them by the hand of the executioner, sent the heads of these chieftains to Honorius (A.D. 413), whose sister, Placidia, he had married, and was by his imperial brother-in-law invited to turn his arms against the newly-arrived barbarians in Spain. Accordingly he crossed the Pyrenees, took Barcelona, and is reckoned with the Visigothic monarchs of Spain, whose order runs thus:

Ataulphus	414-415	Athanagild	554-567
Singeric, 7 days	415	Liuva I.	567-572
Wallia	415-419	Leovigild	572-586
Theodoric I.	419-451	Recared I.	586-601
Thorismond	451-452	Liuva II.	601-603
Theodoric II.	452-466	Witteric	603-610
Euric	466-485	Gundemar	610-612
Alaric II.*	485-507	Sisebut	612-620
Giselric and Amalaric	507-510	Recared II.	620 621
		Suintilla	621-631
Amalaric alone	510-531	Sisenand	631-636
Thiodes	531-548	Chintilla	636-640
Agila	549-554	Tulga	640-641

amusement of those gentlemen, in particular, who may have the honour of residing in that valuable fortress of Gibraltar, one of the richest jewels that adorn the British crown."

* Alaric I. was the great conqueror who took Rome, brother-in-law of Ataulphus, the first of the Visigothic Kings of Spain.

THE VISIGOTHIC KINGS.

Chintasvinthus	641-653	Egica		687-701
Recesvinthus	653-672	Witiza		701-710
Wamba	672-680	Roderic		710
Ervigius	680-687			

In one year after the accession of Roderic the kingdom of the Visigoths, which had then endured three hundred years in Spain, passed away.

These were the kings of the Suevi in Spain; we give their names only:

Hermanric	408-438	Maldra	457-460
Rechil	438-448	Frumarius	460-464
Richiarius	448-457	Remismund	464-469

In the reign of Remismund the Visigoths conquered this nation, and in that of Leovigild the peoples were incorporated.

The Kings of the Vandals were as follow, so far as regards Spain, which they entered under Gonderic, in 409. This chief was succeeded by Genseric, in 428. The latter reigned until 477; of him we presently speak further. Hunneric succeeded to the dominion which Genseric established in Africa. Gundamund followed, then Thorismund, Hilderic, and Gelimer completed the line of this anomalous sovereignty. The last was overthrown by Belisarius, in 534.

The reign of Ataulphus, the Visigoth, was short indeed. He was assassinated at Barcelona by a partisan of Sarus, whom he had brought to death at the overthrow of Jovinus. Singeric, brother of Sarus, was, during a tumult, made king; and he had but just time enough, in his reign of a week, to murder the children of Ataulphus, and insult Placidia so terribly as to make her, the sister of the Emperor Honorius, walk a dozen miles by the side of his horse. Wallia succeeded on the slaying of Singeric, which took place during another revolt. Gibbon quotes from Sidonius Apollinarius the following lines, which have direct reference to Gibraltar and the thirst of Wallia for further conquests to be made in Africa :

> " Quod Tartessiacis avus hujus Vallia terris
> Vandalicas turmas, et juncti Martis Alanos
> Stravit et occiduam texere cadavera Calpem."

This brought the Visigoths into opposition to the new owners of Bætica. Baffled by storms and the repeated shipwrecks which took place before his sight, near Gibraltar, Wallia agreed to the proposals of the Roman envoys, gave up Placidia, received a donation of corn, and attacked the Lilingi with such terrible effect that he exterminated those barbarians who had, in their short term of possession, ruined, or nearly ruined, the long-peaceful province. This was not effected, however, in less than three campaigns. The Alani were utterly defeated, and their king slain; the Vandals proper succumbed with the Suevi, and were ultimately absorbed into the Visigothic power. Here, in short, was fought out the ancient feud of the two main streams of invaders, and the foolish Honorius flattered himself that in the victory of one of them he had seen the end of his national troubles. Wallia professed to be the General of the Roman Emperor, and, according to the view which Gibbon took of the matter, soon gave the Andalusians cause to regret the loss of the Vandals, to whose rapacity there seems to have been a limit, while none was found for that of the Visigoths, in dealing with the Romanised Spaniards.

The inhabitants of the Peninsula were, by this time, composed of very many distinct races of men. The Goths were of many tribes, including Visigoths or Western Goths, and the Ostro or Eastern Goths; the latter were at least as busy as their fellows, but in the ancient Eastern Roman Empire. Besides the former, the Alani, Suevi, and Vandals were in Spain. In Spain there were also the descendants of the aboriginal Iberians, Phœnicians, Carthaginians, Romans, and the mixed race, or Spaniards. Even the Romans had never wholly overcome the Iberians. The Gothic tribes, to use the general name of the second Germanic invaders, fought against each other. In this part of the world at least, they continued opposed to the Romans, so that Genseric, the illegitimate brother of Gonderic, although he brought a fleet into the Bay of Gibraltar, with an army to fight against the Suevi, did not omit, after his victory was secured, to proceed to Africa to the aid of the rebellious Boniface, Count of Africa, who was then fighting the General of Placidia, the Roman Empress, and his former mistress, as regent for Valentinian III. From her the united chiefs, Genseric and Boniface, extorted peace of a hollow sort, with the promise of tribute, so that the conquests of Genseric in Africa remained nominally Roman, but were really Vandalic. The Western Goths, or Visigoths—forgetful of their common cause and neighbouring origin—who had settled in Spain, now cast eyes of desire upon the inheritance of the Vandals in Andalusia, and under the command of their king, Rechilus, attacked the province with disastrous effect, defeated the *quasi*-Romans, and united the country with their own.

Under Liberius, Justinian led an army into Spain, and took possession of all the maritime towns on the Mediterranean coast, from Gibraltar to Valencia. These submitted gladly, says the historian, in order to deliver themselves from the tyranny of Agila the Visigoth, a degraded wretch, and a heretic, whom Liberius defeated, and his own subjects slew. Until A.D. 614, this part of the country remained thus in the hands of the later Romans; then King Sisebut attacked them, and was so far successful that the coast reverted to the Visigothic power in Spain.

How they dealt with each other, and what was the mutual faith of these tribes, let Gibbon tell, as he condensed the tale. After the death of Gonderic, the Vandals "acquired for a king his bastard brother, the terrible Genseric, a name which, in the destruction of the Roman Empire, has deserved an equal rank with the names of Alaric and Attila. The King of the Vandals is described to have been of middle stature, with a lameness of one leg, which he contracted by an accidental fall from his horse. His slow and cautious speech seldom declared the deep purposes of his soul; he disdained to imitate the luxury of the vanquished; but he indulged the sterner passions of anger and revenge. The ambition of Genseric was without bounds, and without scruples; and the warrior could dextrously employ the dark engines of policy to select the allies who could be useful to his purpose, or to scatter among his enemies the seeds of hatred and contention. Almost at the moment of his departure (to join Boniface) he was informed that Hunneric, King of the Suevi, had presumed to ravage the Spanish territories, which he was resolved to abandon. Impatient of the insult, Genseric pursued the hasty retreat of the Suevi as far as Merida (the ancient Emerita), precipitated the king and his army into the river Anas, and calmly returned to the seashore to embark his victorious troops. The vessels which transported the Vandals over the Straits of Gibraltar, a channel of only twelve miles in breadth, were furnished by the Spaniards, who anxiously wished their departure, and by the African General (Boniface) who had implored their formidable assistance." With him were the Alani, whom the Vandals had overcome in 419 A.D. Count Boniface repented, when it was too late, of the treachery of which he had been guilty. The Vandals settled in Africa, as our list of their kings shows, and the gates of Calpe and Abyla had again opened to permit the passage of a conqueror. We need not follow the dreadful road of Genseric and his tribes.

The capital of the Visigothic power was originally at Toulouse. There the ambassador of Ætius found Theodoric I., when he invoked aid to repulse Attila in besieging Orleans; he obtained it, and the Romans marched once more with the Goths, this time against the Huns. Thorismond and Theodoric, the successors in power to their father, were with him in this march, and at the tremendous day of Chalons, which commemorated the delivery of the West from the new horde of barbarians. Here they fought against the Ostrogoths, their kindred tribe, as well as against the Huns, Burgundians, Franks, and Thuringians. Theodoric I. was slain on that memorable day, and Thorismond was the champion of the shattered Roman civilisation in the west. Theodoric murdered Thorismond, the champion, and reigned in his stead. It was he who backed Avitus on the Imperial throne. The description given by Sidonius, and quoted by Gibbon, of the court and mode of living at Toulouse is elaborate, even to the after-dinner nap of this powerful monarch, the greatest man in all the west, and is one of the most curious accounts of a royal household that we know; in referring to the fifth century it is doubly interesting through its being unique. Euric assassinated Theodoric II., and defeated the Suevi. This Euric was one of the most eminent and successful men of his age and race, he was the antagonist of Clovis, his children reigned a short time after his death; but the superior fortunes of the Frank compelled a dissolution of the Visigothic power in Gaul, so that in the reign of Thiodes (531—548) the authority of their king was concentrated in Spain, and the Suevi finally overcome. Here they remained, almost shut out from the world by the same means which had nearly isolated the inhabitants of the same land in the Roman time— means which are effectual to this day; these means of isolation are the Pyrenees and the sea. It has been customary to style the period which now follows as the Dark Age of Spain; it appears, however, more just to call it the Silent Age. The religious history of the country has been sketched by Gibbon with his usual power, no less than with his common mocking spirit. It must not be imagined that the Roman Empire had entirely lost hold of the Peninsula; on the contrary, it was not until far in the seventh century that parts of the eastern and western coasts departed from the Imperial rule of the Eastern Empire. Thiodes, the Visigothic king, directed an expedition against Ceuta, and used the Bay of Gibraltar for its immemorial purpose of invasion. He was repulsed, however, by a sally which, as it took place on a Sunday, and found his soldiers engaged in prayer, points to the strict *Christianity* of the Visigoths. The king himself barely escaped with his life.

CHAPTER VII.

THE VISIGOTHIC KINGS.

WE have but to give a slight sketch of the Visigothic monarchs, such as might have been presented to the astonished eyes of Roderic, last of the line, when he had the wonderful vision of them, passing one by one, in the Vault of Destiny, to the recounting of which we hasten. To do this in a connected manner we must return to Euric, who murdered his brother, Theodoric II., and conquered a large portion of Spain, which had not already fallen into the hands of his people, and became almost sole monarch of the Peninsula. He extended, it is alleged, his acquisitions as far as Arles and Marseilles, defeated Riothamar, the chief of the Bretons, but was himself checked in Auvergne by Ecdicius in 470, yet in four years after contrived to obtain the cession of that province; and, lastly, by way of extending the power of his kingdom, obtained from Odoacer a relinquishment of all the countries south-west of the Alps. He died in 485, leaving his kingdom extending from Gibraltar to the Loire and Rhone. He was succeeded by Alaric II., his son, who seems to have been of a very peaceful disposition, and was a good lawgiver. He married Theudigotha, daughter of the Ostrogoth, Theodoric the Great, but his territories tempting the ambition of Clovis, he was attacked by that Frankish leader, defeated, and slain in battle at Vouglé, near Poitiers. At Narbonne, where the defeated Visigoths halted, they quarrelled about a new king, whether Giselric, the elder, but illegitimate, or Amalaric, the legitimate son of Alaric II., should succeed him. The question was settled by the choice of both, and they were proclaimed joint kings of the Visigoths, with Thiodes, or Theudes, as their guardian, a post which had been originally given to him by the father of the princes. Another authority says that Giselric was elected, that Theodoric the Great sent an Italian army to assert the rights of Amalaric, and that Thiodes was commander of this host, who defeated Giselric, compelled him to return to Africa, and become guardian of the rightful heir. This office he performed well, and Amalaric, when he became of age to rule, was proclaimed King of the Visigoths. To make himself secure, he married Clotilda, daughter of Clovis, but treated her very badly. In revenge for this, her brother Childebert, King of Paris, attacked Amalaric, and a tremendous battle between the Franks and the Visigoths took place in Catalonia. The latter were beaten, and Amalaric, who fled, was killed. In strict speech we should say that the Visigothic kingdom ceased with this event, for Thiodes, who was elected to succeed, was, as we said above, an Ostrogoth. The people remained distinct, however, from the Ostrogoths; hence it would be mere pedantry to say that the Visigothic kingdom expired with Amalaric. It was Thiodes who besieged the fortress of Ceuta; he was slain at Barcelona in 548. Agila succeeded, and reigned until 554, when Athanagild, a military leader, revolted against this ruler, who is described as a monster, obtained aid from Justinian, defeated and killed Agila near Seville. Athanagild tried to get rid of his *quasi*-Roman allies, but failed to do so, and his kingdom was much crippled in consequence of their usurpation. This king is interesting to all readers on account of the histories of his two daughters, Galeswintha the Fair, and Brunehault the Proud. The former married Chilperic I., King of Soissons; the latter Siegbert, King of Metz, sons of Chlotaire, and grandsons of Clovis. Fredegonda the Furious, concubine of Chilperic, hunted Galeswintha to death, and invoked the implacable hate of her sister, Brunehault, who roused up Siegbert of Metz (Austrasia) against Chilperic, his brother; the means of this horrible business were frequent fraticide, murder, fire, perjury, and ruthlessness of the most frightful kinds. Brunehault was tied to the heels of a wild horse, and Fredegonda, the worst of bad women, to whom, according to the report of her enemies, for that is all we have, Lady Macbeth was a lamb, died queen and in peace some years before the death of Brunehault. Liuva I. succeeded Athanagild, and associated with himself Leovigild, his brother, who reigned alone until 586. Of this monarch and his family, Gibbon gives us this strongly characteristic account:

"Spain was restored to the Catholic Church (the country had been Arian) by the example of a royal martyr, who, in our calmer reason, we may style an ungrateful rebel. Leovigild, the Gothic monarch of Spain, deserved the respect of his enemies and the love of his subjects. The Catholics enjoyed a free toleration, and his Arian synods attempted, without much success, to reconcile their scruples by abolishing the unpopular rite of a second baptism. His eldest son, Hermenegild, who was invested by his father with the royal diadem and the fair principality of Bætica (Andalusia), entreated an honourable and orthodox alliance with a Merovingian princess, the daughter of Siegbert, King of Austrasia (Metz), and of the famous Brunehault. The beauteous Ingundis, who was not more than thirteen years of age, was received, beloved, and persecuted in the Arian court of Toledo; and her religious constancy was alternately assaulted by the blandishments and violence of Goiswintha, the Gothic queen, who abused the double claim of maternal authority.* Incensed by her resistance, Goiswintha seized the Catholic princess by her long hair, inhumanly dashed her against the ground, kicked her until she was covered with blood, and at last gave orders that she should be stripped and thrown into a basin or fish-pond. Love and honour might excite Hermenegild to resent this injurious treatment of his bride; and he was gradually persuaded that Ingundis suffered for the cause of Divine truth. Her tender complaint, and the weighty arguments of Leander, Archbishop of Seville, accomplished his conversion; and the heir of the Gothic monarchy was initiated in the Nicene faith by the solemn rites of confirmation. The rash youth, inflamed by zeal, and perhaps by ambition, was tempted to violate the duties of a son and a subject; and the Catholics of Spain, although they could not complain of persecution, applauded his pious rebellion against an heretical father. The civil war was protracted by the long and obstinate sieges of Merida, Cordova, and Seville, which had strenuously espoused the party of Hermenegild. He invited the orthodox barbarians, the Suevi and the Franks, to the destruction of his native land; he solicited the dangerous aid of the Romans, who possessed Africa; and his holy ambassador, the Archbishop Leander, effectively negotiated in person with the Byzantine court. But the hopes of the Catholics were crushed by the active strategy of a monarch who commanded the troops and treasures of Spain; and the guilty Hermenegild, after his

---

* Goiswintha successively married two kings of the Visigoths: Athanagild, to whom she bore Brunehault, the mother of Ingundis; and Leovigild, whose two sons, Hermenegild and Recared, were the issue of a former marriage.

vain attempt to resist or to escape, was compelled to surrender himself into the hands of an incensed father. Leovigild was still mindful of that sacred character; and the rebel, despoiled of the regal ornaments, was still permitted, in a decent exile, to profess the Catholic religion. His repeated and unsuccessful treasons at length provoked the indignation of the Gothic king, and the sentence of death, which he pronounced with apparent reluctance, was privately executed in the Tower at Seville. The inflexible constancy with which he refused to accept the Arian communion as the price of his safety, may excuse the honours which have been paid to the memory of St. Hermenegild. His wife and infant son were detained by the Romans in ignominious captivity; and this domestic misfortune tarnished the glories of Leovigild, and embittered the last moments of his life. His son and successor, Recared, the first Catholic King of Spain, had imbibed the faith of his unfortunate brother, which he supported with more prudence and success. Instead of revolting against his father, Recared patiently expected the hour of his death. Instead of condemning his memory, he piously supposed that the dying monarch had abjured the errors of Arianism, and recommended the conversion of the Gothic nation."

In this Recared succeeded, and the Visigothic people became proper Catholics. This monarch had been to war with Gonthran, King of Burgundy, and defeated him at Carcassonne in 588. He died in 601. Liuva II. succeeded Recared I., and was himself assassinated by Witteric, who usurped the throne in 603, and was slain in 610. Gundemar, who followed, reigned but two years. Sisebut, the next king, was a vigorous ruler. He persecuted the Jews, compelled ninety thousand of them to be baptised, tortured those who would not accept the rite, and confiscated their fortunes. Ceuta, a point so important in the progress of the flux and reflux of conquest between Europe and Africa, was captured by the Visigoths under this king, in the year 616 A.D., and remained, a fatal capture, in their possession until rather less than a century had elapsed, when Count Julian abandoned it to the Moors in 710. Recared II. inherited the throne from his father, Sisebut, and died in seven months afterwards (620). Suintilla was elected king, for it must be observed that the Visigothic monarchy in Spain was more strictly elective than that of the Franks or the Ostrogoths. He contrived to expel the Romans from the few remaining places they commanded in the country (621-626), and died in 631. Sisenand followed, and reigned five years. Chintilla was recognised king in 636, by the Council of Toledo, for it is noteworthy that the influence of the Church in this kingdom was almost predominant. He died in 640. Tulga succeeded, and was deposed in 641. Chintasvinthus, who endeavoured to encourage learning in Spain, next reigned, reformed the code of laws to a truer likeness of the Roman system, and died in 653. The work of legal reformation was continued by the son of Chintasvinthus, who was named Recesvinthus, a ruler who extended the bounds of his kingdom by the conquest of the Basque provinces, which had defied the Romans themselves. His reign was brief, for it ended in 672. The eight gold crowns or coronets which are now in the Hôtel de Cluny, Paris, were found at a place called La Fuente da Guarrazar, in the environs of Toledo. These extraordinary treasures were dedicated by the Visigothic prince, and are among the few relics of three centuries of rule in Spain. The words " RECESVINTHUS REX OFFERT " are suspended in gold letters and by gold chains from the margin of the larger crown. Hanging from the centre is a splendidly-jewelled cross. They are supposed to have been dedicated by the king, Recesvinthus, his queen, and the royal officers, to the honour of the Virgin, in a chapel called Notre Dame des Cormiers. Here they had been buried, it is presumed, in order to conceal them from the Moors when they entered Toledo in 712. Other crowns have been discovered in the same neighbourhood, and are now at Madrid. Strange, that of Recesvinthus the very name should have been almost forgotten when these votive treasures of his turned up, after they had been in their hiding-place nearly twelve hundred years (712-1858)!*

Recesvinthus died in 672, little dreaming how soon the inheritance of his people was to pass away. Then came Wamba, who was notorious in Gascony and other parts of the South of France. His fate was singular, and he was a very able warrior, for he beat the seafaring Saracens in a great naval battle, as they were attempting to effect a landing in Spain in 675. Wamba had been the victim of an attempt at poisoning, and, in the course of the illness which followed, vowed to adopt the monastic robe and rules; in fact he was invested with this robe, and on recovering was pronounced incapable of reigning. The judges were the clergy, and he submitted to their decision. The matter is very obscure, and appears to refer to a conspiracy and forced deposition; but is interesting as showing the leading influence in the Visigothic kingdom to have been that of men of religion. This is a characteristic which is marked in the whole of the Christian history of the Visigoths, as well as in that of their successors of modern date. To the deposed Wamba Ervigius succeeded and reigned until 687. After Ervigius came Egica, who had

---

* See a very curious note by Gayangos on Al-makkari, about the royal diadems that were found by Taric in the Cathedral at Toledo. "25 gold crowns, one for each of the Gothic monarchs who had reigned over Andalus (Spain), it being a custom of that nation that each of their kings should deposit in that sacred place a gold diadem, having his name, figure and condition, the number of children he had, the length of his life and that of his reign, engraved upon it."

married the daughter of his predecessor. He punished the conspirators against Wamba, reigned a long time, and died in 701. Witiza succeeded Ervigius, and by one side at least was depicted in the most odious colours.

The terrible event, towards which our course has been leading, is now at hand. Witiza was the thirty-second of the Visigothic kings of Spain, and the three hundred years of their tenancy had almost expired. They came to rule while Augustin was writing "De Civitate Dei"—*i.e.* in the year of the revolt of Jovinus, at Metz, three years after the death of Arcadius—and they ceased to rule two years after Offa, King of Essex, abdicated and went to Rome as a monk, *i.e.* in the year of the death of Justinian II., Emperor of the East, while England was yet a heptarchy, and in the first year of Ceolred, King of Mercia. The true history of the portentous event in question appears to be that which we shall give in the first case, reserving the romantic, or rather the questionable aspect of the subject for after consideration. Roderic, son of Theodofred, Count of Cordova, was appointed by Witiza to be General of the Spanish armies. He was unable to resist the temptation of power, and rebelled against his sovereign in the year 710, and, by the aid of the military, deposed him, confined him in Toledo, and deprived his sons of the succession to the throne.* "Their resentment was the more dangerous, as it was varnished with the dissimulation of courts; their followers were excited by the remembrance of favours and the promise of a revolution; and their uncle Oppas, Archbishop of Toledo and Seville, was the first person in the Church, and the second in the State." So, in the ornate style of Gibbon, is the mainspring of the disastrous event revealed. In plainer language, the more modern con-

---

* Gibbon's *Decline and Fall of the Roman Empire*, c. 51. Roderic appears to have been general of the cavalry of Witiza.

clusions of later students are thus condensed by the admirable biographer of Roderic, in the "English Cyclopædia of Biography": "For some time after his usurpation, Roderic had to contend against the sons and partisans of the dethroned monarch, who had taken refuge in the northern provinces of Spain. At last the sons of Witiza, perceiving their inability to cope with the forces of the usurper, crossed over to Africa, where they were kindly received by Ilyan (the Count Don Julian, of the Spanish Chronicle), Lord of Ceuta and Tangiers, and a friend of Witiza, who offered, if assisted by the Arabs, whose tributary he was,* to restore the princes to the dominions of their father. Having communicated his project to Muza Ibn Nosseyr, then governor in Africa for the Caliphs of Damascus, that general, who had long wished to carry his arms into Spain, gladly embraced the opportunity offered to him, and promised his powerful assistance. By his orders, Tarif Abu Zarah, with four hundred Berbers, landed at Tartessus (?) (since called Tarifa, in commemoration of this event); and, after ravaging the adjoining country, returned to Africa, laden with plunder and captives. This happened in Ramadan, A.H. 91 (Sept. 710 A.D.). The success of this enterprise filled the Arabian Emir with joy, and a second and more formidable expedition was, the ensuing year, directed against the shores of Spain. On Thursday, the eighth of Rejeb, A.H. 92 (answering to the 30th April, A.D. 711), Taric Ibn Zeyad, a freedman of Muza Ibn Nosseyr, landed with eight thousand men at the foot of the Rock of Calpe, to which he gave his own name, 'Gebal Taric' (the mountain of Taric), since corrupted into Gibraltar." Here we will leave, for the present, this condensed account of modern conclusions.

---

* This statement appears erroneous, for Ceuta was then in the hands of the Spaniards, and had been so since the year 616 A.D. Julian was the brother-in-law of Witiza.

CHAPTER VIII.

DIFFERING HISTORIES OF THE INVASION.

THE course of the descent of the Spanish crown of the Visigoths until it rested for a brief while upon the head of Roderic, is told thus. The account involves so much of the early career of this king, that we prefer to give it in this form and place to adopting another mode of treatment. Recesvinthus had no children; his brothers were not thought fit to inherit the throne; and accordingly—it might be on account of their age or incapability—they were set aside. The nobles thereupon chose Wamba, who had been a captain of the guard to Recesvinthus. He reigned but a short time, and was, it is said, poisoned by Ervigius; to whom succeeded, as we have said elsewhere, Egica; who died in A.D. 701, and was followed by his son Witiza, a disorderly and infamous prince, who was specially obnoxious to the Visigothic churchmen; his crimes, according to Mariana, were those of promoting a law whereby the Pope was disowned, and permission granted to the clergy to marry. An ecclesiastical or Roman party was soon set up against this audacious innovator,—a party which turned to the descendants of King Chintasvinthus, in order to find a royal rival to Witiza.

These descendants were two sons, brothers of Recesvinthus, Theodofred and Favila, the Dukes of Cordova and Cantabria (Biscay). The latter was captain of the guard to Egica. Witiza, in his youth, as it is alleged, on account of his desire for the wife of this duke, slew him with a club. Pelayas, son of Favila, who seems to have been likewise an officer in the king's service, hearing of his father's death, retired to Cantabria; and Count Julian, who had married the sister of Witiza, succeeded him in military command. When Witiza became king, he, having conceived a great hatred—we are not told why —for Pelayas and his uncle Theodofred, put out the eyes of the latter, who was father to the Roderic with whom the Visigothic line of kings ended. Roderic and Pelayas escaped the wrath of Witiza. This king must—if we are to believe the stories of the Spanish writers—have seemed, in the minds of men then living, an extraordinary fool; for he threw down the walls of the fortresses in his country, pretending that this would secure peace, to which end he also took away the weapons of the people; two incredible tales, the narration of which is accounted for by the after remark of the old writer, that Witiza persecuted Gunderic, Archbishop of Toledo, and the priests of his party, who refused to join the king. After a reign of ten years Witiza died in peace—a phenomenon of note in those centuries — at Toledo (A.D. 711). Yet even in respect to the truth of this assertion we are not assured; for it is possible, we are told, that the hereditary vengeance of Roderic might have contrived this event without reference to the ordinary course of nature.

The sons of Witiza formed, as we stated elsewhere, nuclei of a party against Roderic, with whom centred the hopes of another party in the state. In fact there had been two parties with distinct representatives all along, who, so to say, ran side by side in this matter; one of them received the support of the clergy, who wrote the histories, and gave the colour of their feelings to the facts they were compelled to relate. The briefest possible history of the descent of these parties is thus given. Chintasvinthus, by his wife Riesberga, left Recesvinthus—who succeeded him on the throne—Theodofred (father of Roderic), Favila, and a daughter, whose name is unknown. Recesvinthus died without issue, and, the monarchy being elective, not hereditary, Wamba was chosen to succeed him, to the exclusion of Theodofred, whose pretensions, however, were revived by his son, Roderic. The unknown daughter married Ardebastus, a Greek of courage and ability; a soldier who received the hand of the princess as his reward. Their child was Ervigius, who deposed Wamba. This Ervigius married Liübigotona, and the pair had a daughter named Cixilona, who married Egica, the kinsman of Wamba; by means of which union it was intended to stanch the blood-feud of the rivals. Of this marriage no such remedy or help came, as might have been expected. The fruit of the union were Witiza, the king; Oppas, Archbishop of Seville; and a daughter, who married Count Julian. Witiza's two sons were Eba and Sicabutus. Theodofred, the second son of Chintasvinthus, by his wife, Ricilona, had Roderic, the last of the Visigoths. Favila, the third son of Chintasvinthus, had Pelayas, the famous champion of the Christians, from whom arose the new hopes of their power in Spain. This Pelayas, or Pelagius, as he is sometimes styled, was of character utterly the reverse to his cousin Roderic, " the last of the Goths," whose queen's name was, by the way, Egilona. Pelayas was captain of the guard to Roderic, who, whatever his descent might have been, certainly had sense enough to choose brave and good men for his companions.

To Pelayas himself fame has awarded such honour as none have better expressed than Byron—("Childe Harold," Canto I. xxxv. and xxxvi.):

> "Oh, lovely Spain! renowned, romantic land!
> Where is that standard which Pelagio bore,
> When Cava's traitor sire first called the band
> That dyed thy mountain streams with Gothic gore?
>
> "Where are those bloody banners which of yore
> Wav'd o'er thy sons, victorious to the gale,
> And drove, at last, the spoilers to their shore?
> Red gleamed the cross, and waned the crescent pale,
> While Afric's echoes thrilled with Moorish matrons' wail."

Byron's ideas of the Moors having been "spoilers" of the Peninsula, are to be understood according to his knowledge of the subject, which was "mighty small," as Sancho Panza used to say. It was Byron's object to associate in infamy the French invaders of Spain from the north, and of his own time, with the Moors who entered the country from the south, and many ages before. Here is a case of poetical injustice.

Mariana, the Spanish historian, tells us, in few words, the secret of the successful invasion of his country by the Arabs. The kingdom was torn to pieces by the power of the contending families; their diverse interests misled them in respect to all public measures; the people were effeminate; military discipline was neglected or forgotten; the people were no longer what they had been in the earlier days of the Visigothic race in the Peninsula, but abandoned to "eating, drinking, and lewdness." If any man could be competent to set this country on the safe road, it seemed at first to be Roderic, who was popular, brave, hardy, and handsome. Before him the sons of Witiza seemed to have no choice; it is alleged that they fled to Mauritania to save their lives from his cruelty; but it is clear that in this matter the old hatred of party was breaking out again; we must, accordingly, take these accounts with some hesitation. It is certain that Roderic quieted the commotions of the realm soon after his accession; in course of this proceeding it is most likely that the nuclei of the opposing factions found it wise to leave Spain.

To the good qualities we have already ascribed to Roderic must be added, if some historians are to be believed, many that are not less excellent. He had a noble greatness of soul, generosity of temper; he was witty, capable of carrying on difficult enterprises by means of his powers of application, affable, liberal, and a lover of merit. Strong of body, patient and tried in war, there seemed every hope for the realm over which this man, then in the prime of life, was called to rule. At first the hopes to which these qualities gave origin were brought to fruit; the application and decision of Roderic cleared away many of the disorders which were so injurious in the country. A terrible change soon followed these fair signs. Lust, drunkenness, and debauchery in feasting, were the causes of the ruin which came about.

There is this much to be said for Roderic, that, as Gibbon carefully points out, the Visigothic monarchy was still elective, Roderic had evidently been elected by means similar to those which had been effectual in the cases of so many of his predecessors—the means might have been murderous and rebellious. Gibbon's account, which now follows, places, in his usually perspicuous mode, the matter before the reader. The great historian declares thus in section v. cap. 41 of the "History of the Decline and Fall of the Roman Empire," after recounting the progress of Mohammedan conquests in Africa:

"In the progress of conquest from the north and the south, the Goths and the Saracens encountered each other on the confines of Europe and Africa. In the opinion of the latter, the difference of religion is a reasonable ground of enmity and warfare. As early as the time of Othman, their piratical squadrons had ravaged the coasts of Andalusia; nor had they forgotten the relief of Carthage by Gothic succours. In that age, as well as in the present, the kings of Spain were possessed of the fortress of Ceuta, one of the Columns of Hercules, which is divided by a narrow strait from the opposite pillar or point of Europe. A small portion of Mauritania was still wanting to the African conquest; but Muza, in the pride of victory, was repulsed from the walls of Ceuta by the vigilance and courage of Count Julian, the general of the Goths. From his disappointment and perplexity, Muza was relieved by an unexpected message of the Christian chief, who offered his place, his person, and his sword, to the successors of Mahomet, and solicited the disgraceful honour of introducing their arms into the heart of Spain. If we inquire into the cause of his treachery, the Spaniards still repeat the popular story of his daughter Cava, a virgin, who was seduced, or ravaged, by his sovereign; of a father who sacrificed his religion and country to the thirst of revenge. The passions of princes have often been licentious and destructive; but this well-known tale, romantic in itself, is indifferently supported by external evidence, and the history of Spain will suggest some motive more congenial to the breast of a veteran statesman."

Gibbon then proceeds with the account, which we transcribed above, and illustrated from the Spanish histories, of the efforts of the sons of Witiza, and continues: " It is probable that Julian was involved in the disgrace of the unsuccessful faction,[*] that he had little to hope and much to fear from the new reign; and that the imprudent king could not forget or forgive

---

[*] The reader will have noted before (p. 56) that Julian was the brother-in-law of Witiza, and therefore the uncle of his sons.

the injuries which Roderic and his family had sustained.* The merit and influence of the count rendered him a useful or formidable subject; his estates were ample, his followers bold and numerous; and it too fatally shows that, by his Andalusian and Mauritanian commands, he held in his hands the keys of the Spanish monarchy. Too feeble, however, to meet his sovereign in arms, he sought the aid of a foreign power; and his rash invitation to the Moors and Arabs produced the calamities of eight hundred years.† In his epistles, or in a personal interview, he revealed the wealth and nakedness of his country, the weakness of an unpopular prince, the degeneracy of an effeminate people."

Julian was a man of distinguished birth and vast possessions. He was governor, says Mariana, not only of Mauritania, but of a considerable part of Andalusia; so that he thus commanded both sides of the Straits, and held the keys of the kingdom in a wider sense than that which represents him as custodian of the fortress of Ceuta. Cartela, or its ruins, and Tarifa, or its site, were in his hands; and with the adjoining province, Calpe, itself, then but a barren, monkey-inhabited rock, yet destined to become one of the most famous spots in the world's history: a destiny which was soon to begin to have effect. In the charge of Julian the sons of Witiza found a refuge. In their political and reckless movements we

---

* We have shown before (p. 55) that Witiza had put out the eyes of Theodofred, the father of Roderic.

† As to the *calamities* in question here, it is hard to say where they are to be observed. The state of Spain under the Moors was infinitely better in civilisation than under the Visigoths. The people were ten times more numerous, their arts better, their learning nobler. Their occupation of the country gave the very Gothic people and mixed races an opportunity of recovering public virtues, which had been almost forgotten in luxury during the later part of their tenancy of Spain. (See Gibbon's own account, which follows, of the state of the Visigoths in the Peninsula.)

may find the cause of the Arabian invasion, with or without reference to Cava, Caba, or Florinda, as the daughter of the count is variously called. The political and personal hatreds of the families which derived from Chintasvinthus as their ancestor, and in whose name they contended with a common claim to the elective monarchy of Spain, needed little in the way of intensifying to promote reckless hate of the most furious kind. Julian invited the Arabs in the same manner and for the same purpose, also, as it happened, to the same effect, as the descendants of those invaders sought the aid of the Almoravides against their Moslem fellows in Spain, and brought about a new invasion from Africa (A.D. 1086); in turn, and in a like manner, these new African conquerors fell before their own successors, the Almohades (A.D. 1145). Civil war again split this powerful party, and they were expelled from Spain in 1232, to be extinguished by the Merines in 1278. "Every kingdom divided against itself is brought to desolation;" so wrote the Evangelist.

To resume, in the words of Gibbon, in detailing the condition of the Visigoths, and the effect of the invitation of Julian to Muza Ibn Nosseyr: "The Goths were no longer the victorious barbarians who had humbled the pride of Rome, despoiled the queen of nations, and penetrated from the Danube to the Atlantic Ocean. Secluded from the world by the Pyrenean mountains, the successors of Alaric had slumbered in a long peace; the walls of the cities were mouldered into dust; the youth had abandoned the exercise of arms; and the presumption of their ancient renown would expose them in a field of battle to the first assault of the invaders. The ambitious Saracen (Muza) was fired by the ease and importance of the attempt which Julian urged; but the execution was delayed until he had consulted the Commander of the

Faithful, and his messenger returned with the permission of Walid to annex the unknown kingdom of the West to the religion and throne of the Caliphs. In his residence of Tangier, Muza, with secrecy and caution, continued his correspondence and hastened his preparations. But the remorse of the conspirators was soothed by the fallacious assurance that he should content himself with the glory and spoil, without aspiring to establish the Moslems beyond the sea that separates Europe from Africa. Before Muza would trust an army of the Faithful to the traitors and infidels of a foreign land, he made a less dangerous trial of their strength and veracity. One hundred Arabs and four hundred Africans passed over, in four vessels, from Tangier or Ceuta. The place of their descent on the opposite shore of the Strait is marked by the name of Tarif, their chief; and the date of this memorable event is fixed in the month of Ramadan, of the ninety-first year of the Hegira; or the month of July, seven hundred and forty-eight years from the Spanish era of Cæsar, seven hundred and ten after the birth of Christ. From this first station they marched eighteen miles through a hilly country, to the castle and town of Julian, on which (it is still called Algezire) they bestowed the name of the Green Island, from a verdant cape that advances into the sea. Their hospitable entertainment, the Christians who joined their standard, their inroad into a fertile and unguarded province, the richness of their spoil, and the safety of their return, announced to their brethren the most favourable omens of victory. In the ensuing spring five thousand veterans and volunteers were embarked, under the command of Taric, a dauntless and skilful soldier, who surpassed the expectation of his chief;*

---

* It will be observed that Gibbon makes the leader of the second expedition to be not the same as he who commanded the former experimental journey. This is correct; the most extraordinary confusion has appeared in writings on this subject.

and the necessary transports were provided by the industry of his too faithful ally. The Saracens landed at the Pillars or point of Europe. The corrupt and familiar appellation of Gibraltar *(Gibel al Taric)* describes the mountain of Taric; and the intrenchments of his camp were the first outline of those fortifications which, in the hands of our countrymen, have resisted the art and power of the House of Bourbon. The adjacent governor informed the court of Toledo of the descent and progress of the Arabs; and the defeat of his lieutenant, Edeco, who had been commanded to seize and bind the presumptuous strangers, admonished Roderic of the magnitude of the design. At the royal summons, the dukes and counts, the bishops and nobles of the Gothic monarchy, assembled at the head of their followers; and the title of the King of the Romans, which is employed by an Arabian historian, may be occasioned by the close affinity of language, religion, and manners, between the nations of Spain. His army consisted of ninety or a hundred thousand men; a formidable power, if their fidelity and discipline had been adequate to their numbers. The troops of Taric had been augmented to twelve thousand Saracens; but the Christian malcontents were attracted by the influence of Julian, and a crowd of Africans most greedily tasted the temporal blessings of the Koran. In the neighbourhood of Cadiz, the town of Xeres has been illustrated by the encounter which determined the fate of the kingdom. The stream of the Guadalete, which falls into the bay, divided the two camps, and marked the advancing and retreating skirmishes of three successive and bloody days. On the fourth day the two armies joined a more serious and decisive issue; but Alaric would have blushed at the sight of his unworthy successor sustaining on his head a diadem of pearls, encumbered with a flowing robe of gold and silken embroidery, and reclining on a litter or car of ivory, and drawn by two white mules.* Notwithstanding the valour of the Saracens, they fainted under the weight of multitudes, and the plain of Xeres was overspread with sixteen thousand of their dead bodies. "My brethren," said Taric to his surviving companions, " the enemy is before you, the sea is behind ; whither would ye fly ? Follow your General. I am resolved to lose my life, or to trample on the prostrate King of the Romans." Besides the resource of despair, he confided in the secret correspondence and nocturnal interviews of Count Julian with the sons and the brother of Witiza. The two princes and the Archbishop of Toledo occupied the most important post. Their well-timed defection broke the ranks of the Christians ; each warrior was prompted by fear or suspicion to consult his personal safety ; and the remains of the Gothic enemy were scattered or destroyed in the flight and pursuit of the three following days. Amidst the general disorder, Roderic started from his car, and mounted Orelia, the fleetest of his horses ; but he escaped from a soldier's death to perish more ignobly in the waters of the Bætis or Guadalquivir. His diadem, his robes, and his courser, were found on the bank: but, as the body of the Gothic prince was lost in the waves, the pride and ignorance of the Caliph must have been gratified by some meaner head, which was exposed in triumph before the palace of Damascus. " And such," continues a valiant historian of the Arabs, " is the fate of those kings who withdrew themselves from a field of battle."†

Count Julian had plunged so deep into guilt and infamy, that his only hope was in the ruin of his country. After the

---

* In this description of Roderic the Arabians are unanimous.

† As to the fate of King Roderic *(see post)* his death in battle is doubted ; like those of Harold II., Richard III., and the Portuguese king, Sebastian, who was defeated by the Moors in 1578, and said to have been drowned in the river Elmahassen.

Battle of Xeres he recommended the most effectual measures to the victorious Saracens. "The King of the Goths is slain; their princes have fled before you; the army is routed; the nation is astonished. Secure with sufficient detachments the cities of Bætica; but in person, and without delay, march to the royal city of Toledo, and allow not the distracted Christians either time or tranquillity for the election of a new monarch." Taric listened to this advice. A Roman captive and proselyte, who had been enfranchised by the Caliph himself, assaulted Cordova with seven hundred horse; he swam the river, surprised the town, and drove the Christians into the Greek Church, where they defended themselves above three months. (Four hundred men so defended themselves until the last man died fighting. See *post*.) Another detachment reduced the seacoast of Bætica, which in the last period of the Moorish power has comprised in a narrow space the populous kingdom of Granada. The march of Taric from the Bætis to the Tagus was directed through the Sierra Morena, that separates Andalusia and Castile, till he appeared in arms before the walls of Toledo. The most zealous of the Catholics had escaped with the relics of their saints; and, if the gates were shut, it was only until the victor had subscribed a fair and reasonable capitulation. The voluntary exiles were allowed to depart with their effects; seven churches were appropriated to Christian worship; the archbishop and his clergy were at liberty to exercise their functions, the monks to practise or neglect their penances; and the Goths and Romans were left in civil and criminal cases to the subordinate jurisdiction of their own laws and magistrates." Taric protected the Jews, to whose aid Gibbon would have us observe that the conqueror owed not a little. "From the royal seat of Toledo, the Arabian leader spread his conquests to the

K

north, over the modern realms of Castile and Leon; but it is needless to enumerate the cities that yielded to his approach, or again to describe the table of emerald, transported from the East by the Romans, acquired by the Goths among the spoils of Rome, and presented by the last to the throne of Damascus.* Beyond the Asturian mountains, the maritime town of Gijon was the term of the lieutenant of Muza, who had performed, with the speed of a traveller, his victorious march of seven hundred miles from the Rock of Gibraltar to the Bay of Biscay. The failure of land compelled him to retreat; and he was recalled to Toledo, to excuse his presumption of subduing a kingdom in the absence of his general. Spain, which, in a more savage and disorderly state, had resisted, for two hundred years, the arms of the Romans, was overrun in a few months by the Saracens; and such was the eagerness of submission, that the governor of Cordova is recorded as the only chief who fell without conditions a prisoner into their hands." Gibbon goes on to detail the causes of this wonderful success. He then describes how it was checked, and where was to be laid the foundations of the since prodigious power of the Spaniard. " Yet a spark of vital flame was still alive; some invincible fugitives preferred a life of poverty and freedom in the Asturian valleys; the hardy mountaineers repulsed the slaves of the Caliph; and the sword of Pelagius has been transformed into the sceptre of the Catholic king."

What came of that sword and its valiant employer has been hinted at before, and will appear by and by. Meanwhile, from the Arabian accounts of this momentous business, which Gibbon described with his somewhat monotonous felicity,

---

* Of this precious emerald (green glass) table, see *post*.

there is much to be learned. We take, in the first case, from the "History of the Dominion of the Arabs in Spain," by the Spanish historian Condé, as translated by Mrs. Jonathan Foster, published by Mr. Bohn, 1854. This is by far too animated and picturesque to be omitted here.

After describing the progress of the Arabs in North Africa, our new authority goes on thus:—"At this time certain Christians of Gesiras Al-andalus, which is the peninsula of Spain, offended by their king, Roderic,* who was lord of all Spain, from the Narbonese Gaul even to Mauritania, or the land of Tanja, came to Muza Ibn Nosseyr, and incited him to pass into Spain, which is separated from Africa by a strait of the sea called Alzacane or the Narrow Waters. They represented to him that the undertaking would be free from danger, easy of execution, and offered to aid him therein with all their forces; such was the immoderate desire for vengeance by which these men were moved." Accordingly, and not desiring to risk his soldiers in a possible trap, Muza made inquiries. "We find related on this point that one of the principal Christians of Tanja informed him, with much truth and accuracy, of all that he required to know on the subject—made known to him the state of the people, the injudicious government of King Roderic, his defective mode of administering justice, and the fact that, for these causes, he was but little respected by the nation he ruled, by whom he was in effect considered as the wrongful usurper of the crown of the

---

* "The affront here," says Condé, "alluded to, is without doubt that caused by the amours of the king, Don Roderic, with the daughter of Count Julian, whom certain writers call the Caba, as we find related in the Chronicon General, written by order of King Alfonso the Wise. The names of 'Caba,' of her waiting-maid 'Alifa,' and of all who appear in the account, prove that the whole story was but a Moorish fiction founded on the legends and ballads current among the Christians and Moors."

Goths." Spain was described to the Arab chieftain in the most tempting terms; indeed, Strabo's account is not so glowing as that which was presented to Muza Ibn Nosseyr. "This enumeration (of its merits) they completed by citing the various cities in which remained monuments of the ancient kings and of those Ionians whose wisdom and knowledge had ever been acknowledged by the whole world, relics of their works being yet amply existent in Spain, as these men did not fail to affirm. They instanced the great statue of Hercules in Gezira of Cadiz (?), and the idol of Gallicia, with the vast ruins of Merida and Tarragona, of which the like have never been seen in any other region." Muza obtained the Caliph's permission to "bear into Spain the knowledge of God and Alcoranic law." This permission was granted, and Muza commissioned Taric ben Zeyad,* "a captain of great renown," to make such a reconnaisance as has been before referred to. The second voyage was accordingly undertaken upon the success of the first, and this time with prodigious increase of force, for "there was not an Arab who did not desire to take part in this expedition, which set sail when all had been fully prepared. Crossing the strait without accident, Taric disembarked at Gezira Alhadra, or the Green Island, the situation of which favoured the landing of the troops.† The Christians did, indeed, oppose some resistance to the debarkation, but were quickly beaten, and retired in terror and dismay. Taric now fortified himself with his people on a hill at the extremity of Gezira Alhadra, which, from that time, and in his honour, was called Gebal Taric, or the Mount of Taric;

---

* This is one of Condé's mistakes.

† At this time there were two small islands near the shore and opposite the present city of Algeciras, whose verdant colour obtained for them the name of the Green Isles. They are now almost entirely covered by the sea. The smaller, of which a portion still remains, is called the Isle of Doves (*Las Palomas*)—*Condé* (?).

but it is also called the Mount of Victory, or the Portal or Entrance,* seeing that from that point the way was happily opened to our conquest of Spain. This arrival took place on a Tuesday,† the fifth day of the moon of Regib, in the year 92; and Xerif Edris affirms that Taric burnt his ships to deprive his troops of all hopes of flight.

The passage from the Green Island to the main land was at first defended by seventeen hundred Christians under the command of Tadmir (Theodoric), who was one of King Roderic's most distinguished knights, and with these forces the Arab troops had some few skirmishes during the first three days; but after that time, the Spaniards, having been more than once vanquished and put to flight, no longer dared to present themselves before the Moslemah. We find it related that Tadmir then wrote to King Roderic, demanding succour, and saying, "My lord, there have come fierce adventurers from parts of Africa. Whether they have dropped from heaven, or sprung up through the earth, I know not, having found them suddenly before me, and encountered them on my path. I resisted them with all my power, and did my utmost to maintain the passage, but have been compelled to yield to their numbers and the impetuosity of their attack; wherefore they have finally encamped on our soil, in despite of my efforts. And now, my lord, since the matter is thus, I entreat you to succour us with all speed, and with the largest force you can muster; come yourself also, in person, for that will be better than all." The Gothic forces were assembled from all quarters, and those of Taric, plundering and doing all possible harm, advanced even to the banks of the Bætis, or Guadiana.

---

* This seems to have been a much less ancient title than the former, and derived from the landing at Gibraltar of the great Arab conqueror, Abd-l-Mumen Ibn Ali.

† Another error. It was Thursday, as Gayangos discovered.

We shall put the truth of this momentous invasion before the reader at once, in order that the confusion of many accounts may be obviated as soon as possible. The history of the attacks in question was as follows:—Julian was sent first as an invader of his own country, and after his tender to Muza; this was done not only to sound the way for those who were to follow, but, by compelling him to commit himself against Roderic, to prove his sincerity in inviting the Arabs to the destruction of his people; he met with considerable success, both in making captives of his enemies, and in finding friends. This took place some short time after Roderic's ascent to the throne, *i.e.* in November or December, 709, and was a mere incursion, distinguishable from many that had preceded it, from the coast of Africa to that of Spain, in respect to the creed of its commander and his followers; it was made in two vessels. Next came the attack of Tarif, which was effected in four vessels, with four hundred foot and one hundred horsemen. This took place in August or September, 710, and the landing was made at Tarifa, as the former was upon the coast of Algeciras. The confusion in these accounts is not only of modern date, but existed among the Arabs themselves, as Al-makkari points out when he writes that some historians have made two men out of Tarif Abu Zarah, by divorcing the two parts of his name. Tarif returned laden with spoil. Taric followed in the next year with seven thousand men, "chiefly slaves and Berbers, very few only being genuine Arabs," and with them Julian went again. The whole of this body of troops crossed the Straits in four vessels, which went to and fro until all were carried over. Good omens attended the passage of Taric, both in a dream and in an extraordinary prophecy which was related to him by an old woman of Algeciras, who averred that her husband, who was dead, and had been a diviner, had declared to her that Andalus would be conquered by a man having a prominent forehead, and a black mole covered with hair on his left shoulder. Both of these signs were on Taric's body. When the landing was made by Taric, he was met by the count of the district, Theodomir (Tadmir, whose name long stood for that of his province). Roderic was in the north of Spain at this time, and engaged in fighting against the Basques, near Pamplona. Muza did not follow his lieutenants until the summer of A.D. 712. Al-makkari says he "avoided Gibraltar, where no doubt a camp was."

CHAPTER IX.

LEGENDS OF KING RODERIC.

BEFORE we recount, in the bold words of the Moorish historian, the death of Roderic, it will be well to refer to the picturesque legends with which his downfall has been adorned. These form the basis of several Spanish romances and of whole chronicles in Spanish and Moorish, besides modern poems in English, such as those of Scott, called "The Vision of Don Roderic," and Southey's "Roderic, the Last of the Goths." With allied subjects are Landor's "Count Julian," and other works of men who have been tempted by this dramatic subject.

Here is the story of Cava, briefly told to our hand by Howell in his "Letters from Spain." Count Julian was ambassador in Barbary from King Roderic, and his daughter, Cava, one of the maids of honour to Agilona, the Queen of Spain. Cava was very beautiful, and attracted the passion of the king with overwhelming and irresistible force, so that, finding entreaties unavailing, Roderic employed violence upon the maiden, who, thus deflowered, and not knowing what to do, submitted for a time to her disgrace, and, being assured that any messenger she might send to Count Julian would be watched and his letters intercepted if they referred to her dishonour, wrote to her father in the manner of a parable, to this effect: "that there was a fair green apple on the table, and the king's poinard fell upon it and cleft it in two." Julian receiving this secret message, comprehended its meaning, and, in order to revenge, obtained permission to return home on some ordinary business. This permission was granted by the king, whom the apparent submission, if not the pretended love, of Cava had completely deceived.

Arrived in Spain, Julian continued the deceit, and made himself so agreeable to King Roderic, that the monarch concluded the wrong done was unknown to or acquiesced in by his general and courtier. Julian became his most trusted counsellor and favourite, so that his advice was sought and taken in all things. Actuated by the most crafty and reckless spirit of revenge, the count advised that, as the kingdom was at peace with all its neighbours, there was no need to keep up the military and naval guardianship of the coast, which was as costly as it was alleged to be useless. This treacherous counsel being taken, and the kingdom being left defenceless before invaders, the traitor obtained leave to visit his friends in Tarragona, which was three hundred miles from Malaga, where the royal court was then held. After a little while, during which Cava had been left with the king—and no hint of vengeance given by herself or her father, so that the king's conscience was lulled to sleep with his fears—Julian pretended that his wife, Cava's mother, was dangerously ill, and that the daughter must visit her—it might be to receive her dying breath. Cava went, and the gate by which she departed from Malaga is called after her name in the district. Having thus extricated all his family from the king's power, Julian sailed over to Barbary, laid the secret of his country's weakness before the Moslemah, and thus brought about the change of authority which it underwent with surprising facility.

The story of the Arabs, with regard to this message, is that, despite the watchfulness of Roderic upon his victim, she contrived to warn her father of what had befallen her, by sending him a rotten egg among the articles of a splendid gift, which she despatched to him at his castle of Ceuta. No sooner had Julian received this, than divining what had happened, he crossed over to Andalus, and repaired to Toledo, although doing this was contrary to orders, because it was not yet the time fixed for his presentation, it being then the month of January. When Roderic saw Ilyan (Julian) come so unexpectedly, he said to him "O Ilyan! what ails thee, to come to me at this season of the year, in the depth of winter?" and Ilyan replied, "I come to fetch my daughter, for her mother is very ill, and I fear her death, and she has expressed a strong desire to see our daughter, that she may console her in her last moments." Then Roderic observed, "Hast thou procured us the hawks we told thee of?"* "Yes, I have," answered Ilyan, "I have found thee such as thou never sawest the like of in thy life; I shall soon return with them, and bring them to thee, if God be pleased." Ilyan was all this time meaning the Arabs. He then took his daughter, and returned without loss of time to the seat of his government. " Upon this followed," says the Arabian writer, "the negotiation with Muza Ibn Nosseyr" (Appendix to Gayangos' translation of Al-makkari's " History of the Mahommedan Dynasties in Spain").

The story which is thus variously told may or may not be true, but there is very little doubt that, with or without a Cava or a Julian, some invasion would have been attempted by the Arabs, who had just before that time reached the western extremity of their prodigious line of conquests from

---

* Hawks of Mount Atlas, which neighboured to Julian's province, were famous for fierceness and strength before and long after the time which is in question.

the heart of Arabia. Invasions of comparatively unimportant character had been attempted unsuccessfully during several years before Taric landed at Gibraltar. The story of Cava is told in many ways; that which we have given is commonly accepted, but it has also been dressed in even more romantic guises, of the prose as well as of the poetical sorts. The most effective and coherent of these we next proceed to detail as completely as the occasion and our limits allow.

The crime which is imputed to Roderic has been already indicated as the alleged provocation or justification of the treachery of Count Julian. The conduct of Cava herself has been looked upon in many lights, some of which display her as the victim of the violence or the seductive arts of the king, others as his willing mistress. Her true name was Florinda, which, in memory of this unfortunate holder, is never bestowed upon their children by the Spaniards. They give it to their female dogs, so says Cervantes. The Moors retain her name with the same feeling of abhorrence; for, says Voltaire, they had given to a dangerous promontory on their coast the title of "The Cape of the Caba Rumia," *i.e.* "The Cape of the Wicked Christian Woman." They aver that she was buried on that cape, and consider it unlucky to be compelled to put into the bay it incloses on one side. It should be remembered that the story of King Roderic has been written by his enemies, and that, as with many of the monsters of "history," it is not impossible to see a side of the subject which is less dishonourable than that which is commonly presented to us.

The atrocity of the crime which is charged against King Roderic was heightened by the alleged fact of one of the many versions of this legend, that, at the time Florinda was ravished, Count Julian was defending Ceuta against the Moors. The indignity and the opportunity were, so runs the tale, too powerful for the loyalty, or even for the patriotism, of the count, and he betrayed—as all the histories declare, see those of the Moors, which we have just cited—the fortress in his charge to the besiegers, and led their forces in the most effectual manner against his country, and was revenged upon his king. The story avers that, in the interval of time which elapsed between the crime of Roderic and its punishment, the conscience of the king was awakened by his fears, and the effects of these powers upon a sinful and superstitious nature made him wretched to such a degree that he determined to test an ancient tradition, concerning the so-called Vault of Destiny, which was said to exist among some Roman ruins, at a short distance from Toledo, where King Recesvinthus had an adventure with an enchanted knight, who was transformed from the shape of a stag, which the royal hunter pursued into a cave, and in that cave challenged him to combat. The challenge was accepted, begun, and continued for some time, without a result. At length the enchanted warrior, finding that he could achieve nothing, desisted, and, in the course of conversation, informed the astonished king that he was not the monarch for whom the adventure of the cavern was destined; and, further, predicted the downfall of the Visigothic rule and the Christian faith in Spain, which would attend the discovery of the mysteries of the place. Appalled at this announcement, Recesvinthus ordered the entrance to the cavern to be built up, and secured by ponderous bars of iron. So it remained for half a century, and the adventure was expressed as a popular legend, which haunted the royal house of Spain * with inexpressible terrors.

---

* One of Calderon's plays—*Origen, perdida y restauracion de la Virgen del Sagrario*—comprises this story among its multifarious incidents. See notes to Sir Walter Scott's *Vision of Don Roderic*. The play in question is analysed in Sismondi's *Hist. Lit. Midi.* c. xxxiv.

The story is told by Roderic, Archbishop of Toledo, one of the earlier chroniclers of Spain; and in a much more effective manner by one of the " True Histories of the king, Don Roderic " :

"One mile on the east side of the city of Toledo, among some rocks, was situated an ancient tower, of a magnificent structure, though much dilapidated by time, which consumes all: four estadoes (*i.e.* four times a man's height) below it there was a cave with a very narrow entrance, and a gate cut out of the solid rock, lined with a strong covering of iron, and fastened with many locks; above the gate some Greek letters were engraved, which, although abbreviated and of doubtful meaning, were thus interpreted, according to the exposition of learned men: 'The king who opens this cave and can discover the wonders, will discover both good and evil things.' Many kings desired to know the mystery of this tower, and sought with much care to find out the manner of obtaining an entrance; but when they opened the gate such a tremendous noise arose in the cave that it appeared as if the earth was bursting, so that many of those who were present sickened, and others lost their lives with fear. In order to prevent such great perils (as they supposed a dangerous enchantment was contained within), the gate was secured with new locks, concluding that, though a king was destined to open it, the fated time was not yet arrived. At last, King Don Roderic, led on by his evil fortune and unlucky destiny, opened the tower; and some bold attendants, whom he had brought with him, entered, although agitated with fear. Having proceeded a good way, they fled back to the entrance, terrified by a frightful vision which they had beheld. The king was greatly moved, and ordered many torches, so contrived that the tempest in the cave would not extinguish them, to be lighted.

"Then the king entered, not without fear, before all the others. They discovered, by degrees, a splendid hall, apparently built in a very sumptuous manner; in the middle stood a bronze statue of very ferocious appearance, which held a battle-axe in its hands. With this he struck the floor violently, giving it such heavy blows that the noise in the cave was occasioned by the motion of the air. The king, greatly affrighted and astonished, began to conjure this terrible vision, promising that he would return without doing any injury in the cave, after he had obtained a sight of what was contained in it. The statue ceased to strike the floor, and the king, with his followers somewhat assured and recovering their courage, proceeded into the hall, and on the left of the statue they found this inscription on the wall, 'Unfortunate king, thou hast entered here in evil hour.' On the right side of the wall these words were inscribed : ' By strange nations thou shalt be dispossessed, and thy subjects foully degraded.' On the shoulders of the statue other words were written, which said, ' I call upon the Arabs.' And upon his breast was written, ' I do my office.' At the entrance of the hall there was placed a round bowl, from which a great noise, like the fall of waters, proceeded. They found no other thing in the hall, and when the king, sorrowful and greatly affected, had scarcely turned about to leave the cavern, the statue again commenced its accustomed blows upon the floor. After they had mutually promised to conceal what they had seen, they again closed the tower, and blocked up the gate of the cavern with earth, that no memory might remain in the world of such a portentous and evil-boding prodigy. The ensuing midnight they heard great cries and clamour from the cave, resounding like the noise of battle, and the ground shaking with a tremendous roar. The whole edifice of the old tower fell to the ground, by which they were greatly affrighted, the vision which they had beheld appearing to them as a dream.

"The king, having left the tower, ordered wise men to explain what the inscriptions signified, and, having consulted upon and studied their meaning, they declared that the statue of bronze, with the motion which it made with its battle-axe, signified Time, and that its office alluded to in the inscription on its breast, was, that he never rests a single moment. The words on the shoulders, ' I call upon the Arabs,' they expounded that, in time, Spain would be conquered by the Arabs. The words upon the left wall signified the destruction of

King Roderic; those on the right, the dreadful calamities which were to fall upon the Spaniards and Goths, and that the unfortunate king would be dispossessed of all his states. Finally, the letters on the portal indicated that good would betide to the conquerors and evil to the conquered, of which experience proved the truth."

The Arab account of the legend appears in this form: There was in Tangiers a Rúmi (Roman or Goth) named Ilyan (Julian), who was Al-makaddam (Count of the Marches) of Roderic, King of Andalus, who held his court at Toledo. This monarch was the same under whose reign Andalus was invaded and subdued by the Arabs. One of the causes which is said to have contributed to that event is the following: There was at Toledo a palace, the gate of which was secured with many locks, for every king who ruled over that country added a lock to the gate, and none ever dared to open it, nor did any one know what it contained. The number of the locks had already reached twenty—one for each of the kings who had governed that country—when the said Roderic ascended the throne of Andalus. He then said, "I must have the gate of this palace opened, that I may see what is inside." But his counts and bishops said to him, "Do no such thing, O king! do not innovate upon a custom we have kept most religiously." But Roderic replied, "No, you shall not persuade me; I must have it opened and see what it contains." He then caused the gate to be thrown open, but he found nothing inside save a roll of parchment, on which was pourtrayed figures of turbanned men, mounted on generous steeds, having swords in their hands, and spears with fluttering pennons at the ends. This roll contained, besides, an inscription, "The men represented in this picture are the Arabs, the same who, whenever the locks of this palace are broken, will invade the island and subdue it entirely." When Roderic saw this, he repented of what he had done, and caused the gates to be shut. Andalus is often spoken of by the Arabian historians as an island. With this term, Al-makkari wrote of it in the beginning of his book. The name of Algeciras may be but a particular application to the point of arrival of a name, Al-gesira, which applied to the whole country. Thus, a man said he was going to the island, Al-gesira, or Spain, of which the nearest point ultimately received the name in question.

Scott, in his " Vision of Don Roderic," shifted, or rather adapted, the scene from this legendary spot of the terrible vision to another in the precincts of the Cathedral of Toledo, to which, at his order, the archbishop of that city led the king:

> " By winding stair, dark aisle, and secret nook,
> Then on an ancient gateway bent his look;
> And as the key the desperate king essay'd,
> Low-mutter'd thunder, the cathedral shook,
> And twice he stopp'd, and twice new effort made,
> Till the huge bolts roll'd back, and the loud hinges bray'd.

> " Long, large, and lofty was that vaulted hall;
> Roof, walls, and floor were all of marble stone,
> Of polish'd marble, black as funeral pall,
> Carved o'er with signs and characters unknown;
> A paly light, as of the dawning, shone
> Through the sad bounds, but whence they could not spy;
> For window to the upper air was none;
> Yet, by that light, Don Roderic could descry
> Wonders that ne'er till then were seen by mortal eye.

> " Grim sentinels, against the upper wall,
> Of molten bronze, two statues held their place;
> Massive their naked limbs, their stature tall,
> Their frowning foreheads golden circles grace.
> Moulded they seem'd for kings of giant race,
> That lived and sinn'd before the avenging flood;
> This grasp'd a scythe, that rested on a mace;
> This spread his wings for flight, that pondering stood,
> Each stubborn seem'd and stern, immutable of mood.

> "Fix'd was the right-hand giant's brazen look
> Upon his brother's glass of shifting sand,
> As if its ebb be measured by a book,
> Whose iron volume loaded his huge hand;
> In which was wrote of many a falling land,
> Of empires lost, and kings to exile driven:
> And o'er that pair their names in scroll expand —
> 'Lo, DESTINY and TIME! to whom by Heaven
> The guidance of the earth is for a season given' —
>
> "Even while they read, the sand-glass wastes away;
> And, as the last and lagging grains did creep,
> That right-hand giant 'gan his club upsway,
> As one that startles from a heavy sleep.
> Full on the upper wall the mace's sweep
> At once descended with the force of thunder,
> And hurtling down at once, in crumbled heap,
> The marble boundary was rent asunder,
> And gave to Roderic's view new sights of fear and wonder."

The sights thus presented to Roderic were of the sort such as the Arabian account of the battle can best tell.

Roderic, who was recalled from the north of Spain—where he had been quelling an insurrection—by the news of the landing of the Arabs, arrived on the plains of Sidonia with an army of ninety thousand men, and was accompanied by all the nobles of his kingdom; yet Taric was not intimidated by this numerous host, which appeared to him but as an agitated sea; for he knew that if his Moslemah were inferior in point of numbers, they possessed advantages in valour, in the quality of their arms, and in the dexterity with which they used them. It is true that the first and last ranks of the Christians were armed in coats of mail and cuirasses of proof; but the remainder of the force was without this defence. Yet they, too, were in part provided with lances, shields, and swords; while in the other parts they were lightly armed with bows and arrows, slings, and other weapons, each according to the fashion of his country; some having short scythes, clubs, or battle-axes only.

The Moslem leaders thereupon assembled their scattered bands, and recalled the divisions of their flying cavalry, when, being all united, Taric arranged his forces, prepared them for the struggle, and, full of confidence, stood ready to give the Christians battle.

The opposing hosts first found themselves face to face on the plains traversed by the Guadalete.* The day was Sunday, and there still remained two days of the moon of Ramazan. The earth trembled under the tramp of the forces, and the air resounded with the clash of trumpets, the thunder of the drums, the roar of a thousand other instruments, and the mingled outcries of the vast multitude comprising both the hosts. They met with equal bravery and resolution, although with much disparity of numbers, since the Christians had four men for one of the Moslemah. The battle commenced with the dawn of day, and was maintained on both sides with equal constancy; but without advantage for either party. The carnage thus continued until the arrival of night compelled the combatants to give a truce to its sanguinary horrors. Both hosts passed the hours of darkness on the field of battle, and waited impatiently for the arrival of dawn to renew the fight; and when the first light appeared in the east they recommenced the murderous struggle, yet still with the same results. Nothing decisive was gained on either side, and with the second arrival of darkness only did the slaughter cease.

On the third morning of the cruel strife, Taric observed that the Moslemah began to lose heart, and were yielding ground to the Christians; wherefore, riding through the ranks of his people, he rose aloft in his stirrups and addressed them

---

* The inquiries of Gayangos decide the question which was formerly debated of the site of this momentous conflict. It happened much nearer the sea than was believed, and near the mouth of the river Guadalete.

as follows: "O Moslemah, conquerors of Almagreb!* whither tend your steps? To what end your unworthy and inconsiderate flight? The enemies are before you, but behind you is the sea. There is no help for you, save in your own valour and the aid of God. On, therefore, warriors and Moslemah! on! Do as you see your leader shows you the example!" Saying these words, he spurred his horse directly forwards, cut down all before him to right and left, and so forced his way to the Christian banners. Here Taric recognised the king by his decorations and the horse he rode; wherefore, transpiercing him with his lance, the unhappy Roderic fell dead; for so did God destroy him by the hand of Taric; and thus did he bring aid to the Moslemah. The troops of the Faith then cut down all before them, according to the example of their leader; and the Christians, seeing their monarch, with many others of their principal captains, lying dead, fell into disorder, and fled terrified from the field. The Arabs followed their victory. They pursued the fugitives, and the swords of the Moslemah cavalry drank deep of Christian blood in places far and wide from the plains whereon the battle had been fought. Nay, there were so many slaughtered, that God, who created them, can alone recount their numbers. Thus did the battle conclude. The victory of Guadalete was gained on the fifth day of the moon Xawal; and that district remained covered with the bones of the dead for a very long space of time thereafter.

Taric took the head of King Roderic, and sent it to Muza Ibn Nosseyr, giving him intelligence of his various successes, as well at the passing of Alzacauc (the Straits of Gibraltar) as in the victories that followed, relating at length the sanguinary

---

* Western Barbary.

and perilous Battle of Guadalete, wherein he had overcome all the power of the King of the Goths, and had dispersed his immense army.

In this relation, Taric described to Muza how, on the first day, King Roderic entered into the battle, seated in a chariot of war, adorned with ivory ornaments, and drawn by two large white mules. On his head he wore a crown or diadem of pearls, while a rich chlamys, or mantle of purple, broidered with gold, was the covering of his shoulders. The narrator goes on to tell, in the manner of Eastern literature, how the messenger gave to Muza his own account of those matters, a sort of duplicate, or repetition, such as often appears in Homer, of the subject, with one or two very characteristic additions. "These details were heard with much pleasure by the Wali, who said that he would send the head of King Roderic to the Caliph Walid.* Such," exclaims the sententious narrator, " are the misfortunes that may happen to monarchs when they take a conspicuous place in the midst of the battle!"

Thus far the Arabian historian; but there are several accounts of the fate of Roderic, which differ considerably from his. The Christian writers style the battle, which the Arabs name after Guadalete, that of Xeres (Asta of the Romans), which is two leagues from Cadiz, at the foot of the mountains on the north side of the Guadalete, between Rota and Arcos. The Guadalete was the Chryssus of antiquity.

Mariana's (the famous Spanish historian) account of the battle

---

* It is said that on the same day when the messengers of Muza informed the Caliph of the conquest of Andalus, eleven more messengers, from divers parts of the earth, bore to him news of similar victories gained by the Arabs, and that Walid fell on his knees and praised God.

does not differ essentially as to the beginning of the combat from the above, but it gives these further particulars of its course and termination: " First they began with slings, dirks, javelins, and lances; then came to the swords; a long time the battle was dubious, but the Moors seemed to have the worst till D. Oppas, the archbishop, having at that time concealed his treachery, in the heat of the fight, with a great body of his followers, went over to the infidels. He joined Count Julian, with whom were a great number of Goths, and both together fell upon the flank of our army. Our men, horrified with that unparalleled treachery, and tired with fighting, could no longer sustain that charge, but were easily put to flight. The king performed the part not only of a wise general, but of a resolute soldier, relieving the weakest, bringing on fresh men in place of those that were tired, and stopping those that turned their backs. At length, seeing no hope left, he alighted out of his chariot for fear of being taken, and, mounted on a horse called Orelia, he withdrew out of the battle. The Goths, who still stood, missing him, were most part put to the sword; the rest betook themselves to flight. The camp was immediately entered, and the baggage taken. What number was killed was not known; I suppose they were so many it was hard to count them. This single battle robbed Spain of all its glory, and in it perished the renowned name of the Goths. The king's horse, upper garments, and buskins, covered with pearls and precious stones, were found on the bank of the river Guadalete, and there being no news of him afterwards, it was supposed he was drowned passing the river."

Scott, in describing that part of the "Vision" which supplies so many effective elements to his poem, thus refers to the death of Roderic:

> "' Is not yon steed Orelia?'—'Yes, 'tis mine!
> But never was she turn'd from battle-line;
>   Lo! where the recreant spurs o'er stock and stone!
> Curses pursue the slave, and wrath divine!
>   Rivers ingulf him!'—'Hush!' in shuddering tone,
> The prelate said, 'Rash prince: yon vision form's thine own!'
>
> "Just then a torrent passed the flier's course;
>   The dangerous ford the kingly Likeness tried;
> But the deep eddies whelm'd both man and horse,
>   Swept like benighted peasant down the tide."

It is also said that Roderic was not slain in the battle or drowned in the river, but found refuge in a Lusitanian monastery, where for many centuries a tomb was shown, which was inscribed, "HERE LIES RODERIC, LAST OF THE GOTHS."

The fate of King Roderic, as might be expected, made a deep impression upon the Spanish people; their romantic songs and ballads abundantly refer to it, and the catastrophe with which it is involved. The second part of "Don Quixote" contains, in the chapter about the puppet show, a reference to this event, and the sufferer by the violence of the Don laments his loss with a quotation from one of these ballads, which has thus been admirably reproduced by Lockhart in his "Ancient Spanish Ballads":

> "The hosts of Don Rodrigo were scattered in dismay,
>   When lost was the eighth battle, nor heart nor hope had they;
> He, when he saw that field was lost, and all his hope was flown,
>   He turned him from his flying host, and took his way alone.
>
> "His horse was bleeding, blind and lame—he could no farther go;
>   Dismounted, without path or aim, the king stepped to and fro;
> It was a sight of pity to look on Roderic,
>   For, sore athirst and hungry, he staggered faint and sick.
>
> "All stained and strewed with dust and blood, like to some smouldering brand
>   Plucked from the flame, Rodrigo showed; his sword was in his hand,
> But it was hacked into a saw of dark and purple tint;
>   His jewelled mail had many a flaw, his helmet many a dint.

> "He climbed unto a hill-top, the highest he could see—
> Thence all about of that wild rout his last long look took he;
> He saw his royal banners, where they lay drenched and torn,
> He heard the cry of victory, the Arabs' shout of scorn.
>
> "He looked for the brave captains that led the hosts of Spain,
> But all were fled except the dead, and who could count the slain?
> Where'er his eye could wander, all bloody was the plain,
> And, while thus he said, the tears he shed ran down his cheeks like rain:
>
> "'Last night I was the King of Spain; to-day no king am I;
> Last night fair castles held my train—to-night where shall I lie?
> Last night a hundred pages did serve me on the knee,—
> To-night not one I call my own:—not one pertains to me.
>
> "Oh, luckless, luckless was the hour, and cursed was the day,
> When I was born to have the power of this great seignory!
> Unhappy me, that I should see the sun go down to-night!
> O Death, why now so slow art thou—why fearest thou to smite?'"

Master Peter's lamentation in "Don Quixote" vented itself in the words of Don Roderic in the ballad. The Don had made as short work of his imperial and royal puppets as the Moors of his Majesty's subjects. "The Penitence of King Roderic" is another of these ballads; to it Sancho Panza ("Don Quixote," part ii. book iii. chap. 1) calls the attention of the Duchess. Lockhart reproduced this work as follows; it refers to one of the many legends about the woeful death of the monarch:

> "It was when the King Rodrigo had lost his realm of Spain,
> In doleful plight he held his flight o'er Guadalete's plain;
> Afar from the fierce Moslem he fain would hide his woe,
> And up among the wilderness of mountains he would go.
>
> "There lay a shepherd by a rill with all his flock beside him;
> He asked him where upon his hill a weary man might hide him;
> 'Not far,' quoth he, 'within this wood dwells our old Eremite;
> He in his holy solitude will hide ye all the night.'
>
> "'Good friend,' quoth he, 'I hunger!' 'Alas!' the shepherd said,
> 'My scrip no more containeth but one little loaf of bread.'
> The weary king was thankful; the poor man's loaf he took;
> He by him sate, and, while he ate, his tears fell in the brook.

" From underneath his garment the king unlocked his chain,
  A golden chain, with many a link, and the royal ring of Spain ;
  He gave them to the wondering man, and, with heavy steps and slow,
  He up the wild his way began, to the hermitage to go.

" The sun had just descended into the western sea,
  And the holy man was sitting in the breeze beneath his tree ;
  ' I come, I come, good father, to beg a boon of thee :
  This night within thy hermitage give shelter unto me.'

" The old man looked upon the king—he scann'd him o'er and o'er—
  He looked with looks of wondering—he marvelled more and more.
  With blood and dust distained was the garment that he wore,
  And yet in utmost misery a kingly look he bore.

" ' Who art thou, weary stranger ? This path why hast thou ta'en ? '
  ' I am Rodrigo ; yesterday men called me King of Spain :—
  I come to make my penitence within this lonely place ;
  Good father, take thou no offence, for God and Mary's grace ! '

" The Hermit looked with fearful eye upon Rodrigo's face—
  ' Son, mercy dwells with the Most High—not hopeless is thy case ;
  Thus far thou well hast chosen—I to the Lord will pray ;
  He will reveal what penance may wash thy sin away.'

" Now, God us shield ! it was revealed that he his bed must make
  Within a tomb, and share its gloom with a black and living snake.
  Rodrigo bowed his humbled head when God's command he heard,
  And with the snake prepared his bed, according to the word.

" The holy Hermit waited till the third day was gone—
  Then knocked he with his finger upon the cold tombstone ;
  ' Good king, good king,' the Hermit said, ' an answer give to me,
  How fares it with thy darksome bed and dismal company ? '

" ' Good father,' said Rodrigo, ' the snake hath touched me not ;
  Pray for me, holy Hermit—I need thy prayers, God wot ;
  Because the Lord his anger keeps I lie unharmed here ;
  The sting of earthly vengeance sleeps—a worser pain I fear.'

" The Eremite his breast did smite when thus he heard him say ;
  He turned him to his cell—that night he loud and long did pray ;
  At morning hour he came again—then doleful moans heard he ;
  From out the tomb the cry did come of gnawing misery.

"THE PENITENCE OF DON RODERIC."

"He spake, and heard Rodrigo's voice: ' O, Father Eremite,
He eats me now, he eats me now, I feel the adder's bite ;
The part that was most sinning my bedfellow doth rend ;
There had my curse beginning, God grant that it may end !'

"The holy man made answer in words of hopeful strain ;
He bade him trust the body's pang would save the spirit's pain.
Thus died the good Rodrigo, thus died the King of Spain,
Wash'd from offence the spirit hence to God its flight hath ta'en."*

---

* *Ancient Spanish Ballads: Historical and Romantic.* Translated by J. G. Lockhart, Esq. 4th Ed. London: John Murray. 1853.

CHAPTER X.

SKETCH OF THE HISTORY OF THE CONQUEST.

WITH the progress of the conquest of Spain by the Arabs we propose not now to concern ourselves at length. Upon some points of the subject we shall enlarge further on, and when dealing with another section of our history. A few words about the Arab conquest will suffice here. The rapid advance of this people is almost unexampled in history, for, however overwhelming may have been many like achievements, they have never, to the best of our recollection, been permanently effected, so that long possession followed capture. Gibbon's noble " History of the Decline and Fall of the Roman Empire " will, in its sections appertaining to our theme, supply sufficient materials for study by those who wish to take a general survey of the subject, especially in its bearings upon the state of Europe, Asia, and Africa, during the long period which succeeded the establishment of the dominion of the Arabs in Spain. If our limits and plan were henceforth more comprehensive than is the case, we might here detail the treatment which the jealousy of Muza vouchsafed to his energetic lieutenant Taric, the real founder of the Fortress of Gibraltar, to which he gave his name, and which has preserved that name for multitudes of ears which have never received knowledge of his ungenerous superior, or even of their common master, the Caliph Walid himself. In short, Muza, some time after he heard of the victorious progress of his deputy, crossed the

Straits with considerable reinforcements, and, in the Caliph Walid's name, took possession of the enormous spoils of the country. Deeply offended that his lieutenant had so far exceeded his orders and overrun the kingdom of the Peninsula without further authority than had been given to him, Muza demanded a rigid account of the treasures taken, disgraced Taric, and even, it is said, scourged him with his own hands. Taric appealed with success to the Commander of the Faithful, and was reinstated. Muza was disgraced in turn, accused of vanity and falsehood, fined two hundred thousand pieces of gold, publicly whipped, and set in the sun before the palace gate at Damascus for a whole day. Abd-l-aziz, his valiant son and coadjutor in conquest, having been accused of desiring to set up an independent kingdom, that being the alleged object of his proceeding to marry Agilona, the widow of King Roderic, was slain in the palace at Cordova, and his bloody head spitefully shown to the father, who is said to have died of a broken heart. The sons of Witiza, on whose behalf the invasion was alleged to have been made, were re-possessed of their private estates, and his granddaughter married to an Arabian noble. The treatment of the Spaniards, according to Gibbon, was by no means harsh, although war was constantly urged against such of their fellows who retreated into those northern provinces whence their descendants issued in course of time to the re-conquest of the Peninsula, and presented themselves in the novel character of besiegers of Gibraltar. Meanwhile, the Arabs tolerated the Christians more loyally than the latter had tolerated the Jews, or, during the many stages of the re-conquest, the Spaniards dealt with those Moors who fell under their authority.

Magnificent kingdoms were founded in Spain by the Arabs and secured for centuries by the amalgamation of many races on the soil. In the north, however, Leon and Arragon were set up and maintained by the remnants of the Visigothic subjects. Castile and Navarre followed in the same course. In the south, dynasties succeeded each other; the minor provinces became independent, and were often, nay, almost constantly at enmity. Their weakness grew out of their divisions. The Almoravide dynasty was set up in Cordova in 1091; in 1145 that of the Almohades supplanted them there, and, in 1236, the Spanish Christian power had so far recovered itself that, five hundred and forty-five years after the Arabian conquest, the king, Ferdinand the Third of Castile, expelled the Almohades from the city; and the authority of that ancient family was set up anew in Granada. The Moorish dominion in Spain ended with the capture of the city of Granada, by the soldiers of Ferdinand and Isabella, in 1462 (January 2), seven hundred and forty-one years after the landing of Taric at Gibraltar.

This rapid sketch will serve as a key to much that follows of the general history of our subject.

CHAPTER XI.

THE FORTRESS. CADIZ.

WE come now to the Fortress of Gibraltar, and cannot do better, in giving its history under the Moslems, than refer to what is stated of its aspect in the admirable "History of the Mahommedan Dynasties in Spain," of Ahmed Ibn Mohammed Al-makkari, as translated by M. Pascual de Gayangos—a work which, until the Escurial has been compelled to open its treasure chests to students, will be the text for Hispano-Arabian historical readers.* Part of this account we have already given at the opening of our task, where the reader will find that both the Moorish historian, and the Granadian poet whom he copies, compare the Rock to a shining light spreading its rays over the sea. "I saw the whole mountain shining

---

* So jealous have been the Spanish custodians of the literary relics in the library of the Escurial, that, when M. Gayangos applied for leave to examine these treasures, his request was, "as often as made, positively denied, professedly on the plea that the library could not be opened (a contention having, two years before, arisen between the Government and the Royal Household as to the possession of it), but, in reality, from no other motive than my having publicly avowed the intention of making use of my materials in this country. This remnant of inquisitorial jealousy about its treasures ill suits a country which has lately seen its archives and monastic libraries reduced to cinders, and scattered or sold in foreign markets, without the least struggle to rescue or secure them." What is the state of that library in respect to Arabic texts may be conceived when it is understood that the collection of such works is not the result of public munificence, or royal wealth and judgment, but of so fortuitous an event as the capture by two Spanish galleys of three Moorish vessels which had on board the library of Muley Zidán, Emperor of Morocco. The Spanish Government has not sought to increase the wealth of the collection of MSS. which was thus strangely begun.

as if it were on fire," wrote Abu-l-hasán Ibn Musa Ibn Said. Al-makkari further says that Gibraltar stands as a lasting memorial to the conquest of Andalus by the Moslems; that, being named after Taric, it is also called *Jebalu-l-fatah*, the Mountain of the Entrance, or of Victory, and that it was a dependency on Seville.*

The Arabs had strange notions about the Straits of Gibraltar, and it is especially noteworthy that they connected the Straits, and the Pillars which guarded them, with Hercules,† or rather, from their point of view, with the once famous tower at Cadiz. To this effect Al-makkari wrote: " Cadiz is filled with the remains of buildings, temples, aqueducts, and other wonderful constructions of the ancient kings of Andalus." " The most remarkable of these monuments," says Ibnu Ghalib, in his work entitled " Contentment of the Soul in the contemplation of ancient Ruins found in Andalus," "is undoubtedly the tower and idol at Cadiz, which has not its equal in the world, if we except another of the same shape which stands on a high

---

* There is something peculiarly refreshing in being made to look at a battle or course of other events from a point of view which is unusual to ourselves, and to be called upon to consider famous personages with the aid of strange information and opinions. Thus, take this passage: the Arabian author is giving an account of a war which happened early in the twelfth century: " In the same year (A.D. 1109), Errink (Henry of Besançon) and the son of Ramiro (Alfonso I. of Arragon), (*may the Almighty's curses fall upon the heads of both!*), invaded the territory of Al-musta'in Ibn Húd with an army, the numbers of which are only known to God. Al-musta'in hastened to the defence of his States, but fate had decided against him, and he fell a martyr in an encounter with the Christians. *May God have mercy upon him!*"

† "So late as the sixteenth century the site of the Temple of Hercules, near Cadiz, was strewn with fragments of statues, columns and other relics of Roman or Phœnician work." Note, by Gayangos, to Al-makkari's "History of the Mahommedan Dynasties in Spain," book i. c. vi. The Arabs styled the place "the district of the idols." The relics have been washed away by the sea, or used in the fortifications of Cadiz. *See* Salazar, *Hist. de Cadiz.* So late as 1773, some of the foundations of the temple were still visible at very low tides. The port close to Cadiz is called by the country people *Calzada de Hercules*.

promontory in Gallicia. It is notorious that, so long as the idol on the tower of Cadiz stood, it prevented the winds from blowing across the Straits into the ocean; and that no large vessels could sail from the Mediterranean into the ocean, or *vice versa;* but, on the contrary, when it was pulled down in the first year of the reign of the Beni Abd-al-múmen, the spell was broken, and vessels of all descriptions began to furrow the sea with impunity. This idol, according to the opinions of some writers, held some keys in his right hand, but the contrary has been proved by the author of the *Ja'rafiyah."* It is also stated that, according to ancient belief, an immense treasure was concealed under this idol's feet, and that when Ali Ibn Musa, Admiral of the Sea, revolted against the Kaid, his uncle, he caused the idol to be pulled down, and a search made for the treasures, but nothing was found."*

---

* The story is thus picturesquely given by Al-makkari, book i. c. vi., Gayangos, vol. i. p. 77 : "In this city," meaning Cadiz, "there formerly stood a square tower, upwards of one hundred cubits high, and built of large blocks of stone, admirably placed one on the top of the other, and fastened together by hooks of brass. On the top of the tower was a square pedestal of white marble, measuring four spans, and on it a statue representing a human being, so admirably executed in form, proportions, and face, that it looked more like a living man than an inanimate block. His face was turned towards the Western Sea; he had his back to the north; the left arm extended, and the fingers closed with the exception of the forefinger, which he held in an horizontal position, pointing towards the mouth of that sea which issues out of the ocean, and lies between Tangiers and Tarifa, being known by the name of Bahru-z-zokák (the Straits of Gibraltar). His right arm was close to the body, as if holding his garments tightly; and in the right hand he bore a stick, with which he pointed towards the sea. Some authors pretend that what he held were keys, but it is a misstatement; I saw the idol often, and could never discover anything else but the above-mentioned stick, which he held in his right hand in a vertical position, and somewhat raised from the ground; besides, I am assured by the testimony of trustworthy people, who were present or assisted at the pulling down of this idol, that it was a short stick, of about twelve spans in length, having at the end some teeth like a curry-comb. Who was the builder of this tower, with the idol on the top, does not sufficiently appear. Mas'-udi, in his "Golden Meadows," attributes its construction to Al-abbár (Hercules), the same who built the seven idols in the country of Zini, which

96   HISTORY OF GIBRALTAR.

Thus much of the progress of the Arabs in Spain and of the more remarkable treasures which they found there. It is

---

are one in sight of the other; but the most probable opinion seems to be that it was built by one of the ancient kings of Andalus, to serve as a guide to navigators, from the fact of the idol having his left arm extended towards the Bahru-z-zokák (Straits), and pointing to the mouth, as if he were showing the way. There are not wanting people who thought this idol to be made of pure gold; for whenever the rising or setting sun fell on the statue it sent forth rays of light, and shone in the brightest hues, like the colour of a ring-dove, blue being the colour which prevailed. Thus placed on the top of the tower the idol was a signal for the Moslem navigators to go in and out of the ocean, and whoever wanted to sail from any port of the Mediterranean to places in Al-Maghreb (sic), such as Lisbon and others, had only to approach the tower, and then put up the sails, and make for the port whither they wished to go, whether Salé, Anfa (Anafa), or any other on the western coast of Africa. When, in after times, this idol was pulled down, it ceased of course to be a signal for navigators; its demolition happened thus: In the year 540 (A.D. 1145-6), at the beginning of the Second Civil War, Ali-Ibn-'Isa-Ibn-Maymún, who was Admiral of the Fleet, revolted at Cadiz, and declared himself independent. Having heard the inhabitants say that the idol was made of pure gold, his cupidity was raised, and he gave orders for its immediate removal. The statue was accordingly brought down by dint of great exertions, and when on the ground was found to be made of brass, covered only with a thin coat of gold, which, when removed, produced 12,000 gold dinárs. It is a general opinion among Andalusian and African Moslems that this idol exercised a sort of spell over the sea, but that the charm ceased the moment it was thrown down. They account for it in the following manner: There used to be in the ocean some large vessels which the Andalusians call *karákir*, provided with a square sail in front, and another behind; they were manned by a nation called *Majús*, people of great strength, determination, and much practice in navigation, and who, in their landing on the coasts, destroyed everything with fire and sword, and committed unheard-of ravages and cruelties, so that at their appearance the inhabitants fled with their valuables to the mountains, and the whole coast was depopulated. The invasions of these barbarians were periodical—they took place every six or seven years; the number of their vessels was never less than forty, and sometimes amounted to a hundred; they devoured any one they found on the sea. The tower that I have described was known to them, and following the direction pointed out by the idol, they were enabled to make at all times for the mouth of the Straits, and enter the Mediterranean, ravage the coasts of Andalus (Spain), and the islands close to it, sometimes carrying their depredations so far as the coasts of Syria. But when the idol was destroyed by the command of Ali-Ibn-Maymún, as I have already stated, no more was heard of these people, nor were their *karákir* (vessels) seen in these seas, with the exception of two that were wrecked on the coast, one at *Mersu-l-Majús* (the port of the Majús), and the other close to the promontory of Al-aghar" (Trafalgar, *i.e. Jebal Al-gbar*, or the Promontory of the reported that, almost immediately after the landing of Taric,* the foot of the Rock of Calpe was fortified, and received his name; it is also said that the materials of the ancient city of Carteia were employed in the work, but this latter assertion

---

Cave. Thus wrote the painstaking and appreciative Arabian historian. The invading *Majús* were certainly the Northmen, whose histories, as M. Gayangos points out, and those of all the countries which had been before that time obnoxious to their ravages, declare that they were periodical invaders, and we may add, that they ceased to ravage about the middle of the twelfth century. It is curiously confirmatory of the details of this striking piece of history to find that close to Cape Trafalgar are the port of the Majús and the *Bábu-l-Majús* (Gate of the Majús), in both of which places vessels of the Northmen are reported to have been wrecked. A parallel case to this is oddly afforded by the Port-na-Spanien, on the western coast of Ireland, where certain vessels of the Spanish Armada were destroyed in a storm. The Arabs found, or invented, many wonderful things in Andalus; of these we may refer the reader to the curious legend of the iron pot which hung over a terrible chasm in the rocks of a mountain, from out of which no human cunning or force could remove it, because as soon as the hands of any one touched the pot, it sank into the cavity and disappeared, to rise again when the endeavour to take it was abandoned. There were also the marvellous olive tree, which, like the Glastonbury thorn, blossomed and bore fruit on a certain day of the solar year; the bottomless pit of the Cabra—the crater of an extinct volcano; the water-clocks of Toledo, which continued to tell the time "until the tyrant Al-fonsh (Alfonso) and the Christians (may God send confusion amongst them!) took Toledo," in 1134. All these things were as nothing in wonderfulness compared with the great Table of Solomon, the legend of which even captivated the imagination of Gibbon, and which extraordinary piece of furniture was reputed to be of a single emerald; it was, doubtless, a sheet of green glass, and probably of similar origin to that once so famous chalice of Genoa, which was considered the holiest relic of Our Lord. The table was presented to the Caliph Walid as one of the most precious articles in the world. This table is said to have been found in the tower at Toledo, and to be connected with the spells which protected Spain against the Arabs, until Roderic opened the tower.

* It is important to observe that several of the historians have confounded Taric, the freedman of Muza and most active commander, with the much more dignified personage, Tarif, who landed at Tarifa, to which he gave his name. Taric commanded at the Battle of Guadalete; it was he who quarrelled with Muza and went to the East, where he confronted his former, and now jealous and vindictive, master before the Caliph, and, by producing the missing foot of the Table of Solomon, convicted him of falsehood; this conviction led, say some of the Arabian historians, to the utter ruin of Muza. The expeditions of Tarif and Taric—who are both described

is doubtful as regards the evidence, although more than probable in other respects. The account of Ibnu Hayyán is that he selected a good encampment, which he surrounded with walls and trenches. This was, doubtless, the origin of the place, and it is even probable that no large fortress, in the common sense of this term, existed on the Rock until long afterwards. Thus let us leave it, while we recount the fate of one of the most potent of the invaders, Muza Ibn Nosseyr.

---

by Al-makkari as freedmen of Muza—happened with the interval of a year. Condé, in his " History of the Dominion of the Arabs in Spain," blundered dreadfully in respect to these men, and has been the cause of almost innumerable blunders by others. Drinkwater suppressed Taric (!) and gave all his actions to Tarif. Their names and acts are, generally speaking, so nearly alike that it is hardly to be wondered at that errors have occurred in respect to them. M. Gayangos has carefully distinguished one from the other.

CHAPTER XII.

MUZA IBN NOSSEYR.

WHAT became of Muza, the great conqueror and commander in Africa and Spain, the master of Taric and Tarif, to whom Julian applied in the execution of his traitorous purpose? This is a question which the reader may fairly ask. Whatever may be said about the rights of the sons of Witiza to the Visigothic throne, there can be no doubt that to invite foreigners to the conquest of the country was treason, which is darkened when those invaders are enemies sworn against the faith of the nation; the bringing them by any means, and especially to aid them in destroying the country, was treason against the race as well as against the king.

The question of the end of Muza is not difficult to answer, for we have ample information on the subject, too ample it may be said, for there are, as usual, two accounts, and of very different complexions.

After he had overrun Spain, with the aid of Taric, and, as some say, but doubtfully, even penetrated into France, he was, at the instance of Taric, who appealed to the Commander of the Faithful against the treatment vouchsafed to him by Muza, recalled to the East by the Caliph, and compelled to give an account of his conduct. When he received the irresistible command to stay his conquests, he was at Lugo, in Gallicia; on his journey he met Taric, and the pair went to Seville together. After settling affairs in that place, by appointing his son, Abd-l-aziz,* governor, he departed to that part of the coast of Spain where the troops coming from Africa usually landed,† and crossed the sea three years and four months after the landing of Taric, who accompanied him in this return. He left Africa Proper in the hands of his eldest son, Abdallah, the conqueror of Mallorca; and Maghreb, or Western Africa, in those of Abdu-l-Malek, the youngest of his sons. To another son he gave the command of the coast. He then moved on his journey, attended by an enormous number of men and animals, laden with the spoils of many nations, and among them the before-mentioned and famous Table of Solomon, which was said to have been found in the Tower of Destiny at Toledo; he took also with him thirty thousand captives, but advanced to the seat of the Mahommedan power with a downcast and presaging heart, the melancholy of which was deepened by mortification at having been checked in his career of conquest, for it is alleged of him that one of his schemes was to extend even the march of Hannibal, and, by crossing Gaul, the Alps, and Italy, subduing all as he went, to arrive before the seat of the Eastern Christian Empire in Constantinople.

The people of Africa and Syria were brought to a state of utter astonishment by the spectacle of the prodigious wealth and numberless curiosities which this towering man bore in his train as he progressed towards the city of the Commander of the Faithful, which was Damascus. Muza seems to have been a man of violent temper and imperious habits; thus we learn, from the treatment he vouchsafed to Taric, striking him with a rod before the assembled army, and reviling that conqueror in the grossest manner, because he had gone further

---

* Who married the widow of Roderic. † This was probably Gibraltar.

in victory than was proposed for him. On this journey into Syria he gave another proof of this rude and ill-regulated disposition. The most important of the prisoners who had fallen into the hands of the Arabs in Spain was the Governor of Cordova, a prince of the royal house of the Visigoths.* The prisoner fell into the hands of Mugheyth, a commander of great rank, from whom Muza demanded that the captive should be delivered up to himself; but this Mugheyth refused to do, answering, " Nobody shall present him to the Caliph but myself; he is my patron and master, and to him only will I make homage of my prisoner." Upon this, Muza sprang upon the Goth and tore him out of the hands of Mugheyth. However, some of his friends having told him that if he arrived at court with his prisoner, Mugheyth would undoubtedly claim him before the Caliph, in which case the Goth would not contradict the assertion, he ordered him to be beheaded, and the sentence was immediately carried into execution. In consequence of this outrageous method of treating his subor-

---

* The taking of Cordova by means of an unsecured breach and a fig tree which, *growing close to the walls* (!), afforded the means of ascending to the troops of Taric's lieutenant, Mugheyth, strongly illustrates the condition of the Visigothic fortresses at this time. The city thus captured, the governor fled with his troops to the shelter of the church of St. George, which must have been fortified, as were many such edifices, until a much later date than the eighth century. Besieged there, the Goths held out until the result of a stratagem of the Arab general's, who sent a black man among them, betrayed the source of their supply of water, which he then cut off. The Goths, as it appears, had never seen a black man; and when that specimen of this race, which the Arabs had brought from their southern conquests in Africa, fell into their hands, they set about washing him with the hope of blanching his skin, and, failing in their attempts, desisted, more in consequence of the insufficiency of hot water and a hard brush in the operation than in respect for the outcries of the victim. A week after this the negro escaped to the Arabs, betrayed the secret of the water, and thus brought about the destruction of the church by fire, together with its valiant but assuredly not well-informed defenders. The Arab chronicler says that the spot where this act of sacrifice took place is still called the " Church of the Burning," and held in great veneration by the Christians.

dinates and their prisoners, Mugheyth hated Muza, and did much to injure him in the mind of the Caliph by supporting the charges brought against him by Taric.

When Damascus was reached, this imperious commander was accused of peculation, and the Table of Solomon, which these men seriously believed to be composed of one enormous emerald, was demanded of him and produced. The Caliph said, " Taric pretends that it was he, and not thou, who found it." Now this declaration of Taric's was true, for all Muza's concern with this wonderful prize was in wresting it from the possession of the former, who, however, had artfully removed one of the feet from the stem of the table, and concealed it, pretending to Muza that it was short of one foot when it came into his own hands. He removed the foot with an ulterior object, which now becomes apparent. Muza, believing this story, replaced, as well as his artificers could manage it, the pseudo-emerald foot with one of solid gold.

When the table was brought before the Caliph, and that ruler put the question which we have repeated, Muza, little imagining that his own rapacity had dug a trap for him, replied, " Certainly not ; if Taric ever saw this table, it was in my possession, and nowhere else." Then Taric, addressing the Caliph, requested him to question Muza about the leg that was wanting; and, on Muza's answering that he had found it in that state, and, in order to supply the deficiency, caused another leg to be made, Taric triumphantly produced from under his tunic the original support, which at once convinced the Caliph of the truth of Taric's assertion and of Muza's falsehood. After this he disbelieved everything that Muza stated in his own defence, deprived him of all the enormous spoil, and banished him to a distant place, besides fining him so heavily that he was obliged to beg for bread for subsistence among the Arabs. It is said that he was mulcted of only half the imposed fine, and diverse accounts of his end are given by the writers on the subject. Al-makkari, whose record we have been condensing thus far, exercises much acumen in the matter, and concludes that, as to the truth, "God only knows."

It is further related that, while Muza was escaping from the violence of the Caliph, and was in vain seeking an asylum among the Arabs, he found at last, in Wádu-l-Kora, one of his ancient dependants and friends, who, remembering his former engagements, received him into his house, and fed him, until, finding that Muza protracted his stay, and that his means were thereby exhausted, he determined upon delivering him into the hands of the officers of justice. Muza, however, guessing his intention, went up to him, and addressed him in a very humble tone of voice, saying to him, "Wilt thou, O friend, betray me in this manner?" and the man replied, "Against fate there is no complaint. It is not I who betray thee; it is thy Master, thy Creator, He who gave thee sustenance, who now abandons thee." Upon which, Muza raised his eyes, bathed in tears, to the sky, and humbly besought God to grant him help and favour in his perilous situation. On the following day Muza delivered up his soul.

Another story is that he died at Mecca, in the suite of the Caliph, who said the customary prayer over his body.

The glory of the achievement in which Muza played so important a part was, among the Arabs who descended from the invaders of Spain, so great, that the chief companions of Muza were reckoned and their biographies preserved with pride, much in the same way that the companions of Mahommed were described and their careers recorded. Even the second degree of this relationship to Muza, *i.e.* the persons who, by living to an extraordinary age, were reported to have conversed with these companions, and thus reflected, so to say, their splendour to a later age, were famous and, in some degree, venerated by the Arabs in Spain. To have come over with Muza was something more, in Moslem imaginations, as a foundation to an hereditary claim for honour, than to have " come over with the Conqueror" of yore among the English.

The inheritance which had thus fallen from Christian hands to the lot of the Mahommedans, was indeed a magnificent one. It was, so to say, a prodigious treasure chest, of which Gibraltar was the key, the bridge-foot, the doorway, the watch tower, the beacon, the Alpha and Omega, the arch-stone, and what not else, in the enthusiastic language of the new possessors. So proud were these owners of their unexampled windfall, that their rhapsodies continued from century to century. They were incessantly glorifying themselves on account of it. As these expressions of pride and joy are eminently characteristic and strikingly vigorous, let us quote a few of them in the next chapter.

CHAPTER XIII.

THE SPLENDOUR OF ANDALUS.

THE opinion of the Moslems as to the merits and value of Andalus was most exalted. " But, were there no other thing in favour of this country than the prophecy uttered by the messenger of God, when he announced that it should be subdued by his people, and described the first conquerors from whom we descend," says one of the Arabs, "as angels in armour—as appears in the sacred tradition that we hold from Tarif Abú Hamzah Ans Ibn Málik, who had it from his great aunt, Ummu-el-harám, daughter of Malhán, and wife of Abd-l-Walid 'Obádah Ibnu-s-sámah (may God pour his favours upon them all!), which great aunt received it herself from the mouth of the Prophet—that alone would be sufficient to distinguish this, our country, and make it superior to any other." Thus wrote Ahmed Ibn Mohammed Ar-rázi At-tarikhi, the historian, who proceeds to criticise those claims to the honours of the prophecy in question, which certain persons had put forth in favour of Sicily and Crete, as the countries referred to by the words of Mohammed. The report of Al-makkari upon Andalusia, equals that which we have already quoted from the " Geography " of Strabo.

Of the magnificence in which some of the lords of this country lived, while they were in the full pride of possession, and of the fate which came upon their works, it will suffice to condense the account an Arabian author gives of Az-záhra, the now undiscoverable city of palaces, which stood about four miles from Cordova, and was originally founded for a place of pleasure, among forest-clad hills, and for one of the mistresses of An-nássir; but was afterwards used by that king himself. The lady, remarking on the loveliness of the palace, which had been built thus, compared it to a beautiful girl lying in the arms of an Ethiopian; the latter being a dark, oak-covered mountain, which stood behind the place. Thinking to please her, the king ordered the instant removal of the mountain; and was only dissuaded from an attempt to this end by the representations of his learned men, who declared God alone could effect such a purpose. Therefore An-nássir satisfied himself with cutting down the oaks and planting the entire mountain with fig and almond trees, which, in the right season, spread a delightful fragrance. This palace contained four thousand two hundred columns and fifteen thousand doors; a third of the revenue of the State was lavished upon its construction and service; ten thousand slaves daily laboured to build it, with two thousand four hundred mules, and four hundred camels. To this prodigious work An-nássir devoted twenty-five years of labour; Al-hakem, his son, fifteen years more. Some of the columns came from Rome, others from the country of the Franks (probably Narbonne). The Eastern emperor gave one hundred and forty pillars, and one thousand and thirteen shafts of green and rose marbles came from the cities of Africa. The remainder were quarried in Andalusia. The total cost of the building, during twenty-five years, was three hundred thousand dinárs. It was most gloriously furnished. Its fountains were marvels. An unique pearl, presented by the Emperor Leo, was fixed on the top of one of the fountains, in a great hall, the doors of which were of ivory and ebony. The doors of the building throughout were covered with sheets of iron or polished brass; the pillars were of crystal and transparent marble. Attached to this palace was a mosque of equal splendour. The Sclavonian pages and eunuchs in the palace service were three thousand three hundred and fifty, who ate daily thirteen thousand pounds of flesh, besides game, &c. Another authority says there were twelve thousand of these servants. We may finish this extravagant account with one item that will comprehend all and suffice for all. The daily allowance of bread for the fish in the ponds of Az-záhra was twelve thousand loaves, and a vast quantity of black pulse. To this, as to another palace of the same country, might be applied the verse of the Wizir Hazn Ibn Jehwar:

"I once asked that house, whose inhabitants have now exterminated one another, Where are thy owners, the eminent lords who ruled over us?

"And she answered me,—Here they lived for awhile, but they are now gone; they have vanished without my knowing where."

"For our part," wrote Al-makkari, in expansively rejoicing with glory of his people, "we consider Andalus as the prize of the race, won by the horsemen who, at the utmost speed of their chargers, subdued the regions of the East and West." There is striking truthfulness in this Oriental expression; the conquests of the Arabs were made at a gallop; but it must not for a moment be imagined that the mass of the conquerors, still less the great bulk of the occupiers, of these so-styled Arabian acquisitions, were really Arabs, or even Eastern folks, in the ordinary sense of that term. Such was by no means the case. Taric Ibn Zeyad's whole garrison of the northern coast of Africa, opposite to Spain, while Julian yet commanded in Ceuta, was but ten thousand men at the utmost, and of these a very large proportion were Egyptians, themselves subject to the Arabs proper. The Berbers of Andalus and Africa were sufficiently numerous to give a vast amount of trouble to the Arabs in both provinces, and revolted with signal effect ere the conquest was many decades old.

Tarif himself was a Berber; the seven thousand men with whom Taric landed at the foot of the Rock comprised very few true Arabs. All authorities aver that Berbers were the chief strength of the armies of invasion in Spain. A considerable party of Goths turned against Roderic at the battle of the Guadalete, and we may be sure did not lose anything by means of their ever-loyal allies, the troops of the Commander of the Faithful. The influence of the Jews, which was most potent in the circumstances, was ardently employed against their Visigothic tyrants;* cities were entrusted by the Mahommedan leaders to the control of these people, and they were attached to the Moslem service in many ways. When the conquest was made, there was, as one of the Moorish chroniclers quaintly and candidly relates, a grand packing-up of goods by those of the victorious race who, having little to pack, were the more easily disposed to move into the golden land of Andalus, and take possession of new and readily-acquired estates. The Arabs, if so we must call them, understood the true mode of colonising and holding countries; thus, their promises were inviolable. If the Christian chose to abide in his ancestral city, he had but to pay tribute to the Moslems —tribute of no great weight—and his life and property were safe; he might worship God after the manner of his people, and without fear of molestation. Historians mention more

---

* See many sentences by Al-makkari, and, for the military services of the Jews with the Arabs against the Christians at a much later period than that now in question, the proclamation to the people of the African coast by Jusef Ben Taxfin, as to the Battle of Zalacca, A.D. 1086, Condé, *Hist. Dom. Arab.* part iii. 17.

than one case of bargaining, not taking forcible possession, of the sites of Christian churches in cities that had had Moorish owners for centuries after the coming of Taric. These tribute-payers lived side by side with the Moslems in the cities of Spain, and took no open part with their co-religionists in war against the Arabian lords. Also, it must be remembered that Moors and Christians often fought side by side, and against the political enemies of both, without regard to their religions.* These peculiar circumstances deserve ample consideration by all readers of Spanish history.

* See e.g. Condé, Hist. Dom. Arab. part iii. 8, A.D. 1386.

CHAPTER XIV.

EARLY STATE OF GIBRALTAR.

SUCH was the splendid possession which had fallen to the lot of the new power, or rather of the new faith. One of the noteworthy effects of the conquest of Spain by the Moslems was little dreamed of at the time that event came about; this is to be observed in the history of those extraordinary outbreaks of fanaticism which are styled "the Crusades," and which continued to rage with more or less disastrous effects during several centuries.*

---

* We write not without thought of the Crusades as disastrous, and can see nothing of good in their course or effects, unless in the removal of turbulent spirits from their own countries to those of others, which countries they ruined so thoroughly that recovery seemed impossible. As to the spreading of scientific and artistic knowledge, as referred to these monstrous invasions, it is not to be denied for a moment that the intercourse of peace would have been a thousand times greater and more intimate, and a million times more beneficial, than that which took place during the Crusades. When crazy Peter the Hermit began his furious preachings, the Mahommedan countries had been seated in peace for centuries; their civilisation was infinitely greater than that of their invaders, who brought nothing but horror, havoc, and senseless waste in their hands, and took back some scraps of sciences and arts, which they hardly comprehended, and which needed the cultivation of many generations in the new soil ere fruit came. The sole justification for these incursions, or rather the single consolation which we can derive from their occurrence, lies in the truth that, at the time, the civilisation of the Moslems was inclining to corruption, exactly as had happened before in the cases of the Persians when the Greeks overcame them, —of the latter when the Romans took their place, and of these conquerors of the world when their time was come to fall before the so-called barbarians of Gothic and other races; further, of the Goths, when the Arabs came to Spain. On the subject of the Crusades, it must have struck many students that we often read of Christian prisoners being in the hands of the Moslems, but never yet caught a glimpse of a Moslem prisoner in Christian captivity. What is the inference? We write elsewhere

In these contests the Spaniards alone, among the nations of Europe, had no share; they had enough to do at home in recovering from the Moslems those provinces of their own country which Muza and his lieutenants had conquered.

It was not until Gibraltar had again passed into Christian hands that the Spaniards were secure in the possession of the country as a part of Christendom. Of the intermediate time, the records which treat of the Rock are sparse and few. Its military importance was for the first time recognised by Taric, and the stronghold or camp which he founded there must have opened the eyes of the world to the importance of the site; yet it is more than probable that the erections of this leader were merely sufficient to guard a landing-place for supplies and reinforcements in their passage from Almagreb, or Western Africa, to Andalus or Spain. Had the works Taric constructed been of greater importance than sufficed for what we may call a *tête de pont*,* we should surely have had some better account of them than that which has been here given.

For a long time after the conquest of Spain was completed, so far as the Arabs were to achieve it, we hear nothing of Gibraltar as a fortress; the historians of both sides, in the conflicts which continued to rage in that country, endeavour to satisfy their readers with brief accounts of those contests which were wars as well as rebellions. There must have been a fortress of some sort on the spot, but more than this

---

of the effects of northern invasions upon the provinces of Spain, and cannot but note that the most frightful and hateful part of these troubles was in the devilish and purposeless waste which accompanied them. Like wolves among sheep, the ruthless Northmen did ten times the damage their object of plunder required to make it successful. We need to study the records of the Crusades from the Mahommedan point of view ere it is possible to appreciate at their true value the nature of these inroads by our chivalrous ancestors.

* Ayala—*Historia de Gibraltar*—considers these erections in this light.

we know not. The port which the fort guarded was, no doubt, as Ayala asserts, greatly frequented by troops going in and out of Spain, and emigrants who were attracted to that country by reports of its ancient wealth and the ease with which they might establish themselves there. Such, of course, was equally the case in later times with the droves of new invaders who came to support the causes of the Almoravides, Almohades, and Beni-Merines, or Marines, who successively crossed the Straits to conquer and dispossess the holders of fair Andalus.

Before we proceed farther, a passing glance may be profitably given to the state of Spain under the rule of the Moslems, and while their power was not thoroughly established in the country. It was by no means a peaceful state; the successive depositions of the son of Muza, Abd-l-aziz, and those who followed him in command in the north as well as in the south of Andalus—even the pledges which had been given to Theodomir, that he should enjoy his domains in peace, thereby forming a kingdom in a kingdom—the dissensions between the Arabs proper and their more numerous allies, the Berbers —were all fruitful of trouble. The Berbers first rose in Africa, then in Andalus, and were with great difficulty subdued. They defeated Abdi-l-Malek, who had been sent against them; the Syrians came to control them, under Balj: they defeated them, captured their commander, and put him to death. They also defeated other captains, and were not subdued until Yusif Al-ehri came against them with extraordinary powers. This series of outbreaks began in A.D. 723. In the course of it, Kolthúm, General of the Moslems, escaping wounded from a battle, shut himself up in the fortress of Ceuta, with the Balj before mentioned. They were besieged there, and sent vainly into Spain to the Moslem commander,

Abdi-l-Malek Ibn Kattan, to implore aid, which was refused, through fear that, if granted, it would be but the means of establishing an enemy against himself. This curious fact shows, in a very striking manner, the dissensions of the conquerors of Spain, which came about almost immediately after the event which made them powerful in that country. The result of Abdi-l-Malek's policy was that the Spanish Berbers rose against and defeated him, and, as we have said, beheaded and crucified him. The grandchildren of Witiza turned up to the surface again, and troubled the Moslem rulers with accounts of their common hate and quarrels. Sarah the Visigoth, one of these descendants, appealed in person to the Caliph, Abdi-l-Malek, against the injustice of her uncle, Artabash, as the Arabs called him, with regard to certain estates which had been secured to the family in accordance to the convention of Julian with Muza Ibn Nosseyr, or rather with Taric. In the course of this negotiation, it is made clear that Andalus was not in immediate subjection to the Syrian court of the Commander of the Faithful, but dependent on the Wali of Mauritania, for the Caliph gave Sarah letters to this viceroy, and the latter instructed his lieutenant in Spain to do her justice.

Meanwhile, the very Visigoths under Pelayas (Pelagius) were making head in the north of Spain, whence they had been driven by the first influx of the Moslems, and Roderic's cousin was in the way of earning an immortal name as the first to take steps for the restoration of his country, race, and faith. The Moorish historian, Ibnu Hayyán, called Pelayas " a despicable barbarian," and sneered at the cowardice of his countrymen, who, until the administration of Anbasah, did not recommence to defend their wives and daughters ; " until then they had not shown the least inclination to do either."

The commencement of the rebellion happened thus: There remained no city, town, or village in Gallicia but was in the hands of the Moslems, with the exception of a steep mountain, on which this Pelayas took refuge with a handful of men; then his followers went on dying through hunger, until he saw their numbers reduced to about thirty men and ten women, having no other food for support than the honey which they gathered in the crevices of the rock which they themselves inhabited, like so many bees. However, Pelayas and his men fortified themselves by degrees in the passes of the mountain, until the Moslems were made acquainted with their preparations; but, perceiving how few they were, they heeded not the advice conveyed to them, and allowed them to gather strength, saying, "What are thirty barbarians, perched upon a rock? they must inevitably die." "Would to God," says Al-makkari, "that the Moslems had then extinguished at once the sparks of a fire that was destined to consume the whole dominions of Islam in those parts; for, as Ibnu Sa'id has judiciously observed, the contempt in which the Moslems of those days held that mountain, and the few wretched beings who took refuge on it, proved, in after time, the chief cause of the numerous conquests which the posterity of that same Pelayas were enabled to make in the territory of the Moslems—conquests which have so much increased of late years, that the enemy of God has reduced many populous cities; and at the moment in which I write the magnificent city of Cordova, the splendid capital of the Mahommedan empire of Andalus, the court of the Caliphs of the illustrious house of Umeyyah, has fallen into the hands of the infidels. May God annihilate them!" *

* With this very moderate wish the historian, who lived in the time of which he writes, concludes a very striking piece of history.

To Pelayas succeeded Alfonso, and from him came the long line which ended but the other day in the dethronement of Isabella II. one of the hated Bourbons, but connected with this chieftain. Pelayas's rising happened in 717-8, and its effect went on with few stops until the namesake of Alfonso became the first Christian owner of the fortress of Gibraltar.

Had we records of more important events, it would not be desirable to note that, in the year 737, Ok-bah, the lieutenant in Andalus of Obeydullah, the African wali or viceroy, when conducting war against the Franks, had dealt with them so far off as at Narbonne, built a citadel there, and had stations on the banks of the Rhone, was at Zaragoza when he heard of a rebellion in Africa, and thence returned southwards, sent help to his chief by the route of Gibraltar, and afterwards went himself, with victorious effect, to the aid of his master. It was Abdu-r-rahmán, the predecessor but one of this Ok-bah in the rule of Spain, who was commander of the Arabs in the tremendous Battle of Tours, October A.D. 732. He was slain there, with so many of his troops and fellow believers, that Moorish traditionary grief styled the place of combat Baláttu-sh-shohedá, or the Pavement of the Martyrs; likewise the Battle of Balátt. As'-samah, another chief of this people, had been slain in battle near Toulouse, in a fight which bore a similar name to the above, with a vast number of his compatriots. Of the last fight, said the historian, Ibnu Hayyán there remained even in his time a legend among the common people that, on the very spot where so many Moslems fell, the voice of an invisible Muezzin is daily heard at the hour of prayer, calling to his fellow ghosts, no doubt, and to all true believers, to join in adoration and supplication to the God for whose honour they were created. This picturesque and poetical idea was not, so far as we know, entertained by any other people than the Spanish Arabs. By the failure of these fights it was made evident that Moslem progress over the world had reached its term; the Franks were too powerful for even their enormous hosts or the desperate fanaticism which animated them. Another account, and, we are bound to say, the more probable one, of the death of As'-samah, is that, instead of perishing in the fight at Toulouse, he was merely wounded there, and, receiving news of the successes of Pelayas (Pelagius) in the north of Spain, he returned, and was slain in battle against that chieftain, near the walls of Leon, a city which Roderic's cousin was then endeavouring to recover from the Moslems.

According to Ayala, the next event in the history of Gibraltar was the enlarging of the Moorish castle on the Rock, by the successor of Ok-bah, which was then probably completed. An inscription over the south gate, he says, enables us to determine this point of its erection, or, at least, completion:

"Prosperity and Peace to our Sovereign and Slave of the Supreme God, Governor of the Moors, our Sovereign Abi Abul Hazez, son of Jesid, Supreme Governor of the Moors, son of our Sovereign, Abi Al Walid, whom God preserve." *

For a long time after this we have no account of Gibraltar or its neighbourhood. The next incident in its history refers to the progress of the Spaniards in reconquering their country from the Arabs. Of the former nation, Alfonso VI., King of Castile, was, at the latter part of the period in question, the most formidable and successful champion; his conquests were effectual in breaking in upon the Oriental power in the Peninsula. This good fortune had acted so powerfully in com-

---

* This is Carter's version—*Journey from Gibraltar to Malaga*—as quoted by Bell. The date of this inscription is given as A.D. 742.

mon with the increasing rebellions, wars and treasons of Arabs amongst themselves, that Al-mu-Tamed, king of the province of which Cordova was the capital, determined to invoke the aid of Jusef Ben Taxfin, his fellow in the Moslem faith on the southern side of the Straits of Gibraltar, and, in the course of negotiations to that effect, surrendered into his hands the stronghold of Algeciras, which was a fortified post to secure the arrival or departure of troops. In 1086 this surrender was made, and although the assistance thus obtained was successful for the time, and Alfonso defeated with terrible loss at Zalacca, near Badajos, when thirty-five thousand Christians are said to have been slain, yet the result was the establishment of a foreign Arab dynasty in Spain. This was the famous family of the Almoravides, which lasted until 1145, when the Almohades finally overcame them.*

It was in the course of the third invasion, if such those actions must be called, of Jusef Ben Taxfin, that the submission

---

* The account of this battle and the negotiations that preceded it, which Condé gathered from the Mahommedan historians, is full of fire and dramatic interest, especially with regard to a certain ominous series of dreams which Alfonso had on the night preceding the conflict. This account is too long to be extracted here, but we may note one point in it that affirms the existence of Moslems among the vassals of the Castilian King, and his sending them to an Arab sage, in order to obtain an interpretation of the dreams which afflicted his spirit, although his own diviners and wise men declared that they signified nothing but good fortune in the battle which was at hand. The Moslem sage gave a contrary interpretation, which proved the true one. During the war against the Almoravides we find Alfonso in alliance with Aben Abed, the Moorish King of Seville, and his troops defeated by the intruders. It is almost needless to write that this was during the life of the famous Cid Campeador, who also served with Moslems against the Almoravides. The Moorish historians assert that the Cid, who is commonly considered as a model of chivalry, actually burnt alive Aben Gehaf, Governor of Valencia, in the great square of that city. He was probably one of those champions whom Alfonso sent to the aid (?) of Aben Abed in 1086, who were, in the picturesque language of the Moors, "all clad in their armour of iron"; they styled this king Alfonso Ben Ferdeland, because he was son of Ferdinand I., the founder of the kingdom of Castile.

of Gibraltar took place. Some time afterwards this place was recovered from the Almoravides; to this event we shall refer in due time.

The next subject to which our history must be turned is external to Gibraltar. It took place in the year A.D. 1109, and is recorded in the Heimskringla, or Chronicle of the Kings of Norway, and relates to the crusade or journey to the East of Sigurd, second son of Magnus III., Barefoot, King of Norway, commonly called Sigurd the Crusader, or Jorsalafare, the Pilgrim, who, incited by the tales brought to the north by those who had been to Constantinople and Jerusalem, got together a company of men who seem to have been further actuated by that old fire of wandering which so strongly moved the Scandinavians, and were, moreover, tempted by the offers of the Emperor of the East to look upon his service in the famous Varangian Guard as a means for securing wealth and importance. Of two brother-kings of Norway, it was determined that Sigurd should lead the troops, and Eystein rule the realm during his absence. Sigurd sailed with sixty long ships, and wintered in England with Henry the First.* In the spring he departed again for the west coast of France, and at the end of that year found himself in Gallicia, or Jacob's land, as the Northmen called it, on account of the church of St. Jago de Compostella. Here he fell out with the ruler of the province, and plundered it, carrying off his booty to the ships. Sailing further south he came to the Portuguese coast, at Cintra, then in the hands of heathen folks, *i.e.* Arabs. Sigurd took the castle and killed all in it, because they refused to be baptised, and got there an immense booty; thence he proceeded

---

* Ordericus Vitalis.—*History of England and Normandy*—who refers to this visit, says that Sigurd was the son of Magnus III., by an Englishwoman, one Thora.

to Lisbon, on the border country, between "Christian and heathen Spain;" there he had another battle, gained another victory, and took more booty; at a place called Alkassi, Alcazar, of course a common name in the Peninsula, he was again victorious, and "killed so many people, that the town was left empty." Thus recites the Saga of his next adventure:

"King Sigurd then proceeded on his voyage, and came to Niörfa Sound (Gibraltar Straits), and in the Sound he was met by a large viking force (squadron of war ships), and the king gave them battle; and this was his fifth engagement with heathens since the time he came from Norway. So says Halldor Skualldre:

> "'He moistened your dry swords with blood,
> As through Niörfa Sound ye stood;
> The screaming raven got a feast,
> As ye sailed onwards to the East.'

Hence he went along Sarkland, or Saracen's land, Mauritania, where he attacked a strong party who had their fortress in a cave, with a wall before it, in the face of a precipice; a place which was difficult to come at, and where the holders, who are said to have been freebooters, defied and ridiculed the Northmen, spreading their valuables on the top of the wall in their sight. Sigurd was equal to the occasion in craft as in force, for he had his ship's boats drawn up the hill, filled them with archers and slingers, and lowered them before the mouth of the cavern, so that they were able to keep back the defenders long enough to allow the main body of the Northmen to ascend from the foot of the cliff and break down the wall. This done, Sigurd caused large trees to be brought to the mouth of the cave, and roasted the miserable wretches within. Further fights, an entertainment by Roger, Count of Sicily, a landing at Acre, a visit to Jerusalem, where he obtained an honourable reception from Baldwin, whom he assisted with his ships at the siege of Sidon, and a visit to Constantinople, where the Emperor Alexius paid him great honour,* terminated this remarkable voyage."

The journey homewards by land, through Bulgaria, Hungary, and Swabia, is next recorded. In the latter place he was received by the Emperor Lothaire, so says the writer, obviously in error, because Lothaire II. did not become emperor until A.D. 1125, and this journey happened in A.D. 1111. At the former date he was Duke of Saxony, in which capacity, doubtless, he received the wandering king. Henry V. was then Emperor of Germany. Continuing his long journey, Sigurd was welcomed by Nicholas, King of Denmark, who furnished him with a ship for his passage to his own land.

Taking leave of this strange visitant to the waters of Gibraltar, we return to the history of the place. Following the Moorish accounts, we find that the day of the Almoravides was destined to come to an end about the middle of the twelfth century, and by means of the Almohades, a new and more severe sect of Moslems. Their founder, who was styled El-mehedi, the Teacher, was Mahommed Ibu Abdallah, the son of Tamurt, a lamplighter in a mosque, educated at Cordova, the capital of the Almoravides. He travelled for further improvement in the East. At Bagdad he became a pupil of Aben Ahmed Algazali, a reformer, who had written a book which the learned at Cordova condemned and burnt, alleging it to contain doctrines dangerous to the Faith. The news of

---

* The boastful Norwegian chronicler says that Alexius Comnenus offered Sigurd his choice of a gift, either to receive six skifpound, one ton, of gold, or see the great games of the Hippodrome. The Northman wisely preferred the latter. The cost of the games was said to be equal to the value of the gold offered. Sigurd gave his ships to the emperor, and their splendid prows were hung up in the Church of St. Peter, at Constantinople.

this condemnation having been communicated to the author by the student, they joined in vengeance upon the Almoravide oppressors, as they termed Ali, King of Cordova, and his party. In 1116 Mahommed travelled into Mauritania, and rendered himself conspicuous by the austerity of his manner of living, doctrines, and dress. Here a pupil, who afterwards became famous, and is peculiarly interesting to ourselves, came into the charge of the reformer. This pupil was Abd-l-mumen Ibn Ali, who was trained by El-mehedi, in his own views, and inspired with the conviction that the restoration of the truth should come by their means. The pupil began to preach with all the zeal of a convert, and met with the persecution of a reformer. In vain did Ali the Almoravide banish him from the city of Morocco. He took up his quarters in a cemetery, and attracted many hearers with a prophecy of the coming of a new teacher, El-mehedi, who, as might be expected, was soon proclaimed to be Mahommed Ibu Abdallah, the actual teacher of the new prophet, Abd-l-mumen. Retiring to the mountains he converted to his tenets the whole tribe of Masamuda, who were thenceforth styled Mowahedan or Unitarians, a title which gave rise to the famous name, Almohades. With these tenets the party entered into active war against the Almoravides, and, after many changes of fortune, defeated them in A.D. 1128. On the death of Abdallah " El-mehedi," Abd-l-mumen was chosen chief of the new faith, or Emir-al-mumenin. He took Oran, Fez, and Morocco, and sent a general, Abu-amran, across the Straits into Spain (A.D. 1146). This chieftain landed near Algeciras, and besieged that city with success. Friends from Algarve joined Abu-amran in great numbers. " The Almohade force," says Condé, " having taken Algeciras, then directed its march upon Gebal Taric, which surrendered in like manner, when the troops passed on to Xeres. The inhabitants of this city did not wait to be attacked, but joined the new comers, taking the oaths of fidelity and allegiance to their ruler. Cordova, the stronghold and capital of the Almoravide dynasty, succumbed in A.D. 1148, and Abd-l-mumen became King of the Arabs on both sides of the Straits.*

---

* Of the ferocity with which this war was conducted, at least on one side, that of the Almohades, the reader may be assured by a single incident, as related by the Arabian historians. At the siege of Morocco, by Abd-l-mumen, the Almoravide garrison and people suffered the last extremities of hardship and famine, even to cannibalism, ere a party of traitors, "certain Christians of Andalus," agreed to admit the besiegers, and received in return security for themselves. The Almohade party scaled the walls at dawn, on "Saturday, the 18th of the moon Xawal," overcame the faint resistance of the few who retained strength among the defenders, and spent the rest of the day, "until the going down of the sun," in slaughtering the wretched inhabitants. Among the captives was Ibrahem, last of the Almoravide kings, a mere youth, whom Abd-l-mumen was at first inclined to spare, and ordered his wizir to place him in confinement which should last his life. "But the wizir replied and said, 'O king, do not rear a young lion which may ultimately tear us to pieces, and can scarcely fail to become dangerous.' When King Ibrahem and his xeques (sheiks) were brought into the presence of Abd-l-mumen, the youthful sovereign cast himself at the feet of his captor, entreating from him the safety of his life, since he had in no wise offended him; but a near kinsman of Ibrahem, a xeque of the Almoravides, called the Ameer Syr Ben Alhak, was so much displeased by these submissive words, that he spat in the face of Ibrahem, and exclaimed, 'Miserable creature! dost thou imagine, perchance, that thou art offering thy prayers to a loving and compassionate father who will regard thy moaning? Bear thy lot like a man, for this wretch is a monster that may neither be moved by tears nor satiated with blood.' These words enraged the king, Abd-l-mumen, and, in the heat of his anger, he commanded that the king, Ishak Abu Ibrahem, with all the Almoravide xeques and generals, should be put to death, without sparing the life of any one among them. And on that terrible day, as Aben Iza El Raziz relates, all who yet remained of the principal personages were slaughtered accordingly. Three days of slaughter in the city followed this first; and it is averred that more than seventy thousand persons were slain by the Almohades. The only one of the royal family of the Almoravides who was permitted to live on this occasion was a daughter of King Ali, and granddaughter of Jusef Ben Taxfin. Thus rapidly had the glory of that invader been brought to the dust."

CHAPTER XV.

THE FIRST ENGINEER OF GIBRALTAR.

IT is probable that in Abd-l-mumen Ibn Ali we may find the true founder of the fame of Gibraltar as a fortress. It is certain he constructed large works there, in the year A.D. 1161 (A.H. 555). Thus says Condé, quoting an Arabian authority, and in continuation of an account of a campaign by this monarch, in Western Africa (Tunis): "The king then departed from Telencen, and arrived at Tanja (Tangiers) in the moon Dylhagia, of the year (A.H.) 555. In that month the fortifications which he had commanded his people to construct at Gebal Taric were completed, having been commenced on the 9th day of Rebie Primera, in the same year. These works, thus undertaken at Abd-l-mumen's command, were conducted under the superintendence of his son, Cid Abu Said Othman, Wali of Granada, the master by whom they were directed being Haji Yaix, the great architect of Andalusia (Andalus). At the commencement of the year 556 (A.D. 1162) the king, Abd-l-mumen Ibn Ali, passed over to Gebal Fetah, on the coast of Spain, which is in fact Gebal Taric. There he examined the disposition and construction of that city, and the fortifications just completed by his orders, with infinite satisfaction, approving of all that had been done. He remained there two months, during which he received visits from all the walis and generals of Andalusia, in discourse with whom the king informed himself of all things relating to the condition of

Spain; nay, rather of every province thereof. Every day there came numerous xeques and great men to salute their sovereign, and among them were many alimes, with certain of the distinguished Andalusian poets, who recited to Abd-l-mumen the verses which they had composed to his own praise. One of the poets and orators thus presenting himself to the king, Abd-l-mumen, was Abu Giaffar Ben Said, of Granada, who was a youth of tender age; but, having entered the presence in company with his father and brothers, who had come to salute the king, he recited to him the following verses." Then follow some verses which none of our readers would try to read; mere fulsome panegyric, such as Arabian bards delighted in. The most interesting of these may, however, being few, be read here:

> " Illustrious Taric's deeds shalt thou renew,
>   And noble Muza's—they whose might upheld
> The crescent moon of blest Islam, and threw
>   All other radiance into shade. Ye held
> Zeyad and Ben Nosseyr, no power but knew
>   The lustre of his might, whose arm hath felled
> The Christians of these times—our potent Lord;
>   Nor could your blades compete with Abd-l-mumen's sword."

It is interesting at all times to recover the name of an illustrious architect and engineer; for such the builder of Gibraltar undoubtedly appeared in the eyes of his contemporaries. This Haji Yaix, who, by the way, had more than one way of spelling his name, was the designer of those extraordinary machines which were constructed at Cordova by the command of Abd-l-mumen. The galleries of the great mosque at Morocco, which was constructed by the King of the Almohades, were his work; these being intended for the secret approach of the king. The *mimbar*, or pulpit, of admirable workmanship, and, above all, the great apartment upon wheels, which could be moved from one part to another of the mosque (?), with wings which extended on hinges, and of which the wheels moved noiselessly and with complete certainty, to receive him and his attendants, being, as it appears from the by no means clear account, a sort of moveable chapel or pew. The chronicler distinctly leads us to infer that it was also locomotive, and obedient to the will of the king. A poet thus describes these machines:

> "More shalt thou see —
> Machines that move to meet him as he nears them
> Attentive to his wish, and stealing forth
> Silently to receive their potent lord.
> Nay, when he turns to leave them, they retire,
> Anticipating still the wish he forms."

Whatever might have been the true nature of these curious inventions, there can be no doubt that their author, the engineer of Gibraltar, was a man of extraordinary reputation in his time, for the writer of the above verses, speaking again of the same machines, ascribes to him almost miraculous powers; thus he is addressing some one who might be called to the court of Alb-l-mumen:

> "There, secret most prodigious! shalt thou find
> Machines that reason, or that move as beings
> Endowed with sense and will. Portals are there
> Of fair proportion, opening as the step
> Of their known lord approaches them. They haste
> To give him entrance, nor refuse the same
> To such as he hath graced to follow him,
> His nobles and viziers."

On this very important point in the history of our fortress, the reader will welcome another account of the mode in which the buildings were carried out, taken from one who writes too minutely and circumstantially to be wholly incorrect in his descriptions.

We find Al-makkari describing the construction of a fortress on the top of the Rock, by order of Abd-l-mumen Ibn Ali, who landed at Gebal Taric (Gibraltar), which from that day was called the Mountain of Victory. He traced out the building with his own hands, and remained on the spot for two months, and when that time had elapsed, left his son Abú Said to complete the building. One of the architects was Haji Ya-ysh (the Haji Yaix of Condé) the geometrician, and an excellent engineer, who is said to have constructed many valuable machines during his stay in the place, and, among them, a large windmill, "which stood on the very top of the mountain." This was in A.D. 1162, and refers to the erection of what must have been designed for a keep or central tower higher up on the Rock than any previous erections had stood. This was doubtless the fort referred to by Portillo, about the commencement of the last century, as having resisted the attacks of Alfonso XI. and the Count de Niebla, and only yielding to the latter on account of the starving of the garrison. "It was," says Ayala, "built on a high part of the Rock to command the city or ancient town, and consisted at first, as is customary with Moorish castles, of three walls, stretching down to the arsenal on the beach, and on its southern gate is an inscription, showing the date of its erection. Of its ancient precincts there remain only, said the latter writer, referring to his own time, the Tower of Homage on the first wall, some of the foundation of the second, and part of the third on the north side, which has served to protect the town from the shot fired from the Spanish lines, and which bears numerous marks of the ill-treatment of their balls. "It has within," says Portillo, "a tower called 'Calahorra,' which tradition says was built by Hercules; in front a redoubt called Giralda, of amazing strength, and capable of containing sufficient numbers to defend the place, as was seen in the year 1333, when besieged by Don Alfonso XI., King of Castile.

The date of the works of Yaix, or Haji Ya-ysh of Al-makkari, may be fixed on the reader's memory by means of the following events, and the associations they may invoke. It was the year of Becket's resignation of the chancellorship of England; the year before the foundation of Notre Dame, Paris, when Alfonso II., of Arragon, was reigning, the twenty-sixth year of Louis VII. of France; the tenth year of Malcolm IV. of Scotland; and the ninth year of Richard I. of England.

CHAPTER XVI.

TRANSITIONS.

FROM the third quarter of the twelfth century to the end of the next stage in our historical account is a period of considerable length in time. Very important changes had during the interval taken effect in Spain. This is true not only of the Spaniards, but of their Moorish antagonists; and of the latter in their relationship to the African Arabs, or, more truly to write, Moors; for, as the reader may readily conceive from what has been said before, the Arabs gave the impetus which set the fierce tribes of Northern Africa in motion to overpass the Straits of Gibraltar, but were themselves comparatively few in number. That end had come to pass which might have been expected to accrue from such a state of things as this, as well as from the distance, then so difficult to traverse, between the head of the Moslem power at Damascus—and its succeeding metropolitan cities, and the far west of the Peninsula. In fact, the Moorish power in Spain was practically independent of the Commander of the Faithful—in much the same position with regard to that nominal suzerein as the Egyptian rulers have been to the Porte. The Moorish power in Spain was far more intimately connected with its neighbours on the African coast; indeed some of the minor and later dynasties of the country held both sides of the Straits, and reigned at Morocco and in Granada with equal powers. As with the Almoravides and Almohades, the effects of help from one side to the other of the Straits were not always beneficial to the recipient.

The changes which had taken effect in the position of the Christians in Spain were even more momentous than in those of their neighbours and enemies. Kingdom after kingdom had been founded, and a very large proportion of the Peninsula was again in the hands of the descendants of the Visigoths. The power of Pelayas and his descendants had increased prodigiously; the domain of the Asturias, which the former founded about A.D. 713, was consolidated by Alfonso I. in 739, and Leon became a kingdom by including Castile. Arragon became independent about this time, and, on the Moorish side, Abd-e-rahman established the royalty of Cordova. Navarre became a kingdom in 970. The Ommiades were expelled from Cordova in 1091, when the Almoravide dynasty began in that place, and these were supplanted about half a century later by the Almohades, as we have told; who in turn yielded up their capital to Ferdinand III., of Castile, in 1236; and the Almohades gave place to the Beni Merines, who set up the kingdom of Granada, properly so called. In 1247 Ferdinand III. took Seville, and the boundaries of the Moslemiah in Spain were so far narrowed on all sides that it was easy to foresee that the year was soon to arrive which would become memorable on account of the total expulsion of this people from the Peninsula, of which, it must be owned, they obtained possession on strangely easy terms; for never was a conquest of such immense importance, including changing the faith (?) of by far the greater portion of its inhabitants, made more rapidly, or at a cheaper rate of blood and trouble to the victors Blood and trouble were the sole items of the price of Spain to the Moslems; of cash they gave nought. So evident was the coming fall of the Moorish power in this country that we find the historians predicting it long before it came about; lamenting their coming loss of the fair palaces, rich cities, great public works, and all that garden of the world where this noble race had laboured through centuries of possession to such splendid effect, making it anew the earthly Paradise which the Romans found. Heavy were the curses which these patriotic writers loaded upon the heads of the mail-clad hosts of Castile, and the other Christian kingdoms; deep was the interest which their rulers took in the many changes of what they did not fail to call the "infidel" (non-Moslem) powers. So early as the tenth century Abd-e-rahman helped Sancho I., the Fat, to recover his throne. The changes and counter-changes of Leon and Castile, the vicissitudes of Arragon, even of Navarre, all engrossed their Moslem neighbours. We find frequent alliances between Moorish and Christian powers. Even the Cid, that supposed mirror of chivalry, was, as we saw, no inefficient aid to one of the hated Moorish kings. Notwithstanding all these events, which the Moorish historians duly recorded and judged about, there was one misfortune, nearer perhaps to their hearts than any other, at which they did not guess; this was the almost total loss of Arab learning in the Peninsula. Moorish arts, sciences, and skill of all kinds were destined to a fate which was almost as destructive as that which fell upon the race.

We have seen the rise of the Almoravides, their fall before the Almohades; the third change is now at hand in the passing of the power of the latter dynasty to the tribe of the Merines. This new power rose in Africa, the seat of its predecessors. The Arabian historians who guide us now tell that this people had origin in Abu Bekar, a sheikh or xeque in the land of Zaub, in Western Africa, who came with Yakub Al-manzor to Spain, and fought in the Battle of

Alarcos, A.D. 1295, and died in that year (A.H. 592). His grandson, Abu Sa'id, became Ameer, or Emir, of his tribe, and fought strenuously against the Alarabians of Almagreb, to whom he owed blood feud of a terrible kind. He extended his power over many tribes, taking tribute from or consolidating them with his own people (A.H. 614, or A.D. 1218). Abú Sa'id received service and tribute of Fez and Alcazar, and reigned twenty-three years,* until A.D. 1240, or A.H. 640.

The successor of Abu Sa'id was his brother Abu Maurref Mohammed, to whom the Merine sheikhs took the oaths of fidelity and allegiance, swearing to make war upon all whom he should attack, and defend all whom he should take under his protection. This ruler continued in the steps of his predecessor, and enlarged the authority of his place. He was victorious in many battles, and added new tribes to those who followed his banners. His decorations and ornaments were said to have been armour and weapons; war, his sport. "Once only was he defeated by the Almohades, then he died fighting." Thus it happened: the chief of the Almohades, Abu Sa'id, sent against the Merines a force of twenty thousand men, comprising Alarabians, and "certain valiant generals of the Christians." The two powers met on the borders of Fez, and fought obstinately, so that the battle lasted till near the going down of the sun, when Maurref Mohammed encountered a noble and brave Christian, who thrust his lance through his body; a mishap which is alleged to have been due to the

---

* The Abu Sa'id of Condé is the Abu Abdillah of Gayangos, his name being, in the mode of spelling adopted by the former, Abu Said Abdallah Ben Ozman Ben Abu Chalid. It is almost needless to say that, with regard to the spelling of Arabic and Moorish names, we, with one or two exceptions, adopt that of the authorities from whom we quote. The sound of the words will prevent any difficulty of identifying the same man, even, as very rarely happens here, if he is represented by two modes of spelling his name.

exhausted state of the Merine commander's horse. After this the Merines fled and were utterly disorganised, A.D. 1242. In the year following this, Mohammed I. of Granada gave up Jaen to Ferdinand III. of Castile, and placed his kingdom under the protection of this Christian monarch. So much change had come about in Spain! This protectorate does not seem to have lasted long, or been lucky for the Granadians.

The command of the Beni Merines next devolved upon his brother, Abu Bekar Yahye, an ambidextrous man, who could throw a lance from each hand at the same moment with infinite force and ease (*Condé*). The next chief was Abu Jusef, the fourth son of Abdallah Ben Abu Chalid, a terrible enemy to the Almohades, " whom he cut up as the husbandman roots up weeds, without leaving trace or sign thereof." Fez had fallen to the Merines before this. Morocco became theirs in A.H. 678, or A.D. 1278. Here we will for the present leave this powerful tribe or confederation of tribes under ruthless rulers, coming, as they did, from the desert to conquer district after district of Almagreb, and to be the third great Mohammedan wave, so to say, which was destined to pour past Gibraltar to the conquest of Andalus. It is evident that the successive entrances of the Almoravides, Almohades and Beni Merines, were as truly conquests of Spanish territory as was that of Muza and Taric. It is equally clear that each of these tremendous human waves was weaker than its immediate forerunner had been; accordingly it spread less broadly.

We have next, from Ibnu Khaldún, this account of the position of affairs in Gibraltar and its neighbourhood in the year 1273 and soon afterwards, showing how the new power came into Spain. The Beni Merines had built their empire in Africa upon the ruins of that of the Almohades. One of the most powerful monarchs of this new dynasty was

Ya'-kúb Ibn 'Abdi-l-hakk (Abu Jacob Ben Abd-l-hac), who received an embassy from the Moors of Andalus (Cordova), begging aid against the Christians under Alfonso X. of Castile. This was granted with good effect. Thus, in the year 672 (beginning July 17, A.D. 1273), Mohammed II. (Al-fakih, or The Theologian), hearing that the Christians were about to carry war into his dominions, sent an embassy to the before-mentioned Ya'-kúb, Sultan of Fez, or Western Africa, soliciting aid against the infidels; and that sovereign, having graciously acceded to his request, sent first his own son at the head of an army, and himself followed shortly after. Having taken Algeciras from the hands of a rebel who had gained possession of it, he converted it into a receptacle for his warriors. Mohammed, moreover, gave up to the African sovereign Tarifa and the castles pertaining to it; and, when everything had been arranged, the two kings united their forces, put to flight Don Nuno (Gonzales de Lara), the General of the Christians, dispersed his troops, and routed everywhere the army of the Castilian king (A.D. 1275, September 8), sending large bodies of cavalry to make predatory incursions into his dominions. At last, through fear of the Africans, Mohammed made his peace with the Christians, and Ya'-kúb returned to Africa. In the course of time, however, the kings of Granada recovered Algeciras, Tarifa, Ronda, and all the fortresses which Mohammed had given up to the Beni Merines.

There is no doubt that, among the places thus pledged and afterwards recovered, was Gibraltar; it was reckoned among the dependencies of Algeciras. There appears also to be some little confusion in the account of the Moorish historian we have just quoted. Abu Ya'-kúb, or in common writing Abu Jacob, was one of the sons of Abu Jusef, and the voyage when Algeciras was occupied, was the second of those made by the Beni Merines into Spain. Abu Jusef had preceded Abu Jacob three years before that event. In the second voyage they came together, also another son, Abu Zeyan Mendel; at this period the walls of Algeciras were reinstated (A.H. 681, or A.D. 1282). Successive incursions of the Beni Merines had almost ruined the country of the Granadians, and they hardly knew where to turn for aid; hence the kings seem to have sought to play the Castilians against their co-religionists, and *vice versa*, exactly as the temporary state of affairs dictated. As might be expected, and we shall learn further on, the union with Christians and the old enemies of their race was anything but agreeable to the Moslem people in Spain; they rebelled against their so-called apostate rulers, and ultimately placed the Beni Merines in their seats.

In the year of the Hegira 685 (A.D. 1285-6), Abu Jusef died at Algeciras, after a reign of twenty-eight years and a half. Abu Jacob succeeded him, and died in A.H. 706, or A.D. 1306. Abu Sa'id came next, and had but a brief reign of one year and a quarter. He died in 1308, and was followed by Abu Rebia Zuleman Ben Amir Abu Amir Abdallah, son of Abu Jacob. This king captured Ceuta (1308), and died in A.H. 709-10 (1309). Then came Abu Sa'id Othman, who reigned until A.H. 731 (A.D. 1330). It was during his rule over the Merines that the next event in the history of Gibraltar to which we shall direct the reader's attention came to pass. For this purpose we return to the authority of the Moorish historian and industrious compiler which we have so often quoted. These are the histories of the first regular siege of Gibraltar.

CHAPTER XVII.

THE FIRST SIEGE.

IT was whilst the Fortress was in the possession of the Merines of Africa, as before stated, that the Castilians, in A.H. 708 (1308-9) profiting by the absence of part of the African garrison, invested Gibraltar, and made themselves masters of it without much difficulty.* Another Moslem historian writes of this matter thus: "In the year 709 (beginning June, A.D. 1309), the King of Castile, Herando (Ferdinand IV.), laid siege to Algeciras. He remained before that city from the 21st day of Safar to the end of Shaban, when, despairing of reducing that place, he raised the siege, though not without making himself master of Gibraltar."

The Christian accounts of this affair are more complete than either of the above, and inform us of its history with great minuteness. We condense from Bell's version of Ayala the following description of the causes and results of the matter in question. Mohammed IV. of Granada made a truce for the nonce with the Christians, and when this expired the latter were eager for new wars.

As soon as Ferdinand IV. was enabled by the termination of his truce (1309) with Mohammed IV., Abu Abdallah of Granada, to direct his arms against the infidels, he laid siege to Algeciras. Finding the besieged received continued suc-

---

* Al-makkari, vol. ii. p. 355.

cours from Gibraltar, the king determined to get possession of the Rock, for which purpose he detached Alonzo Perez de Guzman to deprive the enemy of this support. "Accompanied by numerous great personages, to assist as well with their council as their arms, Guzman resolved on a simultaneous attack on all sides; and leaving the Archbishop of Seville and Don Juan Nunez to attack on the north front, he landed the remainder of the forces, and, gaining the heights that command the castle, immediately assaulted it. On this occasion was erected the tower of Don Alonzo (so named from Alonzo de Guzman, and not from the eleventh Castilian king of that name), and with such diligence and strength was it constructed, being furnished with wide and substantial walls, on which were placed two battering engines, that immense stones were immediately discharged against the Calahorra, against the walls of the castle, and against the town beyond it in which was the chief population. Although by these means the houses, the town, and the numerous defences were battered to the ground, the Moors were not intimidated. Only eleven hundred in number, and straitened on all sides, they continued to repair the works, defending the place most gallantly, and retarded the victory a whole month. At length, after a sanguinary and obstinate contest, they were obliged to surrender, stipulating only that they should be allowed their liberty, and be transported to Africa. Thus ended, in the year 1309, the first siege of Gibraltar."

Don Alonzo hastened to communicate this pleasing intelligence to the king, that he might personally take possession of a place of the strength of which he seemed to be altogether ignorant; for on entering it, says Ayala, and observing the peculiarity of its situation, with uplifted hands he gave thanks to Providence for the reduction under his dominion of a Rock and Castle so important, and almost impregnable. He rebuilt the walls and strengthened the fortifications, made provision for the reception of shipping in a harbour which he armed if he did not found it; for this king seems to have been among the first to see the importance of Gibraltar as a naval station. This was very considerable, even in that early time, and we have a hint of one of its chief claims to consideration in the charter of privileges which the king granted to the town, whereby he allowed anchorage dues to be paid to it the same as in the port of Seville, excepting only "galleys or armed vessels that navigate in the service of God against the enemies of the holy Faith." Free of toll or anchorage dues lay in the port of Gibraltar the galleys of the knights of Rhodes—free as the king's own ships. The port must have been of inestimable service to these knights, and their great galleys lay safely under the walls of the town, or within the old Mole, which was guarded by the strong tower that Ferdinand IV., among the other additions which he made, built at the extremity of the Mole.

Further, of the charter of King Ferdinand, the first Christian owner of the Fortress of Gibraltar, Ayala, with other documents, quotes at length a declaration of Alfonso XI., citing a similar one by his father, Ferdinand IV., which is dated 1310, and grants freedom from toll, excise, watching, castle-service, &c., to all inhabitants of Gibraltar, also from customs. "Moreover we order and direct that all those who shall proceed to Gibraltar and shall be inhabitants and dwellers therein, whether swindlers, thieves, murderers, or other evildoers whatsoever, or women escaped from their husbands, or in any other manner, shall be freed or secured from the punishment of death; and that those who shall live and dwell in the town or its territory shall neither be threatened nor have injury done to them; not being traitors to their lord, breakers of the king's peace, or one who shall have carried off his lord's wife, for these shall not be protected, but punished as they deserve." Moors, taken beyond the range of a cross-bow from the town, were to belong to the captor, the king's dues being paid; if captured within that distance, but one-third of the value of the captive was to belong to the captor, "according to the custom of other castle warriors in our kingdoms." The place was made a free port for all, Christians, Moors, or Jews, to buy and sell in, free of charge. All malefactors, except traitors, who resided a year and a day in the town, were to be pardoned and freed from justice, except for crimes committed in Gibraltar.

Ferdinand IV. gave the charge of his new acquisition, the key of Spain, into the hands of Alfonso Ferdinand de Mendoza, who thus became the first Christian governor of Gibraltar, and with it supplied that captain with a garrison of three hundred men, besides those who did " duty in the watch-towers;" also furnished them with ample pay, and even provision for their children. The seal which the fortress now employs was granted by this monarch, and is in itself significant of the opinion which he held about it, to wit, a castle of three towers, embattled, and having a key pendant at its gate, to indicate at once the strength of the place, and its relationship to the rest of the king's dominions. Many privileges, besides those we have quoted, were granted to the place for the public service; thus, a share in the royal tunny fisheries, one-third of the profit of the salt pans in the neighbourhood, and rents of shops, furnished a revenue.

The perilous nature of the lives which had to be led by folks in Gibraltar, subject as they were to attacks by the Moors, who were at hand both by land and sea, are now-a-days hard to appreciate in fulness, but might have been estimated but a few generations since, when descents on the Spanish coasts were by no means uncommon and almost, barring rescue, invariably led to slavery, if not death, in Africa. Gibraltar itself was open to attack and possession by the Corsairs at a much later date than that which is commonly supposed to include the duration of their anomalous power.

The Moors seem to have had an impression that Gibraltar had been surrendered by Mohammed, or its retention connived at by him. When it was captured in 1309 by Ferdinand, the siege of Algeciras was soon afterwards abandoned; as well on account of the difficulty of taking the place, as of the terms of the Moorish king, who offered the towns of Belmar and Quesada, and one hundred thousand crowns if Ferdinand would relinquish the siege. We may readily understand that Gibraltar, being in the Spaniards' hands, Algeciras was of comparatively minor importance to the holders of the more powerful fortress. Also, there was to be considered the uncertainty of getting possession of Algeciras, even at an immense cost of money and blood. Ferdinand therefore agreed to these terms of the Moslem monarch, and abandoned the siege of Algeciras. It is alleged that this surrender of territory and money to the Christians reacted against the Moorish king, insomuch as his brother, Nas'r, conspired against him, and he was compelled to abdicate by a tumult in the city, in the course of which it is noteworthy that the historian refers especially to the destruction of books at the gutting of the house of the Wizir Abú Abdillah, "which was attacked by the mob, and gutted of all its valuable contents, besides the treasures which he had amassed in books, jewels, weapons, &c., which God alone could estimate." This story does not support the account given by Ayala, who makes the dethronement of Mohammed to have happened in

April, 1309, and the siege of Algeciras to have been begun by Ferdinand IV., in A.H. 709, *i.e.* after June 10 in that year, and, consequently, not in the reign of Mohammed III., but in that of his dethroner and brother Nas'r; it was not until the February of 1311 the rumour spread that Mohammed was dead, and his body thrown into a fish-pond in the garden of the palace. This was after an attempt at rebellion by Abú Sa'id, a descendant of the founder of the Nasserite dynasty in Cordova, who proclaimed his son, Abu-l-Walid Ismail, as king (February 18th, 1310). In November, 1310, Nas'r had a fit of apoplexy, and his death was rumoured to have followed this attack, so the friends of Mohammed III. persuaded him to claim the crown again (November, 1310), but they were unfortunately hasty for themselves, for "on entering Granada, what was their astonishment to hear that Nas'r had recovered from his illness. This led to closer confinement for Mohammed; his death, and the rumours to which we have referred of the mode of disposing of his body. It appears, however, from a further statement of the author to whom we now refer, that he did not die, by whatever means, until January, 26, 1314. We have next to consider the second siege of Gibraltar, which took place in the year 1315, under the command of Abd-l-Walid, or Ismail Ben Ferag, another zealous Mohammedan who strove in vain to retard the advance of the Christian power into the lands of his people. He succeeded Nas'r on the throne of Granada in 1313, and was nephew of that monarch.

To show how these great changes came about is so important that we shall be excused if we trace them by other aid than the above.

CHAPTER XVIII.

RELATIONS OF THE NASSERITE DYNASTY WITH GIBRALTAR.
THE SECOND SIEGE.

ANOTHER account of these transactions is more complete than the above. The advances of the Christians into the Andalusian territory had been continuous and successful. In 1293 Sancho IV., King of Castile, laid siege—so far had the progress of recovery been carried—to Tarifa; assaulting it by sea and land, and with machines of many kinds: he entered the place by force of arms, slew a great number of the inhabitants, and appointed Alfonso Perez de Guzman governor of the city. This is, we believe, the first appearance in the neighbourhood of Gibraltar of one of the family to which this commander belonged, a family which thereafter distinguished itself through many generations, and held the Rock and Fortress almost independently of the Spanish kings, keeping for centuries their grasp firmly upon them, and resisting attempts of more than one kind to relax that hold. Of this matter we shall see more presently.

Juan of Castile, brother of Sancho IV.—following in a reverse mode the practice of Count Julian against King Roderic—having a quarrel with his brother, crossed over to Africa and made a friend of Abu Jacob Ben Jusef beforenamed, and induced him to send five thousand horse and a proportion of foot soldiers to recapture Tarifa, which he assured his new ally would be an easy matter.* In this, however, he

---
* Condé, part iv. c. xii.

was mistaken, notwithstanding that Juan set the son of Alfonso Perez de Guzman enchained before the walls of the city, threatening his death if it was not surrendered. But, as the Moorish historian wrote, with a grim approval of such fortitude, which is chivalric from the pen of an enemy: "The Alcalde uttered no word of reply. He silently unbound his sword from his girdle, threw it down to the prince for the fulfilment of his threat, and retired from the wall. Then the Moslemah, furious at the contempt thus expressed, struck off the head of the youth, and, placing it on one of their machines, cast it on the walls, that the father might not be able to doubt his loss." The Spanish story is, that Juan of Castile stabbed the lad with his own hand. Before such constancy as this the Moors and their Christian allies retired defeated to Algeciras. The capture of Tarifa had been made from the Moors of Africa, in whose hands it had been placed under circumstances which have been already described. When Sancho IV. obtained possession of the place, his ally, Mohammed II., of Granada, claimed restitution to himself of the conquest, notwithstanding that it had been ceded to Abu Jusef by Mohammed I., and held as an appanage to the African dominion since that time. Sancho replied to this simple request that the place was his by conquest, and that, if ancient rights were to be alleged against the chances of war, he might claim the whole of Granada. Upon this, quarrels came about between the failing people of Granada and their growing Christian neighbours; incursions followed from both sides, and Sancho took Quesada; "but he did not long enjoy his triumph and the fruits of his cruelty, seeing that God the Omnipotent cast him into Gehennah no long time thereafter;" and the Granadians reconquered the fortresses he had captured on their frontier, repeopling them with Moslems where Sancho had expelled the inhabitants of that faith. Among these places was Alcabdat.

The capture of Tarifa discouraged Abu Jacob for the time in his Andalusian enterprises, so that he shortly after treated with Mohammed and sold him Algeciras itself, which thus returned to the kingdom of Granada; he also endeavoured to buy back Tarifa from the son of Sancho IV., who would, it is alleged, have sold it, but for the interposition of the queen and the De Guzmans. He then attacked the troops of the latter, defeated them with great loss (A.D. 1299), and besieged Tarifa again, but, notwithstanding his energetic efforts, without success. He attacked Jaen soon after this with like fortune. He died while still in the enjoyment of good health, " and in the act of prayer with infinite quietude and tranquillity; no mark of suffering on his countenance, save only on the eye-lashes there was a trace of weeping, as when one hath shed abundant tears."

The sons of Mohammed II. were Mohammed III.—Abn Abdillah, Feraz or Ferag, who conspired against the last, and Nas'r, who has been before mentioned. Abu Jusef Jacob Ben Abd-l-hac was lord of Almagreb at this time—the victor of the Almohades, who made incursions to Andalus as before stated, and died at Algeciras in 1286. Then came Abu Jacob Jusef, who voyaged with his father into Andalus and took the strong places of which we have already written. The Castilian kings were Alfonso X., Sancho IV., and Ferdinand IV. In 1302 Nas'r rebelled against Mohammed III., and was defeated. In the same year the King of Granada proposed to buy Tarifa of Ferdinand IV., or to change it for another place. These proposals were refused. In 1305 Mohammed, bent probably on retaliating upon the African Moors some of their ravages in Granada, sent Feraz Ben

Nas'r to Africa with a powerful army, which assembled at Algeciras, besieged and took Ceuta, with a great treasure which was concealed there *(Condé)*. Next year Jusef Ben Jacob, of the Beni Merines, was assassinated in a mysterious manner, and Abdallah Ben Jusef succeeded him. In 1309 the siege of Algeciras, which led to the capture of Gibraltar by Ferdinand IV., took place, and Mohammed attempted its relief while Sulieman Aben Rabie, in alliance with James II. of Arragon, recaptured Ceuta from Mohammed III. The King of Castile, moreover, captured Gibraltar; and his neighbour of Granada, being thus hardly pressed, came to the terms with Ferdinand which placed Algeciras in safety for the time, and left the Rock in his hands.

The rebellion of Nas'r, accompanied by that tumult in Granada which more than one historian laments, because of the destruction of books which accompanied it, and the abdication of Mohammed III., were followed by the accession of Nas'r, a much more vigorous sovereign than his brother, whose offers for peace with Ferdinand IV. were rejected haughtily. Nas'r, arming himself against the King of Barcelona (Arragon), caused the latter to raise the siege of Almeria, which was on the point of surrendering (1309); the rebellion of Abd-l-Sa'id further disturbed the new occupant of the Granadian throne; this was ineffectual, but the false step of Mohammed III. in returning to the city of Granada on the news of Nas'r's death, and the conduct of the father of the former rebel, showed how unsafe was the new dominion, troubled as it was externally by the warlike acts of Ferdinand IV.

From the last, however, the Moslem power was soon to be delivered. He died before Malaga, and when about to besiege that fortress. There is a picturesque legend of the death of this king, which deserves attention from the students of the history of Gibraltar and its neighbourhood, or biographers of the famous men who have been connected with it. He might well be called the Taric of the Christian hold, as he was the Christian founder of the place.

The legend is that two brothers of the family of Carvazal were condemned to death by him, on account of an accusation that they had murdered one of their own friends. The accused declared themselves wholly innocent of the crime, made the most strenuous efforts, and used the utmost entreaties to avert their doom. Ferdinand paid no heed to this defence, but ordered immediate execution of his sentence. As the brothers were being led from his presence, to fall beneath the sword, they, with one voice and in terrible words, summoned the alleged false judge to the tribunal of God, and averred that he would appear there within thirty days of their own departure. Dying, they persisted in declaring their innocence, and repeated the awful call; the king thenceforth has been called "The Summoned," because, actually dying within the period thus indicated, men believed that he departed in obedience to the voices of the dead.*

The stage of life was thus cleared of Mohammed and Ferdinand, Nas'r and Alfonso reigned in their steads, both, now—at least, legally. Nas'r—as to whom there was not wanting charges that he had pushed, or caused to be pushed, Mohammed into the palace fish-pond—set up a gorgeous mausoleum in his honour, with a tear-invoking inscription of the most pathetic and laudatory kind. Thus he was described as the virtuous Sultan, one of the excellent kings, wise in the fear of God, amiable, austere, humble, the hand of justice, path of confidence, light of the state, portal of the law,

* Mariana accounts for the death of this king by his having over-eaten himself.

friend of humanity and religion, illustrious, defender of his people, clement king and prince of the Moslemah; and, with a finer irony, "the irresistible conqueror of the unbelievers. May God sanctify his spirit, and refresh his sepulchre with the delicious cup of benignity, and exalt him to the highest mansions of the just."! (*Condé*.)

There was no peace in Spain, notwithstanding these changes and the youth and energy of Nas'r, who was, at his accession, twenty-three years of age. Three years after that event, he sought the friendship of Pedro, Prince of Castile, who was expected to succeed Ferdinand IV., solicitations which were fortunate for a brief while. In A.H. 713, or A.D. 1312-13, Feraz Ben Nas'r, Wali of Malaga, an almost independent prince, father of Abu Sa'id, who was called Abd-l-Walid, fomented rebellions in the State, and the latter begun war against the king, his uncle, took some castles, among them that which " stands in front of the Alhambra," and the Alcazar of Granada; he besieged Nas'r in the Alhambra; however the latter besought aid of Pedro of Castile, who was then at Cordova.* He entreated this prince to come without delay to his aid. "Pedro," says the Moorish historian, "began to march for that purpose, but not swiftly enough for Nas'r, was compelled to yield, give up his kingdom, and behold in that misfortune a repetition of what had befallen his brother by his own means." He retired to Gaudix, which was restored to him, and died there A.H. 722, A.D. 1321. Pedro continued his journey, and captured Rute from the Moors.

The conqueror of Nas'r was a man of great note for us, for he reigned twelve years, and besieged Gibraltar. His full

---

* Of Pedro of Castile we shall hear curiously in reference to Gibraltar, and the manner of his death.

style is thus given by the authorities: Ismail, the son of Feraz Ben Nas'r Ben Ismail Ben Mohammed Ahmed Ben Mohammed Ben Hasain Ben Acail El Ansari El Chazezi, called Abd-l-Walid and Abu-l-Sa'id, son of the Wali of Malaga, and nephew, by a sister, of Nas'r. He is sometimes described as Ismail Ben Feraz. Apart from warlike qualities Ismail was a strict follower of the Mahommedan law. When tired of hearing the disputes of the theologians attached to his court (polemics seem to have been rife in the Granadian palaces) he is reported to have said that to believe the omnipotence of God required no reasoning; as to his own arguments, " They are here, said he, laying his hand upon his sword." He enforced the prohibition against wine, much increased the taxes on Christians in his domains, and compelled them to wear a distinct costume.

It was in the year of the Hegira 716, A.D. 1315, that Ismail learnt how the King of Castile was sending a large convoy of stores to Gaudix, where Nas'r then resided and kept up friendly relations with his fellow ruler, Alfonso XI., who, since 1312, had succeeded to the throne of Castile. Now, whether this despatch of provisions was contrary to treaty, or otherwise the cause of uneasiness to Ismail, is uncertain to us; but it appears that he determined to waylay and destroy its escort, a stout body of mail-clad Spaniards. His troops, however, being sent for this purpose, caught a Tartar, and were defeated utterly. This fight is called the Battle of Fortuna, and so far added by its success to the courage of the victors (never remiss against the Moors), that they attacked a line of fortresses on the frontier, and did a prodigious deal of harm to the fields and vineyards of their enemies. Upon this, Ismail Ben Feraz called out the strength of his kingdom (A.D. 1315) and determined to ruin the marauders, who, however, so soon as they learnt what was on the way, retired homewards " with the prey they had taken."

Ismail Ben Feraz, averse to let his troops return without doing something, determined to try to recover " that key of his kingdom," as the Moors already called it, the Rock of Taric, and the Fortress upon it, to wit, Gibraltar. He was also bent on recapturing Ceuta, thus hoping once more to unite the Pillars of Hercules to the realm of a single king. The latter place was in the hands of the Merine lord of Almagreb, Suleiman. Ismail accordingly despatched, said the Moorish writer, a strong force against Gibraltar, and invested the place for some time; but the frontier forces of Seville coming to the succour of the besieged, and the Christians, sending assistance to them by sea at the same moment, the Moslemah were compelled to break up their camp, not being strong enough to risk a battle.*

These are all the records we have of the second siege of Gibraltar, nor does it seem probable that we need to know much more. The important point in the history is the clear recognition by both sides — Moors and Spaniards — of the enormous importance of the place. This is amply expressed by the words of the Arabian authority which we have just quoted, " Gebal Taric, that key of the kingdom of Ismail Ben Feraz," the would-be conqueror of the place. He failed in his attempts both upon Calpe and Abyla, but his successor was more fortunate, and the former reverted to the Moslems for a long time. Our next incident in the history of Gibraltar is little known, and very significant of the opinions which were, at that time, held about it.

* *Condé*, part iv. c. xviii.

CHAPTER XIX.

GIBRALTAR OFFERED AS A RANSOM.

THE new birth of energy in the realm of Granada spread its effects far and wide. We have seen how Ismail Ben Feraz aimed at the recovery of Gibraltar from the Christians, and, at the same time, from the Moslems, or Beni Merines of Africa, Ceuta, a much older, and, as it was then thought, more important, fortress than its sister on the Mount of Taric. This brought him into opposition to the nations on the north and south of his kingdom. As to the former, he had small chance of peace with them, who were in alliance with his dispossessed uncle, and hated himself as only Spaniards could hate Moors. Now, Pedro, Infante of Castile, continuing his attacks on Granada, reached within three leagues of the city of that name, Ismail's capital, burnt some of the neighbouring towns, and retired before the approach of Ismail; but, soon afterwards returning, he stormed Velmez, both town and castle; next the Christians took "Tuscar," and expelled the inhabitants, fifteen hundred men, with large numbers of women and children.

This course was continued with unaltered fortune until the invaders, having taken the suburbs of Illora and burnt them, and done abundance of mischief to the neighbouring districts, found themselves, on the morning of the Festival of St. John,* December 27th, 1319, in sight of Granada. They

---

* If this refers to the Festival of St. John the Evangelist, according to the Roman, Old English, French, Scottish, Spanish, and German calendars, the above is the true

were commanded by the Infante Pedro and his uncle Juan, brother of King Alfonso XI. of Castile. Ismail collected his troops and urged them to behave valiantly in the approaching battle. They were led by Mahragain, "a brave Parthian," while Ismail commanded the reserve. The former attacked the Christians with such force that they soon fled, leaving their camp to plunder, and "the two valiant Princes of Castile thus died fighting with the bravery of lions, both falling in the hottest and most stubbornly contested period of the battle. The conquerors continued the pursuit of the flying force until nightfall, when the unhappy Christians, favoured by the obscurity, first began to conceive hopes of escape from their victorious lances. On the following day the Moslemah soldiers found the field was covered with the bodies of the slain; but the vast riches which they obtained from the camp of the Christians well repaid them for the labour of their burial: Ismail having commanded that all should be interred lest the air should become infected by the emanations from them. The Moslemah cavaliers who died on that day were buried with their vestments and arms as they were found—the most honourable shrouds and mortuary ornaments which the true Moslemah can have from the world. It was obtained at the close of the year 718 (A.D. 1319).*

From Al-makkari we have this characteristic description of this important conflict, which comprises a direct and curious reference to the Fortress of Gibraltar.

---

date. The 24th of November is the Festival of St. John of the Cross in the Spanish and Roman calendars; the 12th of the same month is appointed to St. John the Almoner in the Greek calendar, and the 13th of the same to St. John Chrysostom in the Greek rule; so the 13th of September by that of France, and the 26th September to St. John the Evangelist in the Greek calendar. See what follows, from Al-makkari, making the date the 15th of May, which is the Eve of St. John Nepomucen in the Spanish calendar.   * *Ibid.*

In 1319, Pedro, Infante of Castile, having with him, as it is reported, no fewer than twenty-five Christian princes, marched to the attack of Granada. He secured beforehand the blessing of the Pope, or *Bábá* as the Moorish writer styles him, saying also that the Christians worshipped his Holiness. These preparations terrified the Moors of Granada, and they sought help in the old direction and from Abu Sa'id, the Merine Sultan of Fez, who declined, or at least took no notice of, their entreaties. The Granadines must have plucked up hearts of their own or obtained assistance elsewhere than from the Merines, as Pedro was met by five thousand under their king (Sunday, May 15th, 1319). This army seemed so small to the Christians that they felt sure of victory; yet the Moslems made so desperate an attack that the former fled immediately, and more than fifty thousand of them were said to have been slain, besides those who were drowned in the river. (?) The spoils were prodigious; forty-three hundredweight of gold, one hundred and forty hundredweight of silver, besides armour, arms, and horses. There were seven thousand prisoners. Among these were the wife and children of the King (Infante), and, although she offered for her ransom the city of Tarifa and the fortress of *Jebalu-l-fatah* (Gibraltar) and eighteen more castles in that district, the Moslems would not accept it, and she remained in captivity. As to Don Pedro, he was slain, and his skin, being stripped from his body, was stuffed with cotton and suspended over the gate of Granada, where it remained for years.* This was called the Battle of Elvira.

This very curious reference to Gibraltar appears in the history to which we have so often referred. It seems that the

---

* The Christian writers deny this assertion, and say that the body was carried to the convent of Las Huelgas, Burgos.

Moors could hardly have expected to obtain higher ransom than this for the lady and her children. They were probably detained in order to compel the offering of terms different from the above, or the victors in the great combat might have believed themselves secure of the places by ordinary processes of war.

The further progress of Ismail Ben Feraz displays an incident in the history of warlike operations which is very important, and illustrates the use, if not the first employment, of those terrible arms which have nowhere been employed with more effect and energy than at Gibraltar—we mean cannon. It happened in the year 1325 that Ismail besieged the city of Baza. "He fixed his camp," says Condé, "before the city, and entrenched his position with great care; that done he commenced the attack, assaulting the place day and night with various engines of war; among these machines were some that cast globes of fire, with resounding thunders and lightnings, resembling those of the resistless tempest; all these missiles causing fearful injuries to the walls and towers of the city. These attacks, with the privations endured by the defenders, compelled the latter to submission, and they made their conventions with King Ismail to that effect; Medina Baza being surrendered on the 24th of the moon of Regib, 724* (A.D.

---

* The earliest known document of English origin referring to the use of cannon is much later than the above reference to 1325, being dated 1338, and an indenture between John Sterlyng, Clerk of the King's Ships, and Helmyng Leget, keeper of the same, 22nd June, 12th Edward III., for the delivery of "ij canons de ferr sanz estuff" in a ship called "Le Bernard de la Tour" ('Tower'); also, in the barge "La Marie de la Tour," "a cannon of iron of 2 chambers, a brass one, a kettle, and a sponger:" "iij canons of iron with v chambers, and a hand-gun were in the hulk called 'Christopher of the Tower.'" M. Gayangos, in a letter to Captain Brackenbury, Royal Artillery, quoted by the latter in *Athenæum*, No. 2142, November 14, 1868, refers to such statements as this which we quote from Condé, adding, "I believe the same (artillery) came from China and India." If Condé's authority is unimpeach-

1325)." He also employed such machines as these in the taking of Martos, a place which has further significance in our history, and as we shall see, again at the siege of Algeciras.

---

able and its date exact, this employment of cannon at Baza is the first recorded case of the kind in Europe. M. Gayangos, in referring cannon to the far East, has forgotten the description by Marco Polo, of the siege of Sayanfu (Siang-Yang), 1273, which shows that balistæ and mangonels were then used in China; it does not prove, however, because Kublai Khan employed the more ancient mode of projection in the siege of a Chinese city, that cannon were then unknown to the Chinese.

Since the publication in the *Athenæum* of the letter referred to above, a reply by Mr. Riley was issued, which invalidates the assumptions founded on the alleged dates of the English records. This, of course, does not affect the statements we have quoted from Condé; these must stand on their own merits, whatever those may be.

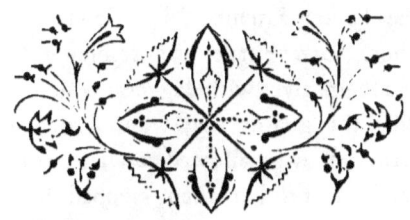

CHAPTER XX.

THE THIRD SIEGE, 1333.

FROM the taking of Martos by such strange means arose an event which changed the course of Moslem history and enabled the son of Ismail to accomplish that achievement for which his father had so strongly striven, *i.e.* the recapture of Gibraltar from the Christians. This event referred to a woman. Among the captives at Martos was a damsel of great beauty whom Mohammed Ben Ismail, son of the Wali of Algeciras, rescued from the soldiery at the peril of his life. Ben Feraz, notwithstanding this, seeing the girl, fell in love with and took her from Ben Ismail, and a great quarrel happened between the men about her. The Wali of Algeciras, it must be remembered, like other personages of that title, was almost independent as a ruler and his son a man of importance, moreover a cousin to Ben Feraz himself; this champion was furious with wrath at the treatment he received, and determined upon taking revenge; for this purpose, having assembled his friends at the gate of the Alhambra, where Ben Feraz was rejoicing for the recent victories, armed themselves with daggers, which they concealed, and after telling the guards they wanted to address the king as he came forth, they were allowed to wait until this happened. Mohammed and his brother then stepped forward, as if to salute their sovereign, and stabbed him in the head and breast, also the chief wizir, who attended, and, in the confusion, escaped. The second wizir was equal to this emergency and dexterously contrived the succession of the crown to Mohammed IV., the son of Ben Feraz. The sepulchral inscription of Ben Feraz declared him to be " the Martyr King, Restorer of the House of the Nas'rs " (A.D. 1324).

Mohammed IV., called Abu Abdallah, was but twelve years old at his accession; later he became a great champion in Andalus. Among the most important of his proceedings was the Third Siege of Gibraltar. He was troubled by rebellions and other distresses, among them, the revolt of his uncle and the General Othman Abn Sa'id, who had had charge of his youth. These called in the aid of the Christians to the ruin of the country, and, further, had help from Africa. Mohammed IV. (it must have been his general, for he was then but sixteen years of age) sent for aid to the Wali of Algeciras, entreating him to prevent the passing of the Straits by the Beni Merines, who, however, not only did this, but took that city of Algeciras itself and others of hardly less importance. Nevertheless did Mohammed, or his advisers, continue this war with energy. Assembling a small but effective force, he took Baena, and after an attack upon Casares, resolved to assault Gibraltar.

The Fortress of the Rock was, say the Moslem authorities, then very poorly garrisoned, by which we are to understand that it was poorly supplied as well as inefficiently garrisoned. The governor was one who had distinguished himself in former wars, and was therefore considered fit to hold so important a place; yet he had one characteristic defect, avarice; for, says Ayala, his principal aim was to accumulate fortune for himself out of the dues and other resources of the fortress. The money thus embezzled he employed to buy houses in Seville. This governor was Vasco Perez de Meira; he neglected his charge, so that the walls were unsound, the place badly provisioned and worse armed. Information to this effect had been carried to the Moorish king, so that "he directed his flying camp on the city, and so closely pressed the siege that, in despite of the machines and engines which the Christians used in their defence, he took possession of the place by force of arms, and occupied it with his troops." The case, however, was not quite of so simple a nature as this summary would seem to indicate. The Moslems captured the arsenal by a *coup de main*, but made slight progress by means of their arms beyond that point, which enabled them to blockade the Fortress, which was so badly stored that a few days must have brought the issue if, as the Christian historians relate, a strange chance had not cast a grain ship ashore and within reach. On more than one similar occasion such wrecks have happened, as when a Danish craft laden with lemons came into the hands of General Elliot's garrison, then suffering dreadfully from scurvy (October 11, 1780) and, in the year preceding, a storm cast abundance of drift wood under the walls, so that, as "fuel had long been a scarce article, this supply," says Drinkwater, " was therefore considered as a miraculous interference of Providence in our favour." The siege under Mohammed lasted but the longer on this account, yet might have been still more protracted if the greed of the Spanish governor had not led the way to his own ruin. He actually fattened his prisoners on the stores which were hardly sufficient to keep his soldiers alive. Shut up in the castle or keep, which had been considerably strengthened since its erection by Abd-l-Mumen Ibn Ali in 1161, the Spaniards, while they ate leather, had the mortification of seeing the food which was needed to maintain their lives and strength, expended in keeping their captives in good condition, and in order that the avaricious governor should, if he and all his men did not become captives in turn, gain higher ransoms for the Moslems. This extraordinary conduct availed De Perez nothing, for—after sustaining the place for nearly five months, during which period the Christian kings of Spain, engaged with intestine troubles, made no effectual efforts to deliver him—the governor was compelled to surrender on receiving safeguard for himself and the few who remained of the garrison. Of course he lost the ransoms for which he had risked, if not sacrificed, so much, and he took good care not to face Alfonso XI., his sovereign, but ended his days in Africa, living on the remains of his plunder and under the contempt of his countrymen. Nevertheless it must be owned that he suffered much in the service, and the siege was, for that age, a lengthy one. Thus ended the third siege of Gibraltar, by means of which it returned to Moslem hands for a time, having been in those of the Christians for about twenty-two years.

CHAPTER XXI.

THE FOURTH SIEGE, 1334.

ALFONSO XI. was not the ruler to allow such a fortress as that of which we are treating to remain unassailed in the power of his enemies. At the moment, however, he was engaged in the northern part of his dominions. Mohammed IV. reconquered Algeciras, which had fallen into the hands of the Beni Merines,* with other cities of this district. This tide of good fortune for the Granadian prince was of brief duration. Alfonso gathered all his forces to recapture Gibraltar, and, as the Arabian chronicler has it, invested the place both by land and sea; so that Mohammed was compelled to repeat the fatal policy of his predecessors, by seeking the aid of the Beni Merines against the enemy of their common faith. The Africans were admitted to the fortress again, and, as soon as it was in their power to do so, annoyed and distressed the rightful garrison almost as much as if they had been their foes. The Granadians were compelled to submit to many indignities from their insolent allies. The Moslem accounts allege that the approach of the troops of their nation compelled Alfonso to raise the siege, and retreat, capturing Teba in the return; but this does not agree with the histories of their antagonists, which declare that it was not until after the failure of a rash attempt that the Castilian king retreated, and but for one day,

* Al-makkari. Condé.

after which he returned with the resolution to free certain of his soldiers who had been taken before the walls, and under the command of Rui Lopez and Fernan de Meira, adventurous captains, who lost much by their rashness. The first thing Alfonso effected was the digging of a trench across the sands, between the Bay of Algeciras and the Mediterranean, thus converting the Rock into an island, a practice which has been partially repeated since his time. His object was evidently to starve the garrison, and keep succour from them. The tenacity of his character displayed itself in this as well as in other circumstances. Not even the death of his son, nor troubles in Castile and the capture of Benimexi by the Arabs, sufficed to change his purpose. Ayala tells us that the monotony and apparent hopelessness of the attempt was relieved by the capture of a distinguished Granadian general, who fell into a trap. Yet there seemed no chance of success. Both parties suffered dreadfully from fatigue and disease, and Alfonso was about to abandon the attack, when envoys came to him from the enemy with proposals for a truce of four years, the Granadians promising to pay annually to Alfonso ten thousand doubloons of gold, the fortress to remain in their hands, with liberty to purchase provisions. Condé condensed the Moorish account of this matter, which is to this effect—that Gibraltar had been usurped by the Beni Merines when they were called to aid, as before stated, so that Mohammed IV. made a virtue of necessity and yielded the fortress, as of free will, to his treacherous ally, whom Alfonso attacked there with such strength that he was about to become master, when the Beni Merines, in their turn, solicited aid from the Granadians; whereupon Mohammed came with a strong army and attacked the Christians so vigorously that he defeated them with great slaughter, and compelled the raising of the siege. This account continues in a manner which looks like truth, to the effect that Mohammed, elated with this success, triumphed over the African general whom he had succoured, boasting that the Christians, like all those born in Andalus, thought the Africans unworthy of their swords, but that the advent of his Granadians saved the hungry and wretched Africans, the Beni Merines, subjects of the Sultan of Fez. Further, that these insults rankled in the hearts of the Merines, who seized the opportunity of Mohammed going to visit their king, Abd-l-Hassan, in Africa, to murder him on the road, A.H. 733, A.D. 1334. It is certain that Mohammed Ben Ismail was assassinated in this manner, and on such an occasion.

It is curious that Al-makkari confounds together the sequence of events in reference to the sieges of 1309 and 1334, for he tells us that " when the news of the former event reached Africa, Abd-l-Hassan (son of Othman) Al-merini, Sultan of Fez, who knew the importance of the Fortress, and spent his treasures upon it in repairing and increasing the fortifications, resolved upon wresting the valuable prize from the enemy. Accordingly, taking with him one of his sons,* he sailed thither with his fleet, and, being joined soon after landing by the Granadians under the command of Mohammed, closely invested the place, and made himself master of it.

No sooner had Abd-l-Hassan reduced Gibraltar † than he began to give his attention to repairing the buildings and increasing the fortifications, spending immense sums of money in building houses and magazines, as well as a *jámi*, or principal mosque, and erecting new walls, towers, and even a citadel.‡

---

* Abd-l-malic (" Abomilique "), who was killed in battle soon after.

† Al-makkari, vol. ii. p. 355.

‡ There is a very elaborate account of these buildings in the " Travels of Ibn Battútah," A.H. 750, or A.D. 1348 *(Gayangos)*.

Before, however, these improvements were fully completed, the Christians invested Gibraltar by sea and land; but their attempt was frustrated by the gallant defence of the Moslems, commanded by the King of Granada, and they were compelled to raise the siege. (This, of course, refers to the fourth attack upon the place.) After this, the Sultan, Abd-l-Hassan, again applied himself further to strengthen Gibraltar, by causing a thick wall to be built at the foot of the Rock, surrounding it on all sides, as the halo surrounds the crescent moon, so that the enemy could discover no prospect of success in attacking it, nor did there appear any way through which he could force an entrance. In the course of time, however, Algeciras became the prey of the infidels, in consequence of the defeat which Abd-l-Hassan, together with Ibnu-l-Ahmar (Abu-l-hijág Yusuf), suffered at Tarifa; and Gibraltar was afterwards taken from the Beni Merines by Mohammed Al-ghani-billah, Sultan of Granada. Soon after the Christians had raised the siege of Gibraltar, continues Al-makkari, Sultan Mohammed was assassinated."

CHAPTER XXII.

THE SIEGE OF TARIFA.

GIBRALTAR thus remained in the hands of the Beni Merines, and was, as usual, *tête de pont* for further conquests. The news of the assassination of Mohammed IV. is said to have come to his army while returning from the relief of the Fortress. (*Condé.*) Jusef Ben Ismail Ben Feraz, his brother, succeeded to the crown, and received the oaths of allegiance from his generals, as they were assembled at Algeciras. He sought peace on all sides, but found none after the expiration of the truce which his brother had made. Even before the lapse of the time, it is alleged that the Merine owner of Gibraltar landed a great force there, which could only be destined for the injuring of the Christians (1338). Alfonso gathered his feudatories, reconciled those to their allegiance who had been in rebellion, engaged allies from Portugal and Arragon and endeavoured to prevent the landing of reinforcements from Africa on the Spanish coast. In this he was unsuccessful; but in the winter of 1339 his troops defeated their enemies. This event seems to have cemented the union of the Granadians with their African neighbours, for both parties gathered immense armies. On the part of the Christians, it was attempted to maintain the command of the Straits of Gibraltar by means of the Castilian and Arragonese fleets. This resulted unfortunately in the first instance, for the African fleet, consisting of one hundred and forty galleys, surrounded those of the Castilians and Arragonese, and destroyed many of them, killing the admiral, Tenorio, and opening the Straits to further reinforcements from the kingdom of Fez. This was towards the close of the year of the Hegira 741, A.D. 1340. Great rejoicings of the Arabs followed this triumph, and their two kings met at Algeciras with the highest hopes. At this conference it was agreed to besiege Tarifa, which was put in practice according to the mode which was referred to here before. "The Moslemah commenced the attack with various machines; among others, those engines of thunder which cast great balls of iron, with *nafta (? naphtha)* whereby a fearful destruction was made in the well-towered walls of the city." *(Condé.)* "Aid was sought in all directions, and the Portuguese as well as the Castilians rushed impetuously to battle; for it seems to have been felt on both sides that the time of a deadly struggle was at hand. Such was indeed the case, for the battle of the Salado, called by the Moorish writers that of the Guadacelito (River Celito) was one of the most terrific combats of which we have records. The Moors made incursions to the Christian territories, and did a prodigious amount of mischief, but were caught on their return laden with plunder. It was then that Abd-l-malek and another general were slain. Meanwhile Alfonso secured assistance in ships from Genoa, Portugal and Arragon, to reinstate his fleet of the Straits; this naval aid was gathered in Tarifa Bay, and in the latter days of October, 1340, Alfonso and his ally and namesake, Alfonso, called the Brave, of Portugal, appeared before the antagonistic hosts in the neighbourhood of the same city. On the 27th of this month, the armies met in combat "near the very spot where, five hundred years later, was fought the Battle of Barrossa." *(Sayers.)* It is needless to enter into details of this terrible conflict; suffice it that at a critical moment the garrison of Tarifa rushed from the place and turned the fortunes of the day to the utter defeat of the Moslems, and the slaughter of a prodigious number of their best soldiers. Some of the vanquished fled to Africa, the King of Fez retreated to Gibraltar, and his ally, of Granada, to Algeciras. The former soon afterwards crossed to Ceuta, and the latter, by sea also, went to Granada. Thus vividly did Al-makkari describe this event: " Abu-l-Hassan landed on the coast of Andalus with the laudable purpose of aiding his fellows of the Moslem faith; he did this with sixty thousand men, and was soon after joined by the Granadian army. ' Alas! God Almighty, whose decrees are infallibly executed upon his creatures, had decided in his infinite wisdom that this proud armament should be dispersed like the dust before the wind, and that Abu-l-Hassan himself should return to his dominions vanquished and a fugitive; that the sharp-edged sword of the infidel should shine over his head, and those of his men. We will not inquire how it happened; but the fact is, that thousands of Moslems won that day the crown of martyrdom, that the ranks of doctors and theologians were frightfully thinned, the law of the sword being executed upon their throats. The Sultan's (of Fez) own son and all his harem fell into the hands of the victorious enemy, his treasures became the prey of the idolators, who from that day thought of nothing short of subjecting the rest of Andalus to their abominable rule.' "

CHAPTER XXIII.

THE SIEGE OF ALGECIRAS, 1342-4.   THE FIFTH SIEGE OF GIBRALTAR.

THIS great victory not only established the supremacy of the Christians in Spain, and inflicted a severe punishment upon their enemies of Andalus and Almagreb, but it drew the eyes of Europe upon the contest in the Peninsula, so that when he sat down before Algeciras, this entrenched camp of Alfonso was the goal of adventurous knights and nobles from many lands. Among these was Henry Plantagenet, Earl of Lancaster, of the blood royal of England, who was son of Edmund (Crouchback), the second son of Henry III., guardian of Edward III., father of the first Duke of Lancaster, and, through the latter, grandfather of Blanche Plantagenet, who married John of Gaunt. This Earl of Lancaster was called "Wryneck," and had been distinguished in opposition to Mortimer, Earl of March, and Queen Isabella, in the days of Edward II. He was wounded in the siege of Algeciras, and died 1345. Besides this lord there came his son, the Earl of Derby, about whom Froissart wrote so much, and the Earls of Salisbury, Lincoln, and Leicester, the King of Navarre, a large body of Genoese mercenaries, French, Portuguese, and Italian knights. The place was defended with the greatest energy; sallies were made; and when the Christians brought forward their wheeled towers of wood, covered with raw hides, the cannons, loaded with *red-hot* balls of iron, with thundering *nafta*, were discharged with terrible effect. We believe this is the earliest recorded instance of red-hot balls being discharged from guns, although, of course, even the Romans employed bolts of incandescent iron in their catapults. If we are correct, it is noteworthy, that at Algeciras was first employed that formidable means of defence which was so serviceable in the Great Siege of Gibraltar. This defence, in a desperate attempt made by the Granadian king to relieve the place by an attack on the entrenched besiegers, was vain; the King of Fez having burnt his fingers before, refused to aid; the blockade which Alfonso kept up at the mouth of the port was by no means ineffectual at any time, and, later, most stringent. Although the besiegers suffered dreadfully, they held to their purpose, and a contribution from the French king, with a loan from the Pope, together seventy thousand florins, enabled Alfonso to keep his troops in the field, and pay his mercenaries. At last Jusef Ben Ismail treated for the surrender of his famous city, and consented to do so, pay twelve thousand gold doubloons, and accept a truce for ten years, besides declaring that he held his crown under the sovereignty of Alfonso and his heirs. Thus, according to the feudal theory, there were no supreme rulers but Christians in Spain, and nominally, the reign of the Moslems expired. The enemy took possession of Algezira Alhadra, an event which occurred, after a siege of twenty months in the moon of Muharram, and the year 744 (A.D. 1344). This was three years before the Battle of Crecy, at which cannon are said to have been first used by the English.

It was recorded by the Arabian historian that Alfonso treated the generals of Jusef Ben Ismail, who had been opposed to him, with great courtesy, and had much consideration for the people who were expelled from their homes in Algeciras. It is noteworthy that this chivalric disposition of the Spanish king was fully appreciated by the Moors, who, as all authorities assure us, put on mourning "in token of respect for him when he died in the course of the next siege of Gibraltar;" and "although he was of a truth rejoiced in his heart at the death of so potent an enemy," as the Moslem chronicler candidly states of his own king, "yet he nevertheless exhibited certain signs of regret, and declared that one of the most excellent princes of the world had been lost in the person of Alfonso Ben Ferdinand, the grandson of Sancho." Meantime, the number of inhabitants on the Rock had been much enlarged by migrations from the neighbouring city of Algeciras, where the expelled could continue with little real disadvantage their old trades in the old channels.

At this time, also, the fortifications had been vastly increased by Abu-l-Hassan, and Faris, his son, the Merine Sultans of Fez, in whose hands Gibraltar still remained. It is clear that although the truce was made between Alfonso and the Granadian king for ten years, yet, either the former broke this condition, or what is more probable, the treaty did not include the Merines; for although Algeciras was taken in A.H. 744 (A.D. 1344), the Castilian again assembled his forces, and was actually "encamped on the sea-shore between Gebal Taric and Algezira Alhadra in the spring of the year 780" (A.D. 1348-9). This was after Ben Ismail had in vain sought to have the truce prolonged to fifteen years. Alfonso would not consent to this, but "came with a great power to lay siege to Gebal Taric so soon as the truce had expired; the loss of that stronghold, which he had once occupied, weighing heavily upon his heart." *(Condé.)* He brought many engines and great machines of war to bear upon the place (no mention here of cannon in Christian hands, so be it noted); but Gebal

Taric, continues the Arabian writer, is so strong by the nature of its site, and the brave garrison defended their hold so well, that he could do nothing effectual against it. In the first case Alfonso began by assaulting the place with the machines that, however terrible in other cases, were comparatively innocuous against the Rock, which, we may be sure, had cannon for its defence. In this attack Alfonso soon found the prodigious advantage that accrued to him by the possession of Algeciras, which city had hitherto been a great hindrance to assaults on Gibraltar. The places defended each other, so to say; but now the Christians were fortunate in having the city as a base of operations against the Rock. Alfonso was comparatively poor, and soon exhausted the money which had been laid up for this war; so, after carrying on the siege for nearly six months he sold part of the estates of the crown to Perez de Guzman for a subsidy which came fortunately to his aid. An Arragonese squadron helped to increase the blockade of the Port of Gibraltar; in fact the siege became a mere blockade, but "it pleased God that this valiant king and unrelenting enemy of Islam, who had hoped to make himself master of all the Moslemah territories in Spain, should himself depart from life."

This happened thus. The plague had been running its common course in the world for two years then last past. In London, in 1348, no fewer than fifty thousand persons were slain by pestilence. In Saragossa three hundred daily died. In Florence more than two-thirds of the people perished. This was the plague which forms what may be called a foil to the luxurious scenes of the "Decameron" of Boccacio. Now, it is not to be wondered at that a camp such as that of Alfonso, pitched in such a place as the sands before Gibraltar, and inhabited by troops so mixed as his, soon became a hole of pestilence, and the terrified people appealed to their general and king that he would abandon the siege of Gibraltar. The women, who were accommodated with quarters in the camp, the very captains, the troops themselves, all besought the king to yield up his purpose, at least for a while, yet, so stubborn was he that not even the kneeling ladies, and urgent counsel, stirred his will; he utterly refused to permit the breaking up of the camp, to give away the advantages of so much cost in blood and treasure. For nearly three months his purpose held, and the sturdy garrison still maintained their hold on Gibraltar; but, says the Arabian writer, " he died of the plague on a Giuma, which was the 10th day of the moon Muharran, in the year 751 " (10th March, 1350).

Thus perished a splendid prince, of whom even his enemies spoke well, says the Moorish historian, writing of his person in this curiously striking portrait: " Alfonso was of middle height, but of well-proportioned figure; his complexion was red and white, his eyes had a tinge of green, with a grave and serious expression; he was robust of person, strong and of a healthy constitution, very elegant and graceful in manner, highly resolute and brave, noble and sincere, and for the misfortune of the Moslemah, very prosperous in war." A Granadian army was then opposed to that of the Spaniards, but such was the chivalric feeling with regard to Alfonso that its commanders refrained from hostilities at the moment of the king's death, nor did they prevent the removal of his body to Seville, whence it was afterwards carried to Cordova.

Thus ended the life of the first Christian captor and repeated besieger of Gibraltar. With his life ended the Fifth Siege of this now famous place.

CHAPTER XXIV.

THE KING OF GIBRALTAR. THE SIXTH AND SEVENTH SIEGES.

THE successor of Alfonso XI. on the throne of Castile was his son, whom we call the *Cruel*, although some of his subjects adopted for him the milder name of the *Just*. The former would appear to be the aptest title for the man who put to death Leonora de Guzman, his father's mistress and the mother of several of his own half-brethren, of whom the famous Henry of Transtamare was afterwards the avenger in blood, and Pedro's successor. Associated as Pedro's name is with so many acts of atrocity, it is not needful for us to do more than recall to the minds of our readers the names of some of his victims. These are, besides Leonora de Guzman, Garcilasso de la Vega, Blanche de Bourbon of the French blood royal, Juanna de Castro, Fadrique de Guzman, his own half-brother, Abu Sa'id or Abu Abdillah, the usurping king of Granada, his guest, whom he killed with his own hand. Bertrand du Guesclin and our own Black Prince were mixed up in the series of revolts which ended in the fratricide by Henry of Transtamare. Mohammed V. of Granada, son of Jusef Ben Ismail, succeeded his father, who was murdered by a lunatic while at prayers, and was himself slain by means of the mother of Ismail, another son of Jusef, 1359.

Meanwhile a striking event in the history of Gibraltar had happened. In the year 756 (A.D. 1354) the Wali of Gebal Taric, Isa Ben Al-hassan Ben Abi Mandel Alascari, took possession of that fortress in his own name, and assumed the title of king. He had power to keep down the faithful inhabitants who would have opposed themselves to his rebellion, but his avarice and cruelty soon rendered him so abhorrent to all the people, that an insurrection ensued, wherein every one declared against him, and he was compelled to shut himself up in the citadel with his son, and but three weeks after the usurpation of the sovereign authority. Being thus besieged by the people, he was, in a short time, reduced to surrender, when his victors sent him bound to Ceuta, and gave him up, together with his son, to the King Abu Anan. That monarch then caused them both to be put to death with the most cruel and unparalleled tortures, as the reward of their disloyalty and rebellion.

The next event of note in the neighbourhood of Gibraltar, for we cannot here take account of the disorders of the Castilian and Granadian kingdoms, was the taking, very easily, of Algeciras by Mohammed V. in 1370, a place which he burnt and dismantled (A.H. 772). In 1379 Henry of Transtamare died suddenly, and, it was averred, by means of certain slippers said to have been poisoned by order of Mohammed V., and sent by him, with other gifts, to his then ally. Juan I. and Henry III. followed consecutively on the Castilian throne. Mohammed V. died in 1407, and Jusef III., his brother, reigned in his stead.

We do not know how Gibraltar came into the possession of the kings of Granada at this time; it is evident that the suzerein of the place, at the death of Isa Ben Al-hassan, was an African prince, for the conquerors of that briefly-reigning monarch sent him to Ceuta. It is clear, from the account in *Condé*, that in 1411 the people of the Rock, weary of the oppressions of their governor and of submitting to the kings of Granada, wrote letters to Abu Sa'id, King of Fez, offering to acknowledge themselves as his vassals if he would aid them in their need and receive them to his faith and protection. The King of Fez was much rejoiced by that embassy, and instantly despatched his brother, also called Abu Sa'id, with two thousand men, to occupy that important fortress, *which is the key to all Spain.* Yet the King of Fez was not moved wholly by his wish to obtain possession of Gibraltar; he was jealous of his brother, who was so much beloved at home that the king fancied he might be dangerous to his own throne. This suspicion seems to have been unjust. The younger Abu Sa'id crossed the Straits with his army, and easily obtained possession of the greater part of the Fortress; the Granadian governor retired to the citadel, and meanwhile succours came to him from his own king, who, in their turn, besieged the troops from Fez, and ultimately made them prisoners of war. The Prince of Granada strengthened the garrison, and returned with Abu Sa'id the younger to his father, who received the latter with honour, and when the King of Fez requested him to destroy his brother, who seems to have been sent to be trapped in Gibraltar, he refused to have anything to do with such wickedness, and sent the letter to the intended victim, who therefore accepted the aid that was proffered by his host, and recrossed the Straits with ample forces and abundant money. The King of Fez was, as may be imagined, intensely astonished at this turn of affairs, which ended in his own deposition and imprisonment. This was the sixth siege of our Fortress.

It was not until 1436 that the peace of the Fortress was disturbed anew by warlike measures; at this time, as if to complete the strangeness of its fortunes, the siege was laid by one of the De Guzmans, so that, after being for centuries the prize of kings, and itself, for a while, a little kingdom, it was then attacked by a private person; this was the first, but not the last like attempt. The new assailant was Henry II., Count of Niebla, who had derived from his grandfather, the first Christian conqueror of the Fortress, a considerable extent of land and valuable rights of tunny and other fisheries on the coast. The constant wars and rebellions of the Arabs caused great injuries to these possessions, so that, in hopes of securing the place, he gathered his vassals and friends from all quarters, and sat down before the Rock in the year we have named. He collected these troops, and ships to aid them, in secret. As before, the Red Sands, to the west of the city, was the point of the land attack. The command was given to the son of the count, and the party flattered themselves that their preparations were unknown to the defenders, whom they believed to be weaker than was really the case. The latter had, with equal secrecy, gathered stores and reinforcements, and added to their defences. The storming party was allowed by the Moors to land where strong defences were already prepared against them; this was a slip of the beach, where the invaders were cramped for room, and exposed to the advance of the tide, which, when the attack began, came in upon them, and, together with the missiles of the besieged, caused the most dreadful losses to the Christians. The boats, which had put off for more soldiers, returned to the aid of those who had first landed, yet it was but to share their fate. The count, who was with his boats, was, after he had got to a safe place, attracted by the entreaties of an old friend; he returned but to be drowned, with forty nobles, by means of the numbers who attempted to get into the boats. An attack, which was planned against the other side of the Fortress, failed also, and the entire army was disorganised, so that both fleet and troops returned homewards utterly defeated. The body of De Guzman was picked up by the Moors, who refused to accept ransom for it, and hung it from the battlements of the citadel for twenty-six years, when Alfonso of Arcos took the place, and removed the corpse of his luckless predecessor. On this occasion the strangely varied fortunes of the Rock were, for the first time, illustrated by the treachery of a born Moor, a convert to Christianity. The death-day of the Moslem power in Spain was now at hand; we shall soon write its epitaph in the mournful yet resigned words of the historian whom we have followed so long through the many turns of this eventful history.

CHAPTER XXV.

THE EIGHTH SIEGE, 1462.

NEARLY an entire generation passed away ere Gibraltar underwent another in the long series of its sieges. The repulse and ruin of De Guzman happened in 1436, and, except such occasional alarms as those to which all fortresses were then liable, and the pain of seeing the hated Christians increase their hold upon the neighbouring country, the Moorish citizens and soldiers of the Rock found safety if not peace upon its sides. The King of Granada was tributary to his royal brother of Castile, yet frontier wars were almost unceasing. The throne of Granada, since we last reckoned its occupants, had passed from Mohammed Ben Jusef, in 1407, to Jusef Ben Jusef, or Jusef III., who reigned until 1422, and was followed by Mohammed VII., called *El Hayzari*, who continued in possession until 1435, and was succeeded by Mohammed VIII., Ben Osman, who ruled until 1454 (A.H. 859). This was the year after the fall of Constantinople under Constantine XIV., and the setting up, under Mohammed II., of the Ottoman Empire in Europe. By this comparison of contemporaneous events we see that although the Moslem dominion in Spain was nodding to its fall, yet, not only was the catastrophe to be postponed until the end of the century, 1492, but the general influence of the followers of the Arabian Prophet was still potent even in Europe, and a mighty power founded with a destiny that was terrible to this continent. When the

Granadian kingdom ended, Constantinople had just fallen after a siege which ranks with those of our Rock under General Elliot; the glorious defence of Charleston by the Confederate States of North America; and, so far as we yet see in historical significance, far surpassed these events, or the destruction of Sebastopol by the French and English.

To Mohammed VIII. succeeded, in 1454, Mohammed IX., Ben Ismail, in the ninth year of whose reign (1462) Gibraltar passed finally into Christian hands. This is how it happened. The place was in the possession of the Spanish Moors, their brethren of Almagreb having, for the last time, parted with it many years before this period; but we know not exactly how. Condé's authority gives the history very briefly, and to the effect that the Duke of Medina-Sidonia attacked the place, and after an obstinate resistance on the part of the garrison, took it—"a great and lasting injury to the Moslemah." This writer also refers to a visit paid to the place by King Henry of Castile. The fact was the Fortress was betrayed to the Christians by a converted Moor, Ali-l-Carro, who repaired to Alonzo of Arcos, the governor of Tarifa, and detailed the almost incapable condition of the Fortress, and thus induced the governor to attempt a surprise, which certainly had so much of the promise of success as lay in its being made at dawn on the very day after the receipt of the intelligence. This attempt was fortunate in leading only to the capture of a small party of Moorish soldiers, who, after being tortured, gave warnings which convinced the governor of Tarifa that more strength than he could employ would be required for success. He therefore sent for aid to Xeres, to the Duke of Medina-Sidonia, to the Count of Arcos, the head of his own family, to Juan, a descendant of the slain De Guzman, and others. Some troops came at once, and with these, rashly as it resulted, the governor made an assault by storm, which the garrison defeated without much difficulty, yet with such effect in dispiriting the assailants, that they would have abandoned their purpose had it not been for further information of the great distress and, what was worse, disputes in the garrison as to whether or not the Rock should be given up, and upon what terms; some would have been content with their lives; others held out for the honours of war; a third party demanded both of these, and safe conveyance for all their properties to the Granadian capital. This news of the state of affairs within was gained by means of a deserter, a second traitor. But for this the attack— it could not yet be called a siege — would have been considered hopeless. While the Christians were weighing the chances of a second attempt which might end in their own ruin or hasten the decision of the Moorish garrison, a party of the besieged sent to offer a capitulation, provided they were permitted to leave the place with all their property. Alonzo of Arcos had hardly looked for so ready a conquest as this implied, yet, strange to say, dissensions were as rife without as within Gibraltar; so he was compelled to evade a reply by declaring his necessity to wait the coming of a greater authority, who was hourly expected in the camp. It was not long before this great personage arrived, being Rodrigo, son of the Count of Arcos, who in obedience to the summons sent by Alfonso, entered the camp with a very welcome reinforcement. The Arab governor of Gibraltar now issued forth to treat for surrender, so eagerly does the hardly-pressed garrison seem to have sought to be rid of the charge which, nevertheless, they had bravely defended by force of arms. The young Count of Arcos, however, such was the condition of the besiegers (!), declared himself unable to grant conditions of any sort without the consent of his own father and the Duke of Medina-Sidonia, who were expected soon to arrive in the camp. This absurd game of hide-and-seek might have continued longer, and the chance of capturing the place lost by the Spaniards, if it had not been for the promptitude of Rodrigo, who sent forward a troop of his own followers and took possession of the city gates; while the garrison, wisely saw that where there was no leader potent enough to give a guarantee, their own safety would be best consulted by continuing to occupy the keep, to which accordingly they retreated, and stood, as it were, at bay within its ancient walls. Thus, as the Rock passed by means of one Roderic to the dominion of the Arab invaders of Spain, so, after seven centuries and a half had elapsed (seven hundred and fifty-one years), it reverted to the Christians by means of a second and more fortunate Roderic.

This Ponce de Leon, bold as he was, incurred the profound displeasure of the Duke of Medina-Sidonia, when this dignitary, who was a little king in his way, joined the Christian army. It was of great importance to the latter that possession of Gibraltar should be his, insomuch as his lands lay largely round about it, and he was more interested in keeping unpleasant neighbours away from a place which had already proved a rock of offence to his power, riches, and dignity. The young Count of Arcos was by no means willing to yield, even to the great Duke, the authority and means for distinction which right of capture would confer upon himself and his family. A violent quarrel ensued on this point between the leaders, and was at one time likely to end in blows. This deplorable result was, however, avoided, rather than decided, by the nobles consenting to enter the fortress at the same instant, and the point of honour was settled by the setting up of their banners at the same moment.

The Spanish historians tell us that a large share of the honour which accrued by the capture of Gibraltar was popularly given to the Alcalde of Tarifa, the King Henry IV. of Castile—who, by the bye, can hardly be said to have deserved his soubriquet of "The Weak"—by way of rewarding him, created him Alcalde of Seville, and when Rodrigo died, in 1477, he was interred in the convent of the Carthusians in that city; on his tomb was engraved the following inscription:

"Here lies interred the much-honoured Alonzo de Arcos, of Tarifa, who recovered Gibraltar from the enemies of our holy faith. He departed this life in the year 1477, having been a great benefactor to this church."*

When Henry IV. learnt that Gibraltar had been conquered, his heart was full of joy, and he appointed the Duke of Medina-Sidonia to the charge of the place, but took care, however, to proclaim it as a fief of his crown, and even, by way of extra security, added to the royal titles that of Lord of Gibraltar. He conferred armorial distinction upon the place by granting the seal which is engraved on the title-page of this book, namely, *Gules*, a castle proper, with a key pendant at the gate, *or*, and the motto, "*Insignia Montis Calpe;*" thus indicating at once the character and importance of the fortress of the Rock, in reference to the kingdom of Castile. In December of the year of the capture the king appointed Pedro de Porras to be his governor of the place, and placed under its jurisdiction the city and district of Algeciras, conferring at the same time many privileges upon such men and their families who chose to settle there, following in this respect the example of Ferdinand IV., whose remarkable

---

* *The History of Gibraltar.* By Lopez de Ayala.

provisions to this end we have already described when treating of the First Siege. Thus: "As, by the grace of God, the city of Gibraltar was taken from the Moors, enemies of our Holy Catholic Faith, and is now belonging to me and my royal crown, and as the city guards the Straits so that there may not pass to the king or kingdom of Granada assistance in men, horses, arms, nor provisions; and as the said city has but few inhabitants, and that to people it I ought to bestow grace and favour on those who choose to go and dwell there, and remain continually, with their wives and children, so that they may be the more disposed to serve me and defend and protect the said city, and guard the Straits; it is therefore my favour to grant as follows." The condition and privileges thus referred to are then recited at length. (*Ayala.*)

Abu Ismail, distressed by the loss of Gibraltar, Archidona and other important places, which happened to him about the same time, applied to Henry IV. to grant him a truce for awhile, and obtained the request. Two years after the capture of the Rock the Castilian king visited the place, and superseded Pedro de Porras, the new governor, in favour of Don Bertrand de la Cueva, Count Laderma, the king's favourite, and alleged lover of the queen, who appointed as his deputy Stephano Villacreces. During this visit Alfonso V., of Portugal, being at Ceuta in the course of an expedition which he had undertaken against the Moors of Africa when he took Alcazar, Seguer, and Tangier, came by the invitation of Henry IV. to see the new acquisition, and was entertained in a splendid manner in hunting and feasting. This display of cordiality was not destined to last the lifetime of the Portuguese monarch, who before his death in 1479 was engaged in a disastrous war with Castile. He died of the plague, and was succeeded by his son John II.

The appointment of Bertran, or Beltran de la Cueva, was significant of his relationship with the king as a favourite. The alleged intimacy of this noble with the queen, and, in consequence, the illegitimacy of her daughter Juana, led to serious insurrections, which had for their object the placing of the king's brother, the Infante Alfonso on the throne. Among the discontented nobles was the Duke of Medina-Sidonia, who obtained from Alfonso a grant of Gibraltar. In pursuance to the rights thus conferred, the Duke undertook the Ninth Siege of Gibraltar; to describe which we shall hasten.

The civil war between the partisans of Alfonso and those of Henry IV. continued until the death of the former in 1468. Alfonso's party then sought to set up Isabella, Henry's sister, in his place, but she refused to deprive her brother of the crown. Finally an accommodation was made, whereby Henry agreed to divorce his queen, to disinherit Juana as illegitimate, and appoint Isabella his heiress in the crown of Castile. She married, 1462, Ferdinand of Arragon and the two united the crowns of Castile and Arragon in 1474.

CHAPTER XXVI.

TERMINATION OF THE ARABIAN REALM OF SPAIN.

HAVING followed the Arabian Realm of Spain through many changes of fortune, and being now arrived near its downfall and the woeful expulsion of the Moors from their seats in Granada—the first to be conquered of the provinces of the Peninsula, and the last to be held—we must spare a little time to trace the further history of this once magnificent and always civilised people. When one looks closely to their history, it is obvious that as they came by war, so they lived in almost constant war, and ultimately perished by war. Wonderful is their history, and it has never been even fairly written; in fact until the records of the Spanish nation are opened without reserve to the student, no hope can exist of doing such a subject justice. Mauro-Arabian history must be observed with greater opportunities, and in a more philosophic spirit than before, ere the Moslem side of the subject is reopened to the reader. So very narrow is the common view now taken that many still believe the conquerors of Andalus to have been in the main Arabs, whereas the fact was that the people of that race who crossed the Straits to victory were mostly Moors and Berbers, *i.e.* natives of the opposite coast of Africa, officered, it may have been, by Arabs; yet, it is interesting to observe that neither Taric nor Tarif were Arabs; that Condé's authority says quaintly that Muza " contrived to persuade the Berbers that they were sons of the Arabs, so that they enlisted in great numbers in his army; also, we know a large part of the garrison of Tangiers in Muza's time was comprised of Egyptians who had been previously conquered by the Arabs. Thus, it is evident that although the impetus of conquest came from the last-named race, and unchallengeable that it was their ardent faith which supplied a new and most powerful motive to the holders of a more ancient belief which must have been strangely effete, yet the Moslem conquests were as waves moving by a central power from Arabia, but it was the power more than the water, or the races, which sped to victory.

The impetus was already dying out long before the conquest of Constantinople was effected. This was quite as much a political as a religious change, for the Turks had already subjugated Moslems ere they came in contact with the remnant of the Roman Imperial power. The very Turkish dominion, fierce and strong as it was at first, and victorious beyond many precedents, so soon began to fade that about 1610 good Sir Richard Knolles, writing his fine old "History of the Turks," little more than a century and a half after the capture of Constantinople by Mohammed II., defined the causes of the ruin of the Ottoman Empire, and described its decay. It was not so with the Moors, Arabs or what you will of Spain, for these were a civilising people, who largely benefited the country they occupied, whereas the Turkish power has been little else than a camp.

After the capture of Gebal Taric by the King Don Enrique, as the Spanish writer has it, the accumulated disasters of the war compelled Aben Ismail of Granada to supplicate for a truce, nor did the former refuse his request. It is even said that Don Enrique (Henry) left Gebal Taric (this refers to the visit which we have mentioned in the last chapter), and repaired to the Vega of Granada, there to hold conference with the King of Granada. He was received with much pomp, and the two rulers banqueted in a magnificent pavilion, where they subsequently arranged the terms of their treaty. They exchanged gifts, and King Henry, when leaving the capital of his strange vassal, was accompanied on part of the road by many of the leading cavaliers of the city. There was peace in the country of Ben Ismail until his death, which happened in the spring of the year 870 (1464). His eldest son, Ali Abu-l-Hassan, who succeeded to the throne, delighted in war, " finding his best pleasures in the perils and horrors thereof; but for that reason he became the cause of the ruin which ultimately befel the kingdom, and brought about the extinction of Islam in Andalus." This king had two wives, the one was mother of Mohammed Ab Nabillah, and the second was Zoraya " daughter of the Governor of Martos, and of the lineage of the Christians. She was the mother of two sons born in an evil hour, seeing that they lent their aid to the downfall of their native country." *(Condé.)* Rash as was Abu-l-Hassan, he was comparatively fortunate in being prevented from carrying out his intention to break the truce which his father had made with Henry IV., by an insurrection which broke out at Malaga, under his own brother, the commander of that city, Abu Abdillah by name. The rebel invited the aid of the Christians, declaring his own ruler to be their enemy. Henry was at Archidona when this matter came about, and received his new would-be ally with favour; promised him aid, and took gifts from him. This conduct exasperated Abu Hassan exceedingly, and he fell upon the Christian territory with fierceness; penetrating even so far as Seville, and desolating the country of Cordova. So greatly had the Moslem territories shrunk, that these cities, formerly in the southern province of their dominions, were now considerably removed from their northern frontier, and at Granada these people might be said to be in sight of the sea they must soon cross.

For successive years these frontiers wars continued, by no means always to the profit of the Moslems. The Christian general who commanded the frontiers of Granada devastated the district of Motejicar, and took that town by surprise. This captain was Rui Ponce de Leon. He was attacked, and afterwards expelled by the Granadine cavaliers. Meanwhile the rebellion of the Wali of Malaga continued, and was effectual in weakening the Moslem power before the Christians.

The infatuation of this people was marvellous, seeing, as they must have seen, that they were not so much settling the claims of two chiefs as ruining the realm which the victor would surely not be able to defend against the ever-watchful enemy, who seemed patient, but was really waiting for the end to come which must put him in possession of the ancient inheritance of his race. Had it not been for the constant disturbances, which reached an amazing degree of violence, in Castile, between the partisans of Henry and Alfonso, that which we should now call " the Moorish question " would have been settled long before it so fell out. It was by means of these dissensions that the next siege of Gibraltar happened, and the Rock passed to the hands of the Duke of Medina-Sidonia. As if to render doubly certain the destruction of the Moorish power in Spain, the crowns of Castile and Arragon were soon to be united in the persons of Ferdinand of Arragon, King of Sicily, son of Juan II. of Arragon, and Isabella, daughter of John (or Juan) of Castile. She had the choice of Ferdinand or Alfonso of Portugal (to say nothing of the French prince, the Duc de Berri); in either case the uniting of two Spanish kingdoms would have been fatal to the Moors. It is hard to say whether the Arragonese with their Sicilian appanage and great interest in the Mediterranean, or the Portuguese with their recent memories of war in Morocco, were the more bitter foes of the Moslemah. The only marriage of this magnificent heiress which could have given respite to the kingdom of Granada might have been with the Duc de Berri. As it fell out the house of Nas'r was doomed, the time only was in doubt; so that the settlement of the Spanish monarchies which followed the death of Henry IV. brought peace to his war-torn kingdom, and the hour of desolation to many a Granadian Moorish hearth. At the same time, it must be observed, that even without the union of the Spanish crowns, the destruction of that of Granada was inevitable under the pressure of three separated, but commonly equal enemies. Whether it had been by Castile, Arragon, or Portugal singly, Granada was certain to succumb: the combining of two rendered the death-throes of the ancient kingdom sharper, and its end swifter to arrive.

We will anticipate the flight of time with Gibraltar, in order to conclude what is to be written here about the latter years of the Moorish kingdom. Henry IV. died in 1474, and a truce was made by Abu-l-Hassan with his successors, as well as with the rebellious (if to such a pretender the so often glorious name of "rebel" can be applied) Wali of Malaga. It was kept with more sincerity by the former than the latter, and seems never to have been more than nominal between the Moslems. To add to these troubles the women of the royal harem quarrelled about their sons, and had parties outside the palace of Granada. Abu Hassan is reported to have been of a hard and cruel nature, and to have estranged the hearts of many, while the gentle manners of his son Abu Abdallah attracted many friends. When the truce expired, a renewal was solicited by the former from Ferdinand and Isabella, who was then at Seville, and these rulers agreed to grant it on condition of receiving a yearly tribute (1476). This condition enraged Abu Hassan, who replied insolently to the envoys: "Go, say to your master, that the kings of Granada who paid tribute to the Christians are now dead; bid them know, moreover, that in Granada we are occupied not in gaining gold for the hands of our enemies, but in the making of sword-blades, and the heads of lances, for their hearts." *(Condé.)*

This preposterous message was followed up in the beginning of A.H. 886 by an attack on Zahara, a fortress between Ronda and Sidonia. As the Arabian writer represented this matter in the picturesque manner of his people, the very elements threatened the foolhardy king; the wind blew hurricanes, and the rain fell in torrents, as if to second the counsel of the captains of Abu Hassan, who in vain protested against the evil course upon which he had entered. By assault and surprise he took the place, and with the boastful spirit of a fool returned to Granada to rejoice in the success of his own audacity. Even as he was thus singing, so to say, the swan-song of his nation, an ancient Alfakir cried out to him, "The ruins of the conquered town shall be upon our own heads." It was vain that his captains, the priests, and wise men of Granada deprecated the suicidal course upon which the king had entered. He renewed the war by attacks upon Castallary and Olbera, which were fruitless of aught but retaliation on his own kingdom. About this time Rui Ponce de Leon assaulted Alhama by escalade and surprise at night, and after " grievous carnage," fighting in every street, and behind barricades, the few remaining Moorish inhabitants were compelled to surrender, the women and children who had taken refuge in a mosque were inhumanly put to death. Abu Hassan made a vain attempt to retake this city, and repeated that attempt with equal ill fortune a few months later. From this expedition he was recalled to his capital by an insurrection among the nobles, who set up his son Abu Abdallah for king. By means of dissimulation Abu Hassan entrapped the young prince and his mother Zoraya, the lady of Christian descent, to whom reference has just been made. He locked up the pair in one of the towers of the Alhambra. The capture of Alhama was a terrible blow to the kingdom of Granada, the more so as Abu Hassan's people attributed the loss to him on account of his having provoked the war which led to that disaster. This place was never recovered.

The escape of Abu Abdallah, contrived by his mother's means, led to a fresh rising against Abu Hassan, and furious fighting in Granada between the loyal and rebellious parties. This ended in the flight of the latter to Almeria, the Wali of which place (the king's brother-in-law) lent his aid for the recovering of the Alhambra, in which he was successful, excepting as regarded one tower, and made an attempt to recover possession of the neighbouring capital which was unfortunate. Compelled to march to the relief of Loxa, then besieged by the Spaniards, Abu Abdallah left the ground free for the partisans of his son, who seized the whole of the Alhambra. The expedition to Loxa was happy in its termination for the Moors, and encouraged the king to think of attempting Alhama again, in which he was obliged to desist; he took Caneti, which was something. Meanwhile, however, he quite lost hold in Granada, his metropolis, and was obliged to retreat to Malaga, where soon after (A.H. 888) he was attacked by the Christians under the Grand Master of Santiago, the Marquis of Cadiz, and the Count of Cifuentes, who plundered the country, cut up the vines, destroyed the flocks and herds, and drove the people of Malaga almost beside themselves with passion and fear as they saw the columns of smoke arise in the air above burning homesteads and farm-buildings. (*Condé.*) The king was too much exhausted to attempt revenge for this incursion, but his brother and Reduan Ben Egas led strong bodies of riders and cross-bow men with such effect that the invaders were utterly routed. This was one of the few late gleams of victory on the once resplendent arms of the Moslems in Spain.

There was no peace to be had in Granada although the mad people saw the Christians at the gates of Malaga, with the southern sea almost at their very feet. New quarrels sprung up; the people saw woeful omens in every event, and declared that the doom of the Abencerages had to be expiated; thus, when Abu Abdallah, the son, set out from Granada on an expedition against the Christians and his lance was broken in the archway, the superstitious folk anticipated evil for his journey.

Never was omen more strictly fulfilled by the event to which it referred, than this one. Abu Abdallah, called *El Zaquir* (the Drunkard) was utterly defeated by the Christians under Diego de Cordova, and after many had been slain by his side, he fled as far as his horse would bear him. This was not far, and, being compelled to dismount, he tried to hide among willows and other trees which grew near the margin of a river. Seeing himself closely followed by three Christians, and fearing to lose his life, this unhappy prince declared his condition, and yielded himself prisoner. He was conducted to the Spanish camp, and treated with respect. This defeat was a terrible affliction to the people of Granada, for in the ruined army was the flower of the city. Such an effect had it that many of El Zaquir's party passed over to that of his father, Abu Hassan. Upon this, the latter left Malaga, took possession anew of the Alhambra, and fortune seemed to smile upon him. (*Condé*.) The Sultana Zoraya, mother of El Zaquir, sent huge sums of money for the ransom of her son, and counselled him to submit to any conditions which the rulers of Castile might impose in exchange for his liberty. Following this advice he agreed to hold his kingdom in perpetual vassalage to the crown of Castile, to pay yearly twelve thousand doubloons in gold, besides presents to be sent at once and three hundred Christian captives to be released at the choice of his own conquerors; he was to answer in person to the summons of the King of Castile, and even offered to place his own son as hostage in the hands of the Christians. In return for these comprehensive promises the Spaniards were to aid El Zaquir in mastering the cities which remained subject to Abu Hassan his father.

These provisoes were agreed to after some dissension, for there were not wanting Spaniards who advised that El Zaquir should not be set free; while the greater number of Christian councillors decided, as the Moslem writers declare, in favour of the conditions in order that the release of the unlucky son of Abu Hassan might, by returning home, increase the civil wars, and spread wider the desolation which was rife in Granada. As the most crafty policy the latter was adopted. Ferdinand received his new vassal at Cordova, embraced him, and treated him as a friend. The treaty was signed, "and then did the star which is most inimical to Islam pour its malignant influence over Andalus, and that decree went forth which determined the conclusion of the Moslem empire in that country."

Further disorders followed the return of El Zaquir to Granada; the party of the father fought against that of the son, and *vice versa*, so that the unhappy country was reduced to a pitiable condition. The city of Granada was the scene of a terrible conflict. The party of the father then proposed that Abdallah El Zagal, " the vigorous," brother of Abu Hassan, and Wali of Malaga, should, by assuming the crown, unite the nation in one. This plan was accepted by the friends of the son. Abu Hassan then abdicated (A.H. 889, A.D. 1483). El Zaquir did not readily agree to this arrangement, and although professing submission, sought the promised aid of the Christians to maintain his power. They came and committed great ravages in the wretched kingdom which it was their object utterly to ruin; and the civil war continued with unabated fury, although one of the original leaders disappeared from the strife. El Zagal called upon the princes of Africa, and even the ruler of Egypt for troops to help him. "But the immutable decree, inscribed on the tablet of the Destinies, had now attained the period of its fulfilment, and from no part did there come succours for the sinking kingdom of Granada." Town after town submitted to the troops of Ferdinand and Isabella. Even Ronda, that strong fortress, perched upon a rock, succumbed at last after a siege during which, as it is asserted, bombs were for the first time used. This was in 1485, May 23rd, says Mariana, yet El Zaquir refused to consult the interests of his people, and come to an accommodation with his rival, so that the treacherous aid of the Spaniards might be dispensed with. Malaga was taken by means of the treachery of the Mohammedan governor, and the people of that city plundered without mercy (1488). Other cities and fortresses fell by force of arms, and although brief gleams of good fortune shone upon the Moslems, the twilight of their power was obvious; its darkness gathering near at hand. More dreadful, perhaps, to the feelings of a true Moslem was the rumour which averred that the Prince

Yahye had become a Christian at the instance of Queen Isabella, and that this conversion was kept secret for reasons of state. Gaudix, Almeria, Baza, fell in turn, the people being allowed to retain their possessions, their allegiance being transferred to the Christian power. "And now the Christians, as well as the Moslemah, found it difficult to believe in the reality of what they saw passing before them, and could not but think it was all a dream." Taberna and Seron followed of their own will, also Almunecaub and Xalerbenia, "both situate on the edge of the sea." Even this was not enough to soothe the animosities of parties in what remained of Granada. El Zaquir had promised to surrender the suzerainty of the capital to Ferdinand when Almeria, Baza, and Gaudix should be taken. Ferdinand now demanded the fulfilment of this condition, and the wretched Arab king was compelled to temporise. Meanwhile, El Zagal finally departed for Africa, having sold, for five millions of maravedis, the last remains of his possessions to Ferdinand; thus the debate lay entirely between the least able Arab competitor and Ferdinand and Isabella the potent Spanish rulers. The former struggled in vain; in vain he preached a Holy War to the mountaineers of Granada; in vain did these simple-hearted men come ardently to his aid. The son of Cid Yahye, a Moslem, but vassal of the Christians, fought and even betrayed his fellows. The city of Granada itself was besieged, and valiantly defended by the able general Musa Ben Abil, who might truly be called the last of the Moors. It was in vain; the city surrendered on conditions which, if truly observed, would have been favourable. Gonzales de Cordova and the representative of El Zaquir signed this capitulation. When the latter produced it to the council of the Arabs, Musa Ben Abil made them a speech so noble in its sentiments, so profoundly moving in its adjurations that it is wonderful his wish for resistance unto death fell on heartless ears. He warned his fellows that the Christian King and Queen would not observe the condition which permitted the free exercise of the Moslem religion, he prophesied the horrors of the Inquisition to them; it was all in vain. Not an arm was lifted, not a voice answered his; so he turned his back on that degraded assembly, and in the highest indignation left the hall.

"*Of the valiant Musa Ben Abil, El Gazani, it is further related that he then proceeded to his own house, took a horse and his arms, mounted, and rode from the city by the gate of Elvira; from that time he never appeared again.*"*

There is hardly need to write more of this pitiful business; let a few words suffice. The place was surrendered, January 2nd, 1492. El Zaquir had an appanage granted to him. He sold that appanage to Ferdinand, departed to Africa, and, as the Moslem writer quoted by Condé says, the unfortunate prince who had not found courage in defence of his own country and kingdom, lost his life in fighting to preserve the crown of another; for his death happened in the battle of the Fords of Bacaba, and while he was a soldier of his cousin, Ahmed Ben Merini, the last Sultan of Granada. Abu Abdallah Mohammed, of the Nasserite dynasty (Mohammed XII.), went to Fez, settled there with his family and adherents, built palaces in imitation of those of Granada, died in A.D. 1538, and was buried in front of the chapel, outside the Gate of the Law in that city. He left two children, whose descendants fell into such poverty that they subsisted upon public alms, the funds of the mosques, "in fact were not better than mere beggars."

* Condé.

The final expulsion of the Moslems happened in A.D. 1610, after many struggles, and, according to the account of their writers, much violence and chicanery endured from the Christians, notwithstanding the conditions of their submission. A large number of these unfortunates settled in Salee, and became the famous "rovers" of that port; others went to Tunis, certain desert cities of which they peopled anew; many found refuge in Syria, Turkey and Egypt.

Praised be God! who exalteth kings and who casteth them low; who giveth power and greatness at His pleasure; who inflicteth poverty and humiliation according to His holy will; the fulfilment of that will as Eternal Justice.

Such is the epitaph of the dominion of the Arabs in Spain.

CHAPTER XXVII.

THE NINTH SIEGE, 1466.

HAVING, except for a few brief words, parted with the Arabs, we may now turn back to our subject, the first of their conquests in Europe, the last place upon which—when, in flagrant violation of the conditions upon which he held their country, Philip II. deported the remnant of the Moslems—their footsteps were permitted to rest.

We have already noted the successive appointments of Pedro de Porras, as royal deputy, or governor of the city of Gibraltar, December 15th, 1462, and of Beltran de la Cueva, the reputed father, by the Queen of Spain, of the Infanta Juana, or "Beltraneja," as she was called, who was married to Alfonso the African, King of Portugal. Beltran had for his lieutenant, or actual governor of the Fortress, Stephano (Estevan) Villacreces, one of the stoutest-hearted of men, as we shall see. Naturally, Count de la Cueva and his deputy were on the king's side during the civil war which ensued with the representatives of Henry's brother Alfonso, whom the Cortes opposed to him in 1465, which contest continued until 1468, when Alfonso died, and his partisans endeavoured to set up his and Henry's sister, Isabella, in his place; this she refused to permit, or oppose the right of Henry to the crown. She married, as we have said, Ferdinand, son of the King of Arragon; this was much against the will of Henry, who threatened to cancel that agreement which, on account of his sister's forbearance, he had made, by which Isabella was appointed heir to the crown of Castile; he further declared that on this marriage he would designate the Beltraneja as his successor. This intention was broken in time, and Henry IV. received his sister and her husband with tolerable courtesy until his death, in 1474.

From Alfonso, the Duke of Medina-Sidonia obtained a grant of the lordship of Gibraltar, both city and fortress, and, naturally enough, sided against the king in the civil war. It was under this pretence that the duke undertook that siege of Gibraltar, which is one of the most memorable of like occurrences in its annals, and, although by no means the longest to endure, was resisted by not less heroic obstinacy on the part of the defenders than any which preceded or succeeded it. Little did Villacreces think that the duke would venture to attack the place which the king had put into his charge, and which was notoriously, even at that time, in its situation at least, one of the strongest fortresses in Europe. It was, until cannon of great calibre came into the service of armies, one of the most hopeless of tasks to assault Gibraltar; the comparatively harmless guns of the fifteenth century made little progress at any time against the Fortress, whatever they might have effected with regard to the city; while the catapults and mangonels of earlier wars were absurdly inefficient. Compared with these, the tremendously potent artillery used by Lord Heathfield and his enemies in the Great Siege evoked such thunders as were never heard before in the Straits, although due to cannon such as we smile at; to wit, 32-pounder, 28-pounder, and 26-pounder guns were the most powerful weapons in use during the dreadful siege to which we have yet to refer.

Such was the strength of Gibraltar against the little guns

which were then in vogue, that at least three-fourths of the modern defences would have been supererogatory then; for what need was there to make galleries in the Rock which could not be armed with guns powerful enough to throw shot or shell with effect upon an enemy, and which were out of reach of an assailant's shot? The means of attack which had been most effective against Gibraltar was blockade, with its result—famine; victory had been given to assailants who, without this, might have pounded at the Rock for a century without profit. Surprise, which has been effectual in a greater or less degree against many garrisons of Gibraltar, has of course been rendered less practicable by successively extending the fortifications and, consequently, increasing the area which the enlarged works brought into view, while they also diminished the number of spots wherein concealment was practicable by an attacking force. We have seen an instance of an attempt upon the Rock by means of surprise, and shall soon meet with another of still more remarkable kind and result. The Ninth Siege was conducted by other means than that of its immediate and less fortunate forerunner; we may conclude that the Duke of Medina-Sidonia did not resort to surprise as a method of assault, as did his ancestor Henry de Guzman, Count of Niebla, whose corpse had hung so long, as they say, from the battlements of the Fortress which he really essayed to capture by that plan. The terrible warning given by the death of this champion, the first of the De Guzmans of Gibraltar fame, not impossibly deterred others of the family from the like mode of attack.

It was not, therefore, by surprise that Stephano Villacreces was to be attacked by one of the principal nobles of his master's Court; a royal vassal, such as the duke, did not by this method make approaches for the conquest of one of the fortresses of the State. This appanage of the Crown, a frontier castle of the highest importance,—such was Gibraltar, not long before wrested from the still-powerful Moslems,—was deliberately assailed, the attacking force was gathered by sound of trumpet and beat of drum, and marched in broad daylight on its astoundingly impudent errand. Neither was that modified sort of surprise employed which is sometimes effectual by the attack of an overwhelming force on a badly prepared citadel. A simple straightforward siege was put in practice in this case, and, marvelling at the audacity of the attack, we cannot fail to see in the event the inherent weakness of the Spanish Crown, broken as its authority was at the time by the civil wars. The union of Castile with Arragon strengthened the throne, yet more serviceable to that end were the bold policy of Cardinal Ximenes and the strong sword of Gonzales de Cordova, the Great Captain. These powers had not, however, yet come into operation, although the tendency of policy in Europe was in the same direction with theirs, as was shown by the life and conduct of Louis XI. of France, who, at the date of the Ninth Siege of Gibraltar, was in the sixth year of his reign; Edward IV. of England was labouring by no means without success in the same road. The course of national life at this period was towards concentration of power in royal hands, and reduction of the authority of the nobles. A more marked example of the need of some such change as this would be hard to find than that of the Ninth Siege of Gibraltar, undertaken as it was by a subject against his king. In Arragon, the nobles had proceeded so far in antagonism to the royal authority that, like their neighbours of Castile, they deposed the king, John II., father of Ferdinand, and invited Pedro of Portugal to succeed him. This was in 1464; in the next year took place that crowning fact of Louis XI.'s career, the Battle of Mont-thèry. There was civil war in nearly every country in Europe—in England, of the Roses ; in France, of the League for the Public Good ; in Sweden, Italy, Naples, Rome, Genoa, Florence, scarcely a land was at peace —wherefore then wonder that new-conquered Granada should find no rest ! Still it is not to be denied that Stephano Villacreces' amazement when he heard that the Duke of Medina-Sidonia was coming against the Crown Fortress of Gibraltar was by no means unnatural. Had the Spanish Arabs or Granadians attempted to recapture their ancient hold, no one would have marvelled ; still less would they have done so if the Sultan of Fez had tried to win again the *tête-de-pont*, which had so often aided African adventure in Europe. John the African, King of Portugal, had by no means broken the power of the Merine Dynasty of Fez, and Almagreb was ever potent on the sea. There, however, had been a treaty with the Moors which assured Stephano of peace from that side ; the Mauritanians could not well attack him unawares on the Rock ; little did he look for danger from homewards and on the land side—a real, terrible danger to last for many months, and treason which was to be successful after all.

Villacreces was, nevertheless, although astonished, not the man either to submit at once to such an assault or to neglect means which might bring help to his garrison. He called in such forces as he could command, gathered what stores were available within his district, which now included the old commune of Algeciras, city and country ; he strengthened his weaker posts so well as it might be done in the few days which intervened to the news and its fulfilment. Above all, he hurried messengers to Beltran de la Cueva, his patron and principal, to King Henry IV. with prayers for aid, which neither was in a position to grant, except by commands to the folks who were settled under the custodian of the Rock and its neighbourhood, that they should aid Stephano de Villacreces by every means in their power, by person as well as by goods. Neither Beltran nor his master were able to leave other troubled parts of Spain, or neglect the task of watching Isabella, Portugal, Arragon, and the rebellious Castilian peers.

Thus left to his own resources, it must be admitted that Villacreces did wonders and showed how worthily he was in command of the great castle. He gathered stores, arms, and men; but as he had not enough of either to justify an attempt to hold the city of Gibraltar, was at once compelled to abandon it, and thus admit the enemy to the advantage of shelter close under his walls. Unavoidable as this must have been, it was the first of many misfortunes to fall on the head of stout Stephano. He seems to have been fairly provided with arms, indifferently well stocked with provisions, and, for the place to be defended, was by no means badly off in the first case for men. But, with all these, he was in no case to oppose a lengthy siege, such as that which was at hand turned out to be. In all these respects Villacreces was far from being equal to his assailants; worse than otherwise was it for him, that, without some turn of fortune in favour of King Henry, there was no chance of help; Henry's luck had no turn until after all was over.

Boldly marched the duke and all his feudal array against the king's castle; without question or debate he took possession of the city of Gibraltar and its mixed population to boot, in his own name, and by virtue of a patent from Alfonso, the nominal head of the rebel party. Meanwhile the king's commander had retreated to the Fortress, which the duke at once attacked with all his power, making assault after assault in the manner of a regular siege, such as, indeed, the matter was; for the duke's armament was of great strength, and amply provided with materials in guns, stores and provisions, besides greatly outnumbering the defenders in men. This siege began in 1406, and was continued with rigour and determination that was equalled by the spirit of the unfortunate garrison, who endured the hardships thus brought upon them with extraordinary courage and fortitude. The place was battered with artillery and such other means of attack as were then employed in regular warfare. All this while the Moors must, with no small satisfaction, have looked on at the distresses and violence of their conquerors; but we do not learn that Villacreces imitated the false policy of so many of his predecessors in charge of the Rock, by calling for the aid of the enemies of his country and faith on either side of the Straits. Having borne the utmost efforts of his foes for about ten months, the captain still held fast to his post; although food became scarcer and yet scarcer in his garrison, there seemed no immediate prospect of a surrender. The main hopes of the defenders looked to the royal power for deliverance, but this came not in answer to the entreaties of Villacreces. Undeterred, therefore, by the failure of his strenuous efforts, the Duke of Medina-Sidonia called to his aid a new body of troops and a larger amount of stores and arms, and placed the whole under the command of Henry his son, the very man into whose hands the successor of King Henry resigned the Rock in days that were soon to arrive, and who thereafter did everything which was practicable to keep the Fortress in possession of his house, as, indeed, it remained for a long period of time. King Henry all this while was disabled from relieving his faithful servant in his need, and hardly powerful enough to hold out against the enemies of his throne. The fresh troops of the De Guzmans left no hour unemployed in their work; they stopped the few supplies which the governor sought abroad for the garrison, and by this means reduced them to extremities of famine and distress. The fresh troops brought cannon of greater power than had been hitherto employed against the Rock, and used them with such fury and constancy that the walls of the castle were at length breached in many places; nevertheless the garrison did not lose hearts of courage, but stood manfully in the gaps where their assailants made assaults at times of their own choosing, and wearied, if they did not master, the valiant defenders. The loss of the city to the latter was of incalculable importance to a body of men who could not replenish their stores or obtain aid of other kinds from without their battered walls. At last a grand attack upon the breaches by an overwhelming force drove the governor from the outer cincture of the Fortress to the innermost defence, or Calahorra, that famous keep which was yet capable of holding its defenders for a while. Bravely the garrison retreated to this their final refuge, and it seemed as if the last man would be slain or starved ere the duke's party got the victory. Five months more, being nearly sixteen months in all, did Villacreces and his men keep hold upon their last retreat; their proper food failed, they devoured the wild shrubs and pitiful herbage which grew in no great store about their walls, and consumed the leather of their boots and girdles ere the less faithful of their number escaped to the enemy's camp. It appears as if these defections broke the hitherto indomitable spirit of Villacreces and his soldiers more than their previous sufferings. At last, in June of the second year of the siege, the surrender was made, and Henry de Guzman took possession, in the name of his father, of the place which had taxed the strength and resources of his powerful and wealthy house. Thus ended the Ninth Siege of Gibraltar; by this means the Fortress repassed into the hands of the most potent noble in the south of Spain, who had been compelled to deliver it as the prize of that sovereign, from whom, by this extraordinary conduct, he again took it.

The duke's triumph—in this world at least—was not destined to last long; in less than twelve months after its achievement he died. Henry de Guzman, the energetic captor of Gibraltar, followed his father in dignity and power as second Duke and fourth Count of Niebla; he became one of the most famous of a famous family, one member of which, in after years, gave the English no small amount of trouble and alarm while commanding the Armada of Philip II. in 1588. If a refined spirit of revenge chose to gratify itself in such a manner, satisfaction might be obtainable in the thought that we English have long held that very Fortress which the second duke bought at so great a price, whose descendant failed completely in ruining our country. The De Guzmans surely owed us something on account of that "Invincible" Armada!

CHAPTER XXVIII.

HISTORY OF GIBRALTAR UNDER FERDINAND AND ISABELLA.
THE TENTH SIEGE.

IT is characteristic of such a sovereign as Henry the Weak, of Castile, that he granted what he had of authority in Gibraltar to the son of the man whose power had been employed to its utmost against himself, and upon that very spot. It seems almost to follow as a matter of course, that this son should have been the active agent of his father in rebellion, the slayer of the king's faithful subject and captor of the royal fortress. The state of Spain under the administration of such a rule need hardly be described; so far as words can picture it, Prescott, the historian of Ferdinand and Isabella and their kingdom, has done so; to his admirable work our readers should turn for an account of what took place in the Peninsula at the period in question.

In less than two years after the Ninth Siege of Gibraltar had deprived King Henry IV. of his royal right in the place, that monarch, if he can be called such, who had a host of masters and at least a score of advisers, actually granted to Henry de Guzman not only a confirmation of, but additions to concessions, which were made before the siege, and as if rebellion did not effect those rights. Thus, the king yielded to the duke's claims on the lordship and gave him possession of the place. No doubt King Henry made this grant with a personal motive, for it was done while negotiations for the marriage of

Ferdinand of Arragon with his sister Isabella were in progress; a marriage which the king knew would blank all his hopes for the Beltraneja's succession to the throne of Castile. The apparent object of the concession was to detach the young Duke de Medina-Sidonia and all his power from the Arragonese party. The grant was made in June (3rd), 1469, or three months before the union of Isabella with Ferdinand took place at Valladolid, and after months of procrastination and the intervention of every obstacle which the king and the party of the Beltraneja could create. This grant, as if to humiliate the donor, was in the following terms, and referred to the original capture of the place from the Moors, which nevertheless was achieved by Ponce de Leon rather than De Guzman, but made no reference to the former as the real winner. "Bearing in mind how Don Henrique de Guzman, my uncle, the Count of Niebla, your grandfather, copying the fidelity and good intentions of his ancestors and descendants, and the royal race from which he sprung, went with all his knights and retainers at his own expense to besiege and attack the city of Gibraltar, then held by the Moors, to redeem it to the faith and service of our Lord and to subject it to my royal crown; how, also, that in that siege there fell a great number of knights and people of his house, and that he himself was buried in the fortress of the said city* (chapel of the Calahorra); and that the same desire being renewed in Don Juan de Guzman, your father,† to conquer the said city, he finally

---

* *Ayala.* No mention here or notice of the hanging out of the De Guzman's body from one of the turrets over the gate of the Barcina, at Gibraltar, a matter, doubtless, too painful to be mentioned, or altogether untrue, yet thoroughly in keeping with the manners of the time and place, and not without historical precedent in that same land; see before of Pedro of Castile.

† No mention here of what Duke Henry, then heir-apparent to the De Guzmans, did before the same place, and at too recent a time to have been forgotten.

got possession of, and reduced it to our holy faith and obedience to me;* that he peopled it, fortified it and provided it with supplies in case of need."† To this follows the grant of the place to the De Guzmans for ever, with all its appurtenances, powers and advantages.

With this prodigious increase of dignity, it is not impossible that the Duke of Medina-Sidonia was, for the time at least, satisfied, and his enmity to the Crown appeased during the civil wars which intervened to the marriage of Ferdinand with Isabella and the death of King Henry. The latter event happened December 11th, 1474, after his Majesty had reigned with almost unparalleled ill-fortune for his subjects and undeniable discredit to himself. His reign lasted twenty years— *i.e.* from 1454 to 1474. The day after the death of the king, his sister Isabella was called to the throne, and, practically, the policy of Castile was guided by Ferdinand of Arragon. From the new rulers the Duke of Medina-Sidonia obtained a further confirmation of his claim, and the title of Marquis of Gibraltar, a distinction which, however apt to the situation of the place, would seem inconsistent with that royal dignity which was likewise derived from the Rock. This Duke Henry took full part in those wars which destroyed the Moorish kingdom of Granada, of which we have already given a sketch.

Ayala tells us that Isabella of Castile, acting, doubtless, with the counsel of her astute husband, whose entire policy was

---

* Not a word about the Ninth Siege, not a hint of stout Esteban de Villacreces and his brave garrison, such a reference being no doubt unpleasant for both parties.

† A striking admission this from the monarch whose proclamation we have already cited with the date December 15th, 1462, or barely three years and a half before the above appears; by virtue of which the district of Algeciras was added to Gibraltar, a district to which it appears the De Guzman had not a shadow of a claim such as he might put forth on account of Gibraltar; the charter, however, states that King Henry followed the laws of his realm in thus rewarding the captor.

opposed to such aggrandisement of a subject as the concession of Gibraltar to the De Guzmans effected, tried every means in her power to induce the duke to surrender the Rock to the Crown, even by offering to exchange for it the city of Utrera. We learn thus much from Ayala, who adds that Duke Henry utterly refused to yield the place on terms which, however profitable and honourable, would have left his great estates in the neighbourhood without that defence and prestige which possession of Gibraltar afforded. It was also a matter of great importance to him to retain Gibraltar as a central depôt for his tunny-fisheries, which extended along the coast in its neighbourhood for a considerable distance. The duke persisted in this refusal until his death in August, 1492, about six months after the surrender of Granada to Ferdinand, and the complete subversion of the Moorish kingdom of that province. The third Duke of Medina-Sidonia, Juan I., was in by no means so fortunate a position as his father had been in dealing with the exigent King of Castile; it was a very different matter to deal with Henry IV., harassed on all sides and hampered by favourites who played with, if they did not insult, the weakness of his character, and to be brought face to face with the astute, victorious, and resolute Ferdinand, to say nothing of his not less statesmanlike wife, Isabella the Catholic. When Duke Juan applied to the latter for a renewal of his grant and privileges in Gibraltar, she undertook to confirm all, but insisted that the Rock and Fortress should be restored to the Crown of Castile. Juan protested against this apparently unreasonable condition, and was successful in his application (*Ayala*). This decision was undisturbed for a long time. The place was used by Ferdinand in 1497 in his invasion of Africa, thus reversing the former service of the Rock; this time the Christians attacked Africa by its means. In 1499 the Moors were expelled from Spain; and the Rock, with the neighbouring forts, saw the last of its ancient masters.

It should here be noted that the neighbourhood of Gibraltar retained its ancient maritime serviceableness and was exalted in fame about this time by means of the voyage of Columbus from Pinto, August 3rd, 1492. Also that Prince Henry of Portugal, one of the most illustrious and successful encouragers of geographical discovery, built on the Cape of Sagres, not far from Cape St. Vincent, a sea-refuge, near to where, it is believed, his famous place of retirement and study was situated. It is further interesting to Englishmen to recollect that about this time, 1501, Katherine of Arragon, daughter of Ferdinand and Isabella, was married to Arthur, Prince of Wales, son of Henry VII., brother of Henry VIII., whom she married for her second husband, with noteworthy effect upon the history of this island and kingdom. In 1510, Ferdinand again attacked the northern coast of Africa.

From Lopez de Ayala's capital history of Gibraltar, to which we are indebted largely in this portion of our history, and which will supply to the inquiring student many curious and important details of the subject, we have knowledge that, by some means not fully expressed, Isabella succeeded in inducing or compelling the Duke of Medina-Sidonia to surrender his rights in Gibraltar. This happened in 1501, when the place was formally yielded to a new governor, Garcilaso de la Vega, Knight of Castile, who, in accordance to a decree dated from Toledo, December 22nd, 1501, arrived at the Fortress in January of the following year, and made known the object of his mission to the authorities, who were assembled in the Orange Court Yard, in front of the principal church. The royal decree was read, ordering the immediate surrender to their Majesties of the city, fortress, and district of Gibraltar, together with all the archives and emblems of justice and authority. The ceremony, accompanied by shouts of "Long live the King," was solemnly performed; wands of office were presented to Garcilaso, and he forthwith took possession of the castle. The keys of all the forts, towers, and gates were surrendered, together with the stores, arms, ammunition, and all other articles, including the wooden coffin of Henry de Guzman, the Count of Niebla, who perished under the walls of the Fortress. Garcilaso next assembled the magistrates of the city and other authorities and nominated Diego Lopez de Haro to be his Lieutenant and Alcalde of the Castle."*

This annexation to the Crown seems to have been very satisfactory to the inhabitants of Gibraltar; at their petition a coat of arms, similar to that which appears on our title-page, was granted to the city, its privileges were renewed, and the principal church rebuilt *(Sayer)*. Anticipating the Spanish practice with regard to modern Ceuta, Gibraltar was devoted to the reception of criminals, who were employed on the walls and other works, maritime and defensive. Not only on this account, but by means of a passage in her will, does the interest of Isabella in Gibraltar become evident. Dying in 1504, her Majesty thus testified her wishes: "It is my will and desire, insomuch as the city of Gibraltar has been surrendered by Don Henry de Guzman, has been restored to the royal Crown, and been inserted among its titles, that it shall for ever so remain. I ask and require of the kings, my successors, that they may hold and retain the said city *for themselves and in their own possession*, and that no alienation of it, or any part of it, or of its jurisdiction, civil or criminal, shall ever be made from the Crown of Spain." It would be difficult to invent a

---

* Lopez de Ayala, *Historia de Gibraltar*; also Sayer, *The History of Gibraltar*.

stronger proof of the great idea of Gibraltar and its importance to the Castilian Crown than that which this last solemn injunction of the queen expresses so unmistakeably. It was Isabella's final command that "no alienation of the whole or part" of the place should be made.

In the disturbances which followed the death of the queen, nothing affected the royal ownership of the Rock. We need not enter into the history of these events, except to remark that their effect was to unsettle men's minds in Spain, and, probably, that to them was in no small measure due the renewed attempt of the De Guzmans on the Rock, which constituted the Tenth Siege.

Gibraltar having been transferred in this very unsatisfactory fashion, Juan de Guzman determined, if he could so contrive, during the troubles which followed the death of Isabella, to retake the place by arms. In 1506 his son Henry gathered the forces of his house once more at the foot of the Rock; but news of his intention having been conveyed to the governor, no surprise was practicable, and assistance was sought from the Captain-General of Granada—*i.e.* the king's officer—a fact which is significant of the changed position of the king and nobles. A *coup-de-main* being hopeless, the besieger blockaded the city during four months, after which, under the advice of the Archbishop of Seville and others, the attempt was given up, and ample reparations made to all those within the district whose property had been injured. Thus ended the Tenth Siege of Gibraltar, the only bloodless one on record.

Charles V. succeeded Ferdinand the Catholic, and with unparalleled fortune united, under his hand, a vast share of the Continent of Europe. He was aware, says a Spanish authority, of the danger to which such a place as Gibraltar was exposed by the revolutionary disturbances to which Spain was then subject. He accordingly employed Rodrigo de Bazan as governor, and wrote in reply to complaints made to him about the blockade by the De Guzmans, thanking the people for their good service to the Crown, promising remuneration* for the losses they had suffered, and urging a continuance in their duty.† There was peace in Gibraltar in Rodrigo Bazan's time; the monastery of St. Francis was rebuilt and much enlarged. Portillo mentions an English monk of that house by the name of Friar Raphael as an exemplary individual. How strongly sounds this word of respect for a countryman of ours who lived in so remote a place and died so long ago!

The trade with Barbary flourished, and Gibraltar benefited by the intercourse of the countries. This comfortable state of things continued, and is as characteristic of the history of a great fortress as the facts that the castle had decayed, and that a petition was sent to the emperor, praying that it might be restored. The wall, particularly on the south side, says Ayala, was greatly dilapidated, the stores were diminished, and the troops too few for the service. Rodrigo Bazan continued in his office until 1553, when Alvaro Bazan, his namesake, if not his relative, succeeded to the post; this appointment marks as clearly as anything can do the growing corruption of Spain. This Governor of Gibraltar was not only an absentee, but too young to perform the duties of his office; "before he was of an age to do that which he was bound to perform," writes the Spanish historian, with humour which might have been uncon-

---

* A distinct reference to Gibraltar appeared on a coin of this reign, and was continued till lately. This coin is still much esteemed in the East, and well known in English trade as the Spanish pillar dollar, so called from its exhibiting the Pillars of Hercules, in conjunction with the royal arms and the motto *Plus ultra*. The old motto was *Non plus ultra*.

† Probably the remuneration referred to here is that which De Guzman supplied.

scious, the place fell out of right keeping; it seems clear that official peculation, for which, ever since the days of Vasco Perez de Meira, until, of course, the present age, the Rock has been famous, was rife there in the reign of Charles V. In reply to remonstrances, plans for repairing and extending the fortifications were prepared; but nothing was done in consequence, and the result was one of the most noteworthy events in our subject's history.

CHAPTER XXIX.

THE ATTACK BY THE CORSAIRS, 1540.

THAT a sovereign, such as Charles V. or his immediate successor, should have allowed our Fortress to be exposed to an attack of a nature such as that to which we now refer, is one of the curiously significant facts of the age in question; into its history we cannot inquire. Great as was the Spanish power on land, it was far less so at sea; the history of the contests between our own country and the Empire shows this even more plainly than the growth and vast extent of the operations of the Corsairs, who, under Hayradin Barba-rossa (Khair-eddin, the "Good of the Faith"), were really among the great powers of that day. It occurred to this chieftain that Gibraltar, of all places, was the best adapted to his purpose of obtaining footing in the west of the Mediterranean. Christian renegades and Moorish prisoners escaped from the Rock, which was, as we said before, a penal settlement, related to him the peculiar advantages of the place, described its defenceless state under Alvaro Bazan and urged an attempt to take it.

The Spanish fleet was in Sicily, the emperor was in Flanders and wrecking the freedom of the city of Ghent, so that the Spaniards were unprepared when the Corsairs made one of their characteristic dashes, hastily fitting out a fleet that was manned at the oars by a thousand Christian slaves and provided with stores by means of promises to pay out of the proceeds of the plunder which was yet to be captured. Armed, further, by two thousand soldiers, this fleet, under the command of the soldier Garamani and the sailor Dali-Hamet, set sail from Algiers on the 24th August, 1540, and approached Gibraltar without interruption. The place was almost defenceless, its walls were neglected, open at all times to attack; and although it seems incredible, we are assured that although warnings had been conveyed to Gibraltar of the destination of the Corsairs, nobody troubled himself about them ere the tornado burst and it was too late to resist. Although it was not until the beginning of September that this event happened, the invaders were allowed, says Ayala, to land at the south of the Rock, to destroy the chapel and hermitage of the Virgin, close to where the lighthouse now stands, plunder the neighbourhood and attack the castle. The city was gutted, the people were seized as slaves and, with their property, put on board the invading galleys ere help came sufficient to repel the marauders from the castle where the few troops retreated and had enough to do to hold their own; the surprised garrison, as it was, suffered greatly. Meanwhile, checked in their attack and bent more on plunder than possession, the invaders took all they could deal with, and keeping along by the Rock with their ships, landed again at the Orange Grove and devastated the place in a savage manner. Thence, making off with the prisoners and booty, the Corsairs were bribed with seven thousand ducats for the ransom of the prisoners—half in merchandise, half in money. On this voluntary ransom, which was borrowed from the Marquis of Tarifa, they stipulated that the Turkish slaves who were confined in Gibraltar should be released, the prisoners taken during the landing set free, and, which was really the most audacious proposal of all, that "their galleys should be allowed in future to take water at the wells of Gibraltar" *(Ayala)*.

These conditions were agreed to; but the difficulty in getting together the money was really or affectedly so great, that the Corsairs, fearing to fall into a trap by means of the Spanish fleet, departed for Algiers (September 12th). Two days afterwards the money arrived from Tarifa and a vessel was sent with it to overtake them, but ineffectually, and the aid of the King of Fez sought with the view to a ransom. The captives were left at Gomera for a price agreed on *(Ayala)*.

Strange as it may seem, all this was effected while the Spanish fleet was not further off than at Carthagena. Don Bernardino de Mendoza, its commander, on hearing what had taken place at his own headquarters, put to sea and, coming up with the Corsairs—who do not seem to have taken much trouble to get out of his way and were, indeed, according to the Spanish account, double the force of their enemies—made an attack upon them, near the island of Arbolan. The principal galley of the Corsairs, with the commanders on board, was defeated; Caramani was killed and Hamet captured, with about four hundred of the marauders. The liberation of more than eight hundred Christian captives was a fruit of this victory and among the more important results was the instilling wholesome fear to the Corsairs' minds. Something was, soon after this amazing event, done towards securing the Rock against similar attacks and by means of rebuilding the Land Port Gate, digging a ditch and erecting a battery; it was not until 1552, twelve years afterwards, that Juan Battista Calvi, of Milan, a famous engineer, "erected two walls at the South Port Gate, from the west upwards to the easternmost point."[*] Other fortifications were proposed, but nothing was effected. Surely one might say, on reading this statement, that Gibraltar was already in Spain.

---

[*] Afterwards called Charles V's walls. *See map.*

CHAPTER XXX.

THE LAST MOORISH HOPES. DUTCH VICTORY IN THE PORT.

THE chastisement inflicted on the Corsairs was effectual no longer than until 1558, when five galleys threatened the place, but were beaten off. In 1567, Prince John Andrea Doria, Charles V.'s Admiral of the Seas, took five Turkish galleys in the Straits and, in the following year, gave a large lamp of silver and endowed it with oil, to burn perpetually before the image of the Virgin of Europa (La Virgen de Europa), which stood in a chapel at the extremity of Europa Point. It is probable that this and other lamps of which Portillo makes mention were really intended to be serviceable as beacons for the Port or Straits of Gibraltar; the commanders of the galleys of Spain and Sicily, says that author, having presented such lamps and provided such supplies of fuel for them. This chapel was near the same spot where now stands the lighthouse *(Ayala)*. In 1571, notwithstanding these repeated dangers, it was found necessary to construct an aqueduct, which, like the fortifications, was so badly done that it soon became useless. In 1575, the engineer, Fratino, inspected the place, ordered the construction of new works and the destruction of others which already existed. These new fortifications were in the directions of the Signal House, the Bastion of Sta Cruz, now called Jumper's Battery, and the battery " del Rosario," also another of which, "King's Battery," occupied the site on the north of the place *(Bell)*. In 1581, the convent of the Mercenarios Calzados was begun on the site of the older chapel of Sta Anna. Next, in 1587, came the monastery of Sta Clara; the hospital of St. Juan de Diaz,—St. John of God,—for sick seamen, was founded by Juan Mateos, a native of Gibraltar. In 1609-10, the last remnant of the Moors, comprising about six hundred thousand persons, was transported by Philip III., and largely by the way of Gibraltar, to Africa. Ayala's excuse for this monstrous transaction must have been ironically made; he says, " that the Spanish clergy could ill-brook the presence of so vast a number of ' infidels,' (as he calls them,) in the country, where their industry, intelligence, and skill in crafts would infallibly become, in a few years, dominant." Representations, founded on justice and common sense, were vainly made, in behalf of this people; at last, exactly nine hundred years after the entry of the Moors by way of Gibraltar, they were expelled thence as a race; as a nation, of course, they had ceased to exist long before. In 1610, Juan de Mendoza, the Spanish admiral, conducted the last transport from the Rock.

In Sully's " Memoirs," book xxv. will be found an account of the transactions of his master Henry IV. of France, with the remnant of the Moors in Spain, stating how that monarch, when King of Navarre, entertained notions of using this people against the Spaniards whom they hated with the hate of a conquered and enslaved race. Also how, at a later time, when exasperated by unwise treatment, that relic of many centuries of antagonism, the Moslems entreated Henry to aid them in a revolt, required only a commander and officers, offered to furnish money and valiant soldiers: further, that they asked only an asylum in France, with freedom for their persons and property, and were not unwilling to embrace the Protestant faith of Henry himself, any other, in short, than that of the hated Spaniards,

2 F

and to colonise the then desert Landes near Bordeaux. Henry inquired into the prospects of success for such a movement as this, and, it may be through fear of his Roman Catholic subjects, was induced to leave his would-be friends to their fate. They broke out in rebellion, which was suppressed with great cruelty, and were ultimately expelled. The expulsion was violently opposed by the Valencian nobles, who considered themselves wronged by being deprived of their slaves, for such had the Moors become!

For the sake of consecutively grouping our materials we have anticipated. Not content with persecuting the Moors who might, with tolerably good management, have been induced to become among the most valuable of his subjects, and who had their places in Spain by virtue of the treaties which Ferdinand made with the later Arab sovereigns, Philip III. so conducted his affairs as to get into one of the hottest of wars with their High Mightinesses the States of Holland, and, further, contrived to enlist against himself the sympathies of his French neighbours. In the wars between the Dutch and their quondam tyrants the Spaniards, a naval action happened in the port of Gibraltar, which ought never to be omitted in its history. Take what Henry IV. of France's minister, the great Sully, wrote about this matter in his incomparable "Memoirs." He had been describing the efforts of the Dutch to secure the French alliance in their wars with Philip of Spain :

"Affairs were in this situation when we heard the news of a great naval action gained, on the 25th of April, by the fleet of the United Provinces over that of the Spaniards, and almost immediately after Buzenval sent us a relation of it which was as follows: Alvares d'Avila, the Spanish admiral, was ordered to cruise near the Straits of Gibraltar, to hinder the

Dutch from entering the Mediterranean, and to deprive them of the trade of the Adriatic. The Dutch, to whom this was a most sensible mortification, gave the command of ten or twelve vessels to one of their ablest seamen, named Heemskerk, with the title of vice-admiral, and ordered him to go and reconnoitre this fleet and attack it. D'Avila, though nearly twice as strong as his enemy, yet provided a reinforcement of twenty-six great ships, some of which were of a thousand tons burthen, and augmented the number of his troops to three thousand five hundred men. With this accession of strength he thought himself so secure of victory that he brought a hundred and fifty gentlemen along with him only to be witnesses of it. However, instead of standing out to sea, as he ought to have done, he posted himself under the town and castle of Gibraltar, that he might not be obliged to fight but when he thought proper.

"Heemskerk, who had taken none of these precautions, no sooner perceived that his enemy seemed to fear him than he advanced to attack him, and immediately began the most furious battle that was ever fought in the memory of man. It lasted eight whole hours. The Dutch vice-admiral, at the beginning, attacked the vessel in which the Spanish admiral was, grappled it, and was ready to board her. A cannon-ball, which wounded him in the thigh soon after the fight began, left him only a hour's life, during which, and till within a moment of his death, he continued to give orders as if he felt no pain. When he found himself ready to expire, he delivered his sword to his lieutenant, obliging him and all that were with him to bind themselves by an oath either to conquer or die. The lieutenant caused the same oath to be taken by the people of all the other vessels, when nothing is heard but a general cry of 'Victory or Death.' At length the Dutch were victorious; they lost only two vessels, and about two hundred and fifty men; the Spaniards lost sixteen ships; three were consumed by fire, and the others, among which was the admiral's ship, ran aground. D'Avila, with thirty-five captains, fifty of his volunteers, and two thousand eight hundred soldiers, lost their lives in the fight; a memorable action, which was not only the source of tears and affliction to many widows and private persons, but filled all Spain with horror.

"This, indeed, was finishing the war by a glorious stroke," writes the French minister, "for the negociations were not laid aside, but were probably pushed on with the greater vigour on account of it."*

* *Memoirs of Sully*, bk. xx. 1607.

CHAPTER XXXI.

OLIVER THE PROTECTOR'S ESTIMATE OF THE ROCK.

ALTHOUGH the nation remained at peace, the people about Gibraltar were, for a long time after this, constantly exposed to incursions of those rovers with whom many of the expelled Moors sought revenge upon their tyrants; to meet these evils watch-towers were erected along the whole coast of Granada "from the easternmost point to the Portuguese territory," the ruins of which are to be observed in many places to this day. A few years before the Old Mole and the Torre del Puerto were repaired, and the king visited the Rock, with no incident of greater importance than that of being compelled, by the narrowness of the gate, to leave his carriage and enter on foot. On hearing complaints that his Majesty had been thus inconvenienced, the governor replied that the gate was not made to admit carriages but to keep enemies out. A fatal pestilence desolated Gibraltar in 1649.

The advent of the English upon the scene was nearer at hand than most folks looked for at this time, for we learn by the letters of Oliver the Protector, that in 1656, April 28th, his Highness wrote from Whitehall to "Generals Blake and Montague, at sea," and engaged in war against what Mr. Carlyle calls "the Spaniards and their Papist Domdaniel." These English chieftains were then "somewhere off Cadiz Bay," with a fleet which might have anticipated the feat of Rooke. After discussing if Cadiz itself might not be open to attack by cutting off the city on the island at the bridge, the Protector proceeded, "Whether any other place be attemptable; especially that of the Town and Castle of Gibraltar—which, if possessed and made tenable by us (to which Mr. Carlyle adds a note of, 'Hear, hear!') it would be an advantage to our trade and an annoyance to the Spaniard; and enable us, without keeping so great a fleet on that coast, with six nimble frigates lodged there to do the Spaniard more harm than by a fleet, and ease our own charge!" It seems that these "sea-generals" thought either of these attempts impracticable with their force in hand. Montague replied to Secretary Thurloe, "I perceive much desire that Gibraltar should be taken, my thoughts as to that are, in short, these,—that the likeliest way to get it is, by landing on the sand and quickly cutting it off between sea and sea (a plan partly carried out ere this, as we showed before), or so secure our men there that they may hinder the intercourse of the town with the main: frigates lying near to to assist them: and it is well known that Spain never victualleth any place for one month. This will want four or five thousand men, well-officered. This is my only thought which I submit at present."

It is evident from this that Oliver clearly saw the value of the place, and that Montague had made search for the best mode of attempting a capture; the former decided that for the present nothing of this sort could be done. The great ships of the English fleet were therefore ordered home under Montague, Blake was instructed to stay out the then coming winter with "a good squadron of frigates, about the number of twenty ships, such as you shall judge proper and fit for that purpose."

After this storm of war with England, and near evil to Gibraltar, the latter place had peace; but it was evident notwithstanding outward signs of prosperity, mere increase of flesh, so to say, the decadence of Spain was going on. Philip IV. died in 1665, Charles II. succeeded him and, although in some respects a reforming sovereign, left his dominions in an even worse plight than he found them; this was by means of the Spanish and the old French enmity. It seems to follow that we should be in alliance with Spain while she was at war with Louis XIV. In 1693 Sir George Rooke, with an English and Dutch fleet, guarding a great convoy of the ships of both nations, fell in, June 17th, with the French fleet under Tourville, not far from Cape St. Vincent, when ensued a desperate fight, during which the convoy escaped, and ultimately reached Gibraltar, where the Spanish garrison, taking to the guns, beat off the French ships which had followed the traders. Upon this Tourville opened a terrible bombardment on the town and Fortress, which lasted nine days, but effected little against the Rock.

CHAPTER XXXII.

WAR OF THE SUCCESSION—CAPTURE OF GIBRALTAR BY THE ENGLISH.

THE peace of Ryswick, 1697, concluded the warlike operations, after the opportune arrival of the English had barely saved Barcelona, three years before that date. Charles II. of Spain died in 1700, November 1st, and left his dominions to Philip of Anjou *i.e.* V. of Spain, second son of the Dauphin Louis, and grandson of Louis XIV. of France. The Archduke Charles, second son Leopold I. of Germany, claimed the throne in the right of his mother, Margaret Theresa, daughter of Philip IV. of Spain. Upon this the War of the Succession began; and England, under William III., with Austria, and Holland, resolving to permit no union between France and Spain, joined against the claim of Philip V. It is famous in our history on account of the campaigns in Holland, Flanders, and Germany, under Marlborough. When William III. died in 1702, March 8th, Anne came to the throne with a resolution to continue the war; this was effected without much result, until in 1704 it was determined to attack Spain at home with the aid of the Portuguese. The English fleet, under the orders of Sir George Rooke, reached Lisbon, and detached Admiral Dilkes to cruise in the Straits of Gibraltar, where he captured two Spanish vessels of war. Rooke was ordered to proceed to the Mediterranean and assist the defenders of Nice and Villafranca, but was induced by the Archduke Charles to attempt the capture of Barcelona; in this he failed and, proceeding on his voyage, missed the French fleet at sea.

Resolved upon doing something important with the forces from which so much was expected, the commanders of the allied fleets and troops—*i.e.* Landgrave George of Hesse-Darmstadt; Rooke; George Byng, Lord Torrington ;* Sir Cloudesley Shovel; Admiral Leake and the three Dutch admirals, being informed that Gibraltar was open to attack, determined on that enterprise, which ultimately placed the Rock in the hands of the English. As usual, the place was weak in troops and stores and needed repairs; the Spanish finances had been diverted to more pressing objects in the war and, although the Governor

---

* George Byng, a distinguished English admiral, was born at Wrotham, Kent, in 1663; entered the navy in 1678; when but fifteen years of age he changed service into the army and was for three years in garrison at Tangiers under Colonel Kirk. There he obtained some knowledge of the character and importance of Gibraltar. He then returned to the navy, made himself famous in action and long service in the East Indies and lent much effective aid to the placing of William III. on the throne of Great Britain in 1688. He was concerned, as we shall see, in the taking of Gibraltar and, while in command of a squadron in the North Sea, compelled the Pretender with a French fleet to depart from the Frith of Forth, 1708 (Burnet, *History of his own Times*). He was sent with a fleet into the Baltic to watch Charles XII. of Sweden, 1717; then sailed for the Mediterranean and, when near Messina, totally defeated a Spanish fleet, October 19th, 1719; was created Lord Torrington in 1721 and died, January 17th, 1733. He had five sons, of whom the first and second succeeded in turn to the viscounty of their father; the third, Robert, had a son who was smothered in the Black Hole at Calcutta, June 20th, 1756; the fourth son, John, was the unfortunate admiral who was shot by order of a court-martial, or rather by means of ministerial cowardice, March 14th, 1757; the fifth son, Colonel Edward Byng, died of convulsions, brought on by the sight of his brother being brought to trial at Portsmouth, 1756. The shameful wrong done to Admiral John Byng is connected with the history of Gibraltar, as it was while refitting his fleet in the port there that he learned the French fleet had quitted Toulon and landed troops for the Siege of Minorca, then in English hands, for the relief of which island the admiral had been sent to sea. In Gibraltar Bay was held the unfortunate Council of War which must have had much to do with dispiriting the hopes of Byng for a victory over the French under the command of the Marquis de la Galisonnière. The indecisive issue of the naval fight which ensued and the history of the English admiral's trial, are well known.

of Gibraltar had entreated means for strengthening the Fortress, nothing was afforded for the purpose.

Such was the position of Gibraltar when fate was about to place it in new hands. The Council of War against the Rock was held on board the Royal Catherine in the Bay of Tetuan, July 17th, 1704. It was then and there decided to make the attempt and, on the 21st of that month, the British fleet came to an anchor in the Bay of Gibraltar and landed five thousand men before the north front of the Rock, so as at once and effectually to cut off the receipt of supplies by the garrison. So little time had been lost in this business that the appearance of the ships took the garrison by surprise. Many of these vessels are famous in the history of our navy. Among them may be named the Essex, Captain Hubbard; the Ranelagh, Admiral Byng and Captain Cole; the Torbay; Centurion; Grafton, Sir A. Leake; Nassau; St. George; Royal Catherine, Admiral Sir George Rooke; Monmouth; Bedford, Sir Henry Hardy; Royal Oak; Kent, Admiral Dilkes; Burford; Nottingham; Orford, Captain Norris; Barfleur, Admiral Sir Cloudesley Shovel, and Hampton Court, Captain (afterwards Sir Charles) Wager. There were in all forty-five ships, six frigates, seven fire ships, two hospital ships, two bombs and a yacht.*

Prompt in all their measures, the commanders of the allied forces sent, on the morning after their arrival, a demand for the surrender of Gibraltar to the Archduke Charles, in whose

---

* As we have now arrived at a comparatively modern part of our history, the reader will find frequent need to consult the map which precedes this text. As to former sieges the old names remain in use; but in a limited degree, nevertheless, it cannot have been difficult to identify many of the localities which have been already named. In studying the Great Siege, the reader will find the map still more serviceable than before and, indeed, indispensable to a fair understanding of the subject. Some of the names of spots in Gibraltar—*e.g.* "Jumper's Bastion"—derive from the siege which we now consider.

cause as rightful king and styled Charles III. of Spain, the Landgrave George of Hesse-Darmstadt appeared in arms. It is said that the garrison consisted of not more than one hundred and fifty men, exclusive of the inhabitants, the stores, however, appear to have been sufficient for the needs of a prolonged siege; the governor, the Marquis Diego de Salinas, was competent to his office and, had he been fitly backed by troops, might never have lost the Fortress. On receipt of the summons a council was held and the answer which the English summons produced recited the oaths of the inhabitants and troops to Philip V. and professed their determination to adhere to its obligations with their lives and fortunes. According to the Spanish authorities, the garrison, all told, comprised not more than five hundred* men; the arms were one hundred pieces of cannon, of heavy make for that day. The Old Mole and the New Mole were garrisoned by citizens and militia, two hundred in the former and a smaller number in the latter, the Land Port Gate was guarded by a weak force of invalids, sixty in all; in the castle were sixty-two soldiers of divers arms.† On the arrival of the valiant reply of the little garrison, which was late on July 21st, so prompt were all motions in these matters, the ships—a tremendous force for that age, carrying troops, which in all amounted to nearly four times the number of the garrison—received orders for the attack which was designed for the next morning, but, owing to the contrary effect of the wind, they were not successfully placed in time. The first offensive step was taken by the captain of the Dorsetshire, of eighty guns, Captain

---

* The Spanish memorial to Philip V. after the capture, stated the garrison to be "fewer than three hundred men, a few poor and raw peasants."
† Ayala: Monte, Hist. de Gibraltar.

Whittaker, who, says Sayer, was sent with boats to burn a French privateer of twelve guns which lay at the Old Mole. More serious demonstrations followed on the morning of the 23rd of July; the fleet, after throwing a few shots into the Fortress and receiving prompt replies, poured out its missiles with unflagging fierceness and maintained the fire until long after noon. Six Dutch ships and sixteen English vessels, the squadrons of Vanderdusen and Byng, fronted the Line Wall between the heads of the Moles; three English men-of-war, under Captain Hicks—a well-known name—being the Yarmouth, seventy guns, under Hicks; the Hampton Court, seventy guns, under the afterwards-famous Captain Wager, and the Tiger, fifty guns, Captain Cavendish—took up stations on the west of the others and the New Mole. The efforts of this great force soon told on the walls; the guns on the New Mole were rapidly silenced and its garrison fled. Sir George Rooke's dispatches state that he ordered Captain Whittaker to make an attack on this Mole with boats, but Captain Hicks intercepted the signal to his more remote fellow-officer and anticipated the execution of the orders it conveyed; with Captain Jumper, of the Lennox, seventy guns, he pushed to the shore, but it was to experience the effects of a mine which was sprung under their first footsteps and destroyed forty men and two officers. Captain Whittaker was more fortunate; he took the New Mole, kept it, repulsed an attack of the enemy and proceeding assailed Jumper's Bastion. The effect of this attack was extended to the Line Wall; this part, the fort on the point of the Old Mole and that defence itself, were successively captured by Whittaker's party and the marines who had been landed soon after the arrival of the fleet.

It was hardly possible to sustain such an attack as this; the besieged offered to capitulate and finally surrendered with the honours of war, the right of retaining their property, six days provisions, three brass guns of different sizes and twelve rounds of ammunition. The garrison had three days allowed for its departure; those, as well as the inhabitants of the Rock, who chose to remain might do so with full civil and religious rights. Oaths of allegiance were to be transferred to Charles III. by those who proposed to remain. The magazines were to be pointed out, as well as all useless arms and provisions. French subjects were to remain as prisoners of war. Few of the inhabitants continued in Gibraltar, the mass removed to St. Roque. Thus in less than three days (July 21st to July 24th, 1704), this famous Fortress once more underwent a change of masters, the Prince of Hesse-Darmstadt took possession in the name of Charles III. Sir George Rooke, however, overrode this proceeding, pulled down the standard of Charles, set up that of Great Britain and proclaimed Queen Anne. A garrison of eighteen hundred English seamen was placed in the Fortress.* The loss of the victors was very small.

Proposals have been made from time to time for the restitu-

---

* This seems a high-handed proceeding on the part of the English admiral, but it was not without strong strategical as well as political and moral authorities that this thing was done. It is certain that the place could not have been kept in Charles III.'s possession during the remainder of the war; the English alone of the parties then present were competent to hold it, for the Dutch force was quite subordinate to that of its allies. At the conclusion of the struggle the Rock was formally surrendered, "absolutely, with all manner of right for ever without exemption or impediment," to England as one of the belligerents in a war which she certainly did not provoke; had it not been thus awarded some equivalent must have been found which would have been acceptable to her. The common talk about our seat in Gibraltar is based upon a foolish notion that we have no right there, whereas our position is as just as that of Spain with regard to Ceuta, better than that of France to Strasburgh, of England to Canada, or of any other holder of a prize of war.

tion of Gibraltar and various specious arguments advanced in favour of that act. We have not here to reason on this matter; let it suffice that the place belongs to us by right of cession, at the Peace of Utrecht, 1711, confirmed over and over again; that, such being the case, if we did give it up, common justice demands that we should be indemnified—first, by an equivalent such as must have been offered at the end of the War of Succession; secondly, for all we have spent upon it during more than a century and a half of ownership, an expenditure which has given to the Rock all its value as a modern stronghold. The foolish suggestion of an exchange being effected of Gibraltar for Ceuta, is one of the most amazing freaks of this day. Ceuta belongs to the Spaniards by an inferior right to our own on its fellow Rock. If Gibraltar belongs to the Spaniards, Ceuta is, by an equal right, the property of the Moors, our old and very faithful allies, whom it is now proposed we should join in robbing. Ceuta is not worth a tenth part of Gibraltar, yet if it were worth ten times as much, the wrongfulness of keeping it would be greater than that of holding Gibraltar as we do. In short, Gibraltar is the coign of vantage for a great maritime power; such as Spain is not, but such as France and the United States are. It would be worth a war with Spain, on the part of France, to have the key of the Mediterranean. If the policy of the United States with regard to European aggression were changed and the Union remained unbroken, it might be worth the while of those who are ardent in the cause of oppressed races to get up a cry for the Spaniards and try to acquire the Rock. To either enemy we should have a reply. A party at home has more than once —as in 1782, when Lord Shelburne's ministry was shot out of office by the indignant nation—proposed to cede the place. Dr. Franklin, when representing our enemies, coolly, but not very logically, averred that Portsmouth might as justly be ceded to Spain as Gibraltar to England. This party still survives and but lately renewed the attempt in the old manner, with the old arguments reduced to that weakest and least conclusive of all—*i.e.* the alleged morality of such a sacrifice. We have briefly entered upon this subject at this place, because it is our purpose to conclude with it at the earliest opportunity. Readers who desire further information will find it amply afforded in the " Parliamentary History " of the discussions in both Houses of the Legislature upon the repeated attempts to have the Rock ceded to Spain; in Coxe's " History of the Bourbon Kings of Spain;" Lord Mahon's " History of England;" " The Memoirs of Sir R. Walpole;" " The Correspondence of the Earl of Chatham " and, for a succinct compilation from these and other authorities, with many otherwise unpublished letters, the excellent chapters on the subject in Captain Sayer's " History of Gibraltar," 1862.

The Spaniards departed from the Fortress they had valiantly won and as valiantly defended; the majority remained at St. Roque, not without hopes of soon returning to their homes; like the Moors whom they had dispossessed, their descendants are said to preserve until this day the records and family documents which form the bases of claims upon property on that Rock which, for more than a century and a half, has known other masters. On the other hand, great as his achievement was and invaluable as was his addition to the power of the British commonwealth, Sir George Rooke received no reward whatever. From the Whigs he obtained, indeed, so much of a reward as is conveyable in vigorous detraction. The captor of Magdala and deliverer of some missionaries, at the price of ten millions of money and one wounded man, has been magnificently rewarded; but Rooke got not even thanks. He landed what troops and sailors could be spared for the defence of his capture and left the prince in command when, about a fortnight after the victory, he once more put to sea (August 9th). On the 10th the prospect of further battle offered for, having stood to the eastward with his ships, the English admiral encountered the vanguard of a great French fleet under the command of one of the ablest seamen of that nation, the Count of Toulouse (Thoulouse) and comprising nearly eighty sail, fifty-two of which were ships of considerable size. At first the French seemed to decline a battle and on the 12th of August they were, as Captain Sayer says, so far off as to be out of sight. On the following day the enemy again appeared and offered battle. The fleets were almost equally matched in numbers and, except that a large proportion of the English ammunition had been expended upon the Rock, there was at least equal chances in their favour; besides which Rooke had the wind, which Toulouse endeavoured to gain and so brought on a vigorous combat. Rooke, Sir John Byng, and Admiral Dilkes were placed to bear the brunt of the battle with the Dutch ships astern of them and Leake, with valiant Sir Cloudesley Shovel as leader, before all, in the old Barfleur, that ship which has retained a glorious name in the English navy. This was then a very large vessel and powerfully handled by Sir Cloudesley, the former cabin-boy, and long before this battle off Malaga one of the best and bravest of English captains. The battle began fiercely and was continued firmly; the English suffered greatly at first, the admiral's ship, the Royal Catherine, being one of the first to fight and be attacked. The French ships were most violently assailed by Shovel, who went nearly alongside his antagonist, and there concentrated his fire with terrible effect. The combat continued until late in the evening and ended in a drawn battle, so far as its consequences were apparent at the time; but the Count of Toulouse withdrew in the early morning with all his ships, having suffered terribly in masts, sails and rigging, with more than three thousand men killed and wounded—among the latter were the count himself, one of his commodores and nearly one hundred and fifty officers of various grades. Another French commander, the Bailif of Lorraine, was killed, with many more. The whole French fleet retired from the scene of action, notwithstanding that the Englishmen followed as well as they could until the 16th of August. When he had lost sight of his enemy Rooke returned to Gibraltar, partly to look for the French, partly to refit his battered ships. Meanwhile Toulouse was making for harbour at Toulon, which he reached in due time and used for refitting the Armada, an operation that was not complete until the year had almost expired; whereas Rooke's ships were at sea and ready for another fight in less than ten days when, no enemy appearing, the greater number of the vessels were sent home and only Admiral Leake's squadron remained in the Spanish waters. Such was the great battle off Malaga, which cost the allies two thousand seven hundred and ten men in killed and wounded, including Sir Andrew Leake, the captain of the Grafton (seventy guns).*

---

* Some notion of the fierceness of the English sailors in combat may be gained from the following passage in a letter from Sir Cloudesley Shovel, as quoted by Captain Sayer :—" We having the weather-gauge, gave me an opportunity of coming as near as I pleased, which was within pistol-shot, before I fired a gun ; through which means and God's assistance, the enemy declined us and were on the run in less than four hours, by which time we had little wind and their galleys towed off their lame ships

These achievements would seem to form claims for rewards and distinctions at the hands of those who were trustees for the nation in distributing them to the deserving, yet Rooke got nothing of this sort from the powers that were; in fact, although ere very long the importance of the capture of the Rock was popularly recognised, the government, swayed by the passions of party, absolutely ignored the transaction; the House of Lords declined to address the queen and although the Lower House was more active in procuring rewards for the combatants, Rooke consulted the interests of his party and his own dignity by retiring from the public service. He was never in favour with the Lords and, for reasons that only party spirit could vitalise, had been the object of inquiry on the part of their house after the failure of the expedition to Cadiz, in respect to which, however, his extraordinary triumph in capturing the Spanish galleons and war ships at Vigo (a feat which may compare with some of the achievements of Sir Francis Drake) stood him in stead. (*See* Smollett's abstracts of accounts of these transactions in his continuation of Hume's "History of England.") The queen, influenced by the Duchess of Marlborough, absolutely resented the placing of Rooke's name in juxtaposition with that of the Duke of Marlborough, then recently victorious at Blenheim. The duke got Woodstock—the admiral nothing. Yet it seems pro-

---

and others as they pleased." (These row galleys, then manned by convicts, often played important parts in Mediterranean warfare, even so late as the middle of the last century.) "I set my sails and rowed," says Shovel, " with three boats a-head, to get alongside with the admiral of the White and Red; but he, outsailing me, shunned fighting and lay alongside of the little ships. Notwithstanding the engagement was very sharp, I think the like between two fleets never was seen in any time." He meant "my time," as to which in the fighting way at sea there was no better judge living than stout and honest-hearted Sir Cloudesley Shovel.—*See* Smollet's Continuation of Hume's *History of England*.

bable that in the long run Gibraltar has been more valuable than the glories of half the duke's victories put together. Sir Cloudesley Shovel succeeded Rooke in command of the fleet, with the title of Vice-Admiral of England. Sir George returned to his seat at St. Lawrence, near Canterbury, where, January 24, 1709, aged 58, he died and was buried in the neighbouring cathedral.

CHAPTER XXXIII.

THE TWELFTH SIEGE.

THE next event which we have to record in the history of the Rock is the effort which the Spanish king and his French allies, before the year 1704 had expired, directed by land and sea against the English. The latter had done much in fortifying the hold, especially by a new battery above the monastery, and placed a garrison of three thousand men within the walls which, although victualled for not more than two months, was a much more potent force than the ancient owners had maintained, as the latter now found to their cost. So swift was the backward blow of the losers that within three months after the surrender (Oct. 9), the place was again attacked and trenches opened against it, from which, a few days later, heavy guns did damage at a short distance and dismantled the old round tower *(Ayala)*. A French fleet of twenty-two ships aided these operations and it was feared by the garrison would, if the sea and land forces were combined, wear them out; the troops alone were four times more numerous than the besieged. The Battery of St. Paul was cannonaded on the 28th of October and the civil governor killed. More troops, both Spanish and French, were landed, but for a considerable time their efforts were ineffectual; the elevation of the Rock gave to its holders important advantages in placing guns and mortars and viewing with ease all the operations of their enemies.

The arrival of succours from England had an important effect upon the spirits of the two parties. Sir John Leake came into the Bay on the day after the Battery of St. Paul was attacked, drove four French ships ashore and stopped the advances of the soldiers on that side of the Rock which was exposed to his guns; thus friends were substituted in that quarter for foes. The next attempt was by escalade and proved fatal to a great number of those who, under the guidance of a native goatherd, one Simon Susaste, actually ascended the Rock and reached so high as the signal station, where English troops were sent to capture them; they inflicted serious loss on the latter, but, after losing nearly one hundred and sixty men, became prisoners of war. It seems that among the causes of this failure was a dispute between the commanders of the besieging forces and the neglect of the Spaniards (*Sayer*). The firing continued with increased force and effect until a large number of the Rock guns were disabled and the ammunition of the besieged was running low; the stores of other kinds were scanty, disease was prevailing and the men's hearts sinking, when news came that active measures for succouring them, including the despatch of an entire relief of the garrison, engineers, stores and tools, were in hand. Thus heartened, the English, although reduced to about half their original force, kept their posts as well as they could and defeated the enemy when, as was frequent, they assaulted the works. On the 7th December, two months after the beginning of the siege, part of the English help arrived; thus strengthened, a sortie was made and much damage done to the enemy; on the 20th a second sally was effected with even more effect. A month later the besiegers made a great assault on the King's lines, the weakness of which had been betrayed to them; this was for a time successfully executed, but the garrison sent a party under Colonel Moncal which soon reinstated the holders. Hard as was the existence of the English, that of their enemy was even worse and their sufferings must have been intense through the trenches filling with water, the cutting off of supplies by inland floods and the progress of disease in their camp. Marshal Tessé, a famous commander, was appointed to conduct further operations and the hopes of the besiegers revived with the reinforcements which, on a great scale, he conducted to them. A violent assault was made upon a breach which was hardly enlarged enough to warrant success and ended in the useless sacrifice of more than two hundred lives. Another attack, this time by the combined armies and navies, was frustrated, so far as the latter were concerned, by the wind shifting to the south, converting that part of the Rock which had been appointed for the naval assault into a lee shore. A letter which Captain Sayer quotes from the *Memoire de Tessé* gives a somewhat humorous account of the state of the besieging army before Gibraltar, the marshal avers that the dilatory proceedings of the Spaniards spoiled everything—the cannon did not arrive when it was wanted, a vast supply of powder could not be heard of; meanwhile a French fleet under Pointé arriving in the Bay, was caught there by Leake, who captured three of the ships and destroyed that of Pointé. The English admiral sent his reinforcements ashore and thus placed the garrison in a position nearly equal to that it occupied before the siege begun ; whereas, as Tessé told the Prince de Condé, the allies could not continue the attack and yet were unable to quit the place except at the sacrifice of all their stores and materials of war. Having lost ten thousand men, the French commander raised the siege on the

18th April, 1705, *i.e.* six months after the task was begun amid hopeful declarations.

All this time the War of the Spanish Succession, which had dragged us into the European battle-fields, continued to rage with varying success, yet, so far as Spain was concerned, with a general leaning to the establishing of Philip V. on the throne. The archduke's cause was further aided by Charles Mordaunt, the Earl of Peterborough—Pope's friend—who conferred upon him a wider immortality in two verses than the earl's own laurels could secure. "Almost as quickly as he conquered Spain," one of the famous lines in question, might have been supplemented by a statement of how rapidly he lost his ready gains. He made an attack on Barcelona and Prince George of Hesse, one of the captors of Gibraltar, was slain. This disastrous war continued until 1711, when the death of the Emperor Joseph II. simplified the cause of contest and led to a settlement at the Peace of Utrecht. This treaty is noteworthy for our present subject on account of the formal cession to England by Spain of the Rock and Fortress, "in all manner of right for ever." For this Spain received, according to the conditions of the treaty, a full consideration; upon this, even more than the right of conquest, the British claim has since rested.

CHAPTER XXXIV.

THE THIRTEENTH SIEGE.

THIS defeat, with the terrible losses of men and money which attended it, was not sufficient to check the desires of Spain for the restitution of that portion of her territory which she had ceded to England.

Another siege was undertaken after many attempts had failed to obtain by negotiation that which force had not succeeded in winning. These attempts involved some of the most amazing declarations and tergiversations on the parts of the Spaniards and the English Government. The latter must be understood as distinct from the people, who made it a point of national pride to insist on retaining the place and held to it with such force of will that more than one ministry, which would, if left alone, willingly have temporised, if not yielded, dared not propose in the House of Commons a cession of the Rock. The history of these efforts and their failures may be read in Lord Mahon's "History of England;" Archdeacon Coxe's "Memoirs of the Bourbon Kings of Spain;" the "Memoirs of Sir Robert Walpole;" the "Parliamentary History;" and briefly, Captain Sayer's "History of Gibraltar." At one time (July, 1725) matters went so far that in a conference with Philip V. and his queen, the high-handed Isabella of Parma—who, since the return of her husband from the monastery of St. Ildefonso, had been actual ruler—Mr. Stanhope, the English minister, was told by the lady, "Either relinquish Gibraltar, or your trade with the Indies;" and a demand had been stated beforehand making the cession the alternative of instant war.

Conduct of this sort was much less likely to be successful than such pathetic appeals as have been recently in vogue; it was impossible that the English nation would surrender the place which had been retained at considerable cost of blood and treasure. A promise on the part of George I. was alleged for its restoration and admitted by him, but with a qualification that he would endeavour to obtain the consent of Parliament in the matter. The Spaniards seem to have been unable to master the fact that since the execution of Charles I. no English king has been allowed to do what he pleased with the possessions of the nation; hence their disgust is less difficult to understand at what they called the withdrawal of George I. from his word.

In December, 1726, the Spanish ambassador made a new formal demand for the restitution of the Rock, with the understood alternative that peace or war between the nations depended on the answer. The English preferred war, the House of Commons strengthened the king's hands. After further squabbling war began and Gibraltar was again assailed, January, 1727. Stores had been previously gathered, materials brought together and a large force assembled near Algeciras in the December previous to the attack. These preparations gave warning to the garrison of the storm to come. So fierce was the Spanish Government at the outset of the siege that the heavy guns and the stores of Cadiz were taken before the Rock, peasants were pressed to dig the trenches and the business pressed without stay.

The history of this attack is striking on account of the

evidence it affords of the utter lack of judgment on the part of those assailants who attempted a regular siege of the Rock without securing command of the sea, or so thoroughly exhausting their enemy that he could not supply the garrison. The latter feat being out of the question in this instance and the former so impracticable as never to have been attempted at the Thirteenth Siege, it is evident that experience of former failures, as with Algeciras while it remained open to the sea, was thrown away upon that Spanish queen who sent what was for that time a vast force of artillery and a great army against Gibraltar. Insufficiently prepared as was the Fortress, her Majesty might as well, if a *coup de main* failed, have pounded the Rock. This was the feeling of the beleaguers, who took the extraordinary step of protesting to their government their despair of succeeding in the task upon which they were employed. Practically the attack became a great land duel with artillery, no powerful assaults of other kinds having been made by either party.

Admiral Hopson was stationed for a while in the Bay, but was compelled, says Drinkwater, to overlook the preparations of the Spaniards in transporting provisions, artillery and ammunition from Algeciras to the camp at St. Roque. This compulsory neglect also affected Brigadier Kane, who was despatched from Minorca with troops. Neither of these officers could interfere because they were ignorant of hostilities having begun between the countries. Nevertheless, what reinforcements for the garrison could be spared were sent from Minorca, likewise fresh troops and considerable supplies from England, ere the attack could be said to have been begun, and the garrison was never really distressed for lack of reliefs of men or stores. Sir Charles Wager, whom we met at the capture of Gibraltar in command of the Sea Horse, was now an admiral and led six ships with reliefs to the Rock. The trenches were opened on February 10, on the western beach near the old windmill, on the Neutral Ground, that is, at a spot which the bounds set by the treaty prohibited to Spain. General Clayton, the lieutenant-governor, says Drinkwater, remonstrated with the Spanish commander, Las Torres, and was answered in a manner which expressed the intentions of the besiegers. This was before war had been declared and the Spanish proceedings were, to say the least, irregular. These excavations produced the hostilities they challenged, in the evening of the 11th February, the English commander fired at the workmen from the Old Mole and Willis's Batteries, two of the lower defences of the Rock. The first offensive operations by the Spaniards were undertaken, but with slight effect, from Punta Mala, against the ships of the English which lay in the Bay. The trenches had been begun in the night before, were directed towards the Inundation and wrought by a large force and with great energy during the night. In the morning the garrison observing this effort endeavoured, but with no result, to check further advance in this way. Here, first of all, was presented a proof of the importance of the command of the sea to either party. The admiral sent two vessels into Blackstrap Bay, which cannonaded the troops as they gathered on the following night in the new works at the foot of the Rock and drove them with great loss from their hiding-places. The creation of a battery by the Spaniards between the Devil's Tower and Santa Barbara, where ruins still exist, stopped this means of defence and compelled the ships to retreat. Thus protected from this side, the trenches were continued and the Old Mole Head, Landport—on the west of the Inundation—and the works on that side were assailed with a vigorous cannonade. Approaching nearer at every turn of their trenches, the assailants gathered force and built battery after battery, armed with mortars as well as guns, which more or less commanded the whole of the lower fortifications at the north-west angle of the place. So close did they approach that pieces of rock were cast down from above upon the works and great injury inflicted upon the labourers. On the part of the defence all the available workmen and civilians of the town were employed under military direction in repairing damages, carrying shot and powder. Further reinforcements came in with stores, which strengthened the English greatly. Their position was also much improved by the disastrous effects of a violent storm, which not only swamped the besiegers' works, but powerfully affected their communications.*

All this time the English ships were active in intercepting the stores of the enemy and carrying them to the use of the garrison. Notwithstanding these impediments, the trenches were pushed forward so vigorously that in the second week in March (the 10th says James, the 3rd of March says Drinkwater) the works were carried to one hundred paces of the place and the Old Mole much injured by the fire which followed this stage of the operations. Among the other offensive attempts mentioned by the "Officer" and James was that of driving a gallery under Queen Anne's and Willis's Batteries (on the "Lines" which still bear that officer's name): this was begun with the very ill-considered object of blowing up these works. As Captain Sayer commented, this was a waste of forces upon the intractable limestone of the Rock. This author tells us that, on the 12th of March, the enemy had reached so near Landport Gate as to be within musket-

---

* *Journal of an Officer* ; James's *History of the Herculean Straits*, the best portion of which work refers to this siege ; Sayer's *History of Gibraltar*.

shot of that defence. The Spaniards progressed thus far at great cost to themselves and with little loss to their antagonists; they were suffering dreadfully through dysentery and fatigue—desertions were very numerous. The arrival on the 27th March of further reinforcements to the besieged, comprising Colonel Middleton's regiment, six companies and a half of that of Colonel Hays, besides engineers, artillerymen, ammunition and provisions, made the attack even less hopeful than before; to these discouragements must be added a second storm, which did at least equal injury to their works to that of the first hurricane. The frequent arrival of troops and stores showed the earnestness of the British Government in defending the Fortress and acted with reversed effect upon the minds of those who saw their enemy's craft approach and discharge cargoes at the New Mole, or where it now stands. On the 2nd of April, the admirals prepared to bombard the enemy in Algeciras, but a calm prevented the attempt. On the 10th April, the Solebay came in with five hundred men from Minorca; on the 12th of the same month the admiral finally departed, leaving a squadron under Commodore Davies. Thus strengthened and encouraged, General Clayton, on the 16th, made a feint of a sortie to drive the Spaniards from their trenches at night and expose them to the fire of his guns as they got into the open plain ("Officer," Drinkwater). This scheme failed through a mistake of orders. More troops came from England, under Lord Portmore, the governor, on the 21st, and raised the garrison to nearly five thousand five hundred men, besides civilian working parties; stores of powder soon afterwards came from Lisbon and shells from Port Mahon. "Daunted but not subdued," the attacking forces opened a new battery against Willis's and the Prince's Lines; gathered strength of guns and mortars in all their batteries for a tremendous cannonade, which was effected, says the "Officer," "so that we seemed to live in flames." This bombardment continued for nearly a fortnight (until May 12th), with few intervals in its fury and did such prodigious damage to the English works that it was hardly possible to maintain them; the greater number of the guns were silenced, yet comparatively little loss of men was inflicted. New guns were mounted as occasion permitted, the ruins cleared away and breaches temporarily repaired; so that, for the nonce, the Rock was as strong as ever, while the besiegers had exhausted themselves, wasted a vast amount of ammunition, damaged their artillery beyond serviceableness and were correspondingly depressed. It was now the turn of the English to inflict damage; a powerful fire was maintained, great mischief done to the Spanish works and the efforts of their builders so completely frustrated, that, as James relates, and the "Officer" confirms, the final retaliatory measures of the British commander seem to have been almost superfluous, except so far probably as might have affected the Spaniards with gladness, when news arrived of the progress of negotiations for peace between the belligerents. The news was communicated to the garrison by Colonel Fitzgerald, an Irish mercenary in the Spanish service. These arrangements were completed on the 23rd June, five months after the opening of this the Thirteenth Siege of Gibraltar. Thus, after the settlement of details, ended this memorable attack; the English being much better off at the end than the Spaniards were at the beginning of their disastrous venture. The latter lost, it is said, three thousand men from all causes. As it was, however, their government retired sullenly from the attempt and on more than one occasion it seemed likely that fighting would begin again. (*See* Archdeacon Coxe's "History of the

Bourbon Kings of Spain;" "Memoirs of Sir R. Walpole;" "Journal of an Officer during the Siege," British Museum; James's "History of the Herculean Straits;" Sayer's "History of Gibraltar;" and Drinkwater's "History of the late Siege of Gibraltar," 1790.)

CHAPTER XXXV.

FURTHER NEGOTIATIONS.

ONE would think that the temper of the British people had been sufficiently pronounced during the last detailed siege to have put an end to further schemes on the part of those at home who, for an equivalent, as they said, would have surrendered the Rock, as well as to the hopes of the Spaniards which had for their object the regaining of this key of the Mediterranean. Such was not the case, however. All sorts of crooked negotiations were entertained, the truth of which has never, so far as we can see, been arrived at. There is a good account of these in Captain Sayer's "History." In 1729 a "feeler" was made in the Houses of Lords and Commons; the history of this business may be read in the journals of Parliament and the newspapers of that day; the negotiations which were concluded by the English envoy at the end of the year 1729 contained no reference to the Rock; things, therefore, in respect to it remained as before. Soon afterwards (1732) the Spaniards drew lines of fortifications across the neck of the Peninsula, so as, if possible, to isolate the Fortress, and constructed the Forts San Felipe and Santa Barbara, of twenty-four guns each. At their extremities, which are nearly a mile asunder and a mile from the Rock, these now remain in ruins and appear on our map. They were effective in Drinkwater's time. The former commanded the best anchorage in the Bay. In 1754, war having broken out between France and England,

Minorca, then the next English neighbour to Gibraltar, was besieged by the former. The object of this attack is reported to have been that of securing a bait powerful enough to obtain the alliance of Spain for the French. Admiral Byng was sent at the last hour to the relief of the island; he failed; his disastrous fate is well known. Minorca was taken by the French. The English Cabinet, whose supineness had permitted this mishap, or disgrace, was expeditiously turned out of office, and Pitt brought into power. Meanwhile France, to secure the desired Spanish alliance, offered to cede her new capture and aid in another attack on the Rock (Coxe, " History of the Bourbon Kings of Spain "). On the other hand, Pitt, dreading the success of this scheme, offered (Aug. 23, 1757) to cede the Rock to Spain as the price of an alliance with England, in exchange for the lost island of Minorca, which the Spaniards were to aid in recovering from the French. This curious and promising scheme was proposed too late; the French offer was not accepted by Spain, which, however, remained neutral in the contest. Great dissatisfaction existed both at home and on the Rock with regard to the maintenance, management and cost of the garrison. The governor was accused of all sorts of misconduct, plundering and tyranny. A spirited defence was made by Lord Tyrawley before the House of Lords as to his own conduct; he was one of the warmest advocates for surrendering the place. The emoluments of the governor's office amounted to twenty thousand pounds per annum, exclusive of his salary, and were shared by knaves at home. During the governorship of Lord Home (1760), a plan was arranged by a mutinous party of the garrison for the seizing of the Fort, plundering it and its surrender to the Spaniards. This traitorous design was discovered and R.ed, the ringleader, shot on the Alameda.

The successive governors of Gibraltar after Lord Portmore were (1730) Lieutenant-General Sabine, Lieutenant-General Columbine, Lieutenant-General Hargrave, General Bland (1749), Lord Tyrawley, Earl Home—who died at Gibraltar in 1761, Lieutenant-General Cornwallis—who was succeeded by General the Right Honourable George Augustus Elliot, afterwards Lord Heathfield, who won his peerage on the Rock, as we have soon to tell.

The revolt of the North American colonies soon involved England in new wars with her old enemies France and Spain, and produced another enemy not less bitter and formidable than they have so often proved. The French openly joined the revolted colonies in 1778 (February 6th); the Spaniards joined the French in the following year. Both European nations combined their strength against Gibraltar with armies and fleets of the most powerful kind. It is noteworthy here that Ayala's "History of Gibraltar," which was written and published about this time and evidently in anticipation of the event, makes no secret of the height of the author's hopes as to the result of the then impending siege. This "History" is a capital work, especially useful for the local details of the population, fortifications, dimensions, &c. which it comprises, and invaluable to the student in our subject. Bell's translation (1845) is unfortunate in being void of many of the historical documents of the original; it contains, however, a curious plan of Gibraltar from a MS. in the British Museum. In this national collection are many MSS. and a large number of printed books, tracts and essays, concerning the Rock and Fortress.

CHAPTER XXXVI.

THE FOURTEENTH SIEGE—THE GREAT SIEGE, 1779-1783.

TO attempt a detailed account of the tremendous conflict which next comes to our hands would not only be impracticable within the limits of this work, but it is superfluous to do so at length. Drinkwater's account of this event, " the Siege of Sebastopol " of the last century, at which he was present, supplies abundance of particulars which readers can study with pleasure in the straightforward and simple style of the English officer. This excellent volume, the text-book of the subject, has been supplemented by more than one other. In Captain Sayer's " History," all the important matters relating to the grand action have been drawn together with considerable skill and research, which produced much that was unknown to the worthy " Captain of the late 72nd Regiment, or Royal Manchester Volunteers." It is noteworthy that Colonel James a laborious, but terribly confused and uncritical writer— Captain Drinkwater and Captain Sayer, all held appointments on the Rock (the last as civil magistrate); their opportunities were therefore excellent. In the following abstract we shall chiefly depend upon Drinkwater's work as not only the most complete of contemporary histories, but because his style is simple and clear in a marked degree. This author gives a very good sketch of the fortifications and appearance of the Rock in his time, which, of course, is much more valuable than that of the Spaniard Ayala, although the historical researches and national character of the latter render his production more precious to the student of the history of Gibraltar at large. Taken together, we have in these descriptions abundance of material for those who wish to reconstruct the place of three generations since, when old systems of fortifying and old artillery still obtained. Our space does not admit more than a reference to these sources. Nor are the charts, plans and views of Drinkwater without extreme interest.

Drinkwater points out the artful plan of the Spanish Court in endeavouring to cut off supplies to the Rock by procuring a right to farm the African ports which generally supplied our garrison with food. A strict alliance of damaging effect to England was afterwards concluded between Spain and Morocco. Thanks to the perseverance of the governor, the great Elliot, the place was less badly off than it might have been in common hands; but it was very insufficiently garrisoned, armed and supplied to resist the terrible efforts which were now bending against it with unsuspected force. The French fleet, twenty-eight sail of the line, was at sea and waiting off Cape Finisterre for that of the Spaniards, ere a chance revealed to the captain of a Swedish brig the near approach of the conflict, of which he conveyed news to the governor and thus confirmed suspicions which had been roused by accounts of gatherings at Cadiz and elsewhere and transmitted by British agents. On the 21st of June, 1779, communication with Spain was forbidden to the garrison. Upon this, preparations were made to meet the coming assault. These were small enough, for the best accounts agree that, notwithstanding the fine speeches of the Earl of Chatham in Parliament two years before, to the effect that he regarded Gibraltar with very different eyes than those of the William Pitt who had offered to forego the place, next to nothing had been done to second the entreaties, objurgations, and remonstrances of Elliot. War was practically declared by Spain against England, June 16, 1779, this was at home; before Gibraltar, cannon were brought from St. Roque—and other threatening arrangements made. *Five companies of artillery only* were in the garrison, which Elliot declared should consist, all told, of not fewer than eight thousand * men! To supply the deficiency as well as possible, one hundred and eighty men were trained in the management of what were then great guns. On July 5 a Spanish squadron, of considerable force appeared from the westward and lay-to off the Rock. Three privateer cutters came in from the westward and were followed and watched by a schooner under Portuguese colours. At this vessel the first guns were fired in this grand siege and from Europa batteries. On the 6th July news of the declaration of war reached Gibraltar; on the 11th the first hostile shot was fired, at a boat, by the Spaniards in Fort St. Barbara; on the 16th the enemy blocked up the port of Gibraltar by placing a strong squadron off Algeciras. The minute accounts which Drinkwater gave of the arrivals of row-boats now and then, the little bits of gossip and hearsay with which his memoirs are enriched, are characteristic and expressive of the suspense of the garrison throughout the siege. Now came a Moorish row-galley, then a Portuguese boat and a schooner, next a settee was captured; the one with fowls, another with cattle, a third with charcoal, the next with fruit. A Venetian, two Dutchmen, a friendly Swede and smaller craft came in as well as they could. Drinkwater noted them, one by one, not without anxious welcomes. A Spaniard, in an

---

* Five thousand three hundred and eighty-two, all told, was the strength of the garrison at the opening of the siege. Of these, more than one thousand were Hanoverians. At first the enemy mustered about fourteen thousand men, besides crews.

open boat laden with onions, came to Waterport and was looked at with eyes askant and threatening. One almost hears the dash of the long dead waves about his little craft.

On the 22nd soldiers were observed from the Rock, tracing lines for a camp; then the garrison knew, without doubt, that they would be the prime objects of attack in the war. Nothing was decisive of their doubts before this ominous appearance. On the 26th a camp was formed at St. Roque. The original design was to starve the garrison. This scheme was promising of success if it could be maintained in operation. Elliot discerned it and took his best means to baffle its effect. There were but forty head of cattle in the place: active preparations were seen by day and night in the camp. The garrison cleared itself from such encumbrances as could be shaken off; those who remained did so at their own risk. On the 20th a new camp was formed under the Queen of Spain's Chair. Fort St. Philip had been armed on the 17th. High in the air the sentry of the British guard saw arrive, day after day and night after night, fresh stores, fresh men, timber, fascines, guns; "two waggons, drawn each by twelve mules," appeared in broad daylight on the 8th, reached the lines and were not inaptly guessed to bring "fixed ammunition," *i.e.* mortars; events of ugly significance grew more and more frequent and the governor thought it was time to interfere. One sometimes wonders what he would have done with a modern, say Armstrong, gun or two at command. As it was he called a council of war on the 11th September and the result was a determination to open fire from the batteries on the north end of the Rock, namely Willis's, Queen Charlotte's and a recently formed one called Green's Lodge (one thousand feet above the sea). This was done and produced its intended result, a stampede of the enemy, horse, foot and Miquelets (customs' officers). "A lady fired the first shot," says Ancell. It will be remembered that the galleries which now supply the more important defence were not then formed. A 24-pounder, then a great gun, was (Oct. 12) hauled up the face of part of the Rock, to its very summit on this side (one thousand three hundred and thirty-seven feet high) and called "The Rock Gun," as now. It was twice dismounted.

Drinkwater notes the expedient of Captain Mercier, of the 39th Regiment, as that which has since almost revolutionised the practice of artillery; it was, to fire out of *guns* five and a half inch shells, with short fuses. This plan was tried on the 25th and answered well. The shells were despatched with much precision and the fuses so exactly calculated that the missiles often burst over the enemies' heads and wounded them before they got to cover. Less powder than before was thus used and the foe more seriously injured; the former was a most important matter, it accounted for the extraordinary number of shells expended during the siege, which was no fewer than one hundred and twenty-nine thousand one hundred and fifty-one.* In October the besiegers were computed at fourteen thousand men. Lieutenant-General Don Martin A. de Soto Mayor was in command of these. Moderate firing continued against the enemy during the period now in question and effectually disturbed their workmen. In reply, new batteries, bearing on "Willis's" and our lines, were opened between the Spanish lines and Fort St. Philip. On our side new works were contrived

---

* Besides these missiles, fifty-seven thousand one hundred and sixty-one solid shot were fired, twelve thousand six hundred and eighty-one discharges of grape shot, nine hundred and twenty-six carcases, and six hundred and seventy-nine light balls. Total, two hundred thousand six hundred rounds, and four thousand seven hundred and twenty-eight shot from gun-boats. Eight thousand barrels of powder were used.

and executed. Rice was now sold for £3 12s. 6d. the cwt. and marked the scarcity of provisions. Small-pox appeared among the Jews and added to the difficulties of the defence; nevertheless, the Royal Battery, below the Rock Gun, was armed with four 24-pounders on the 31st October. Provisions got dearer as November passed; mutton was 3s. 6d. a pound already; a goose was worth a guinea. The governor, by way of experiment, lived on four ounces of rice per diem for eight days. The daring running of privateers to the Rock enlivened the garrison, brought news and small stores. These acts Drinkwater notes with charming freshness and spirit. One act of this sort, performed by the "Buck," Captain Fagg, occupied unsuccessfully the Spanish admiral and twenty-one of his craft. In this case the bold ship came for provisions (!). She got what could be given, went out on the 20th December and was sunk by a French frigate. A storm brought large quantities of wood, cork, &c., down the Palamones to the Rock. "This supply was considered a miraculous interference of Providence in our favour" and was sorely needed for fuel. Deserters informed Elliot that forty mortars were mounted and all the batteries completed in the Spanish lines, January 6, 1780. A polacre, with six thousand bushels of barley, was driven into the port and captured—a visible blessing to the besieged. A woman died through want; meanwhile, though seven months had passed, no relief from home arrived. French fleets passed out of the Straits. The first person injured by the enemy's fire was a woman, January 13th. The first ship that came in with aid was an ordnance brig, which, at first, with others, was seen to be sailing through the Straits eastwards; but, suddenly altering her course, ran in under the enemy's guns to the huge joy of the English—joy that was increased by her news that a large convoy had started with her a month before for the Rock. Ere these arrived, a deserter stated that preparations for bombarding were complete against Gibraltar. Next came an English brig with intelligence that Admiral Rodney had captured off the Portuguese coast a Spanish 64-gun ship, five ships of 30 and 28 guns and seventeen merchantmen; also that twenty-one English sail of the line and the expected convoy were coming. One of the prizes dropped in next, January 18, with news of a fight off Cape St. Vincent between Rodney and Langara, in which one of the Spanish line-of-battle ships blew up and six others and Langara himself were captured. The Straits were now clear of foes and on the 21st January the whole convoy and stores came in; on the 25th the prizes. This was a most opportune relief; but for it the Rock must have been surrendered. A great victory and ample relief were enough to make the defenders frantic with joy—joyful indeed they were.* Their joy was only damped by the result of a blunder on the part of the English officers, who despatched already-laden ships to convey the great stores that had been gathered at Tangiers for the garrison. The wind changed, the ships could not be fitted to take the provisions and the latter were practically lost to us. Dread of a bombardment grew upon Elliot's mind and deserters confirmed the fears; obdurate and valiant, he, however, prepared for the worst by sending away all families that were unprovided with a year's provisions; about one thousand men, all told, of the 2nd Battalion, 73rd Highlanders were diverted from Minorca to reinforce the garrison of the Rock. Rodney sailed with his fleet on the

---

* Prince William Henry, afterwards William IV. of Great Britain and Ireland, was then a midshipman on board the Prince George.

13th February, 1780. The Spanish admiral in command at this siege, who had, while Rodney remained at the Rock, protected his vessels at Algeciras by means of a strong boom, now ventured out again and re-established the blockade, thus again shutting up Gibraltar. Nevertheless, small craft contrived to bring stores and news of Rodney sailing stoutly off Cape St. Vincent. Soon after the blockade became effectual and scurvy, the foe to garrisons, was so rife as to destroy in all ten times more than the enemy's shot. March, April and May passed on without events of note. An attempt to destroy our squadron with fire-ships failed in June and the hulls of the fruitless craft became firewood for the garrison.

About the end of the year 1779, the British Government, anxious to relieve the country of its embarrassing position in war, sounded the Spanish authorities with a view to the probable effect of a cession of Gibraltar upon the Franco-Spanish alliance. An exchange for Porto Rico and another station in the Mediterranean was suggested or discussed. The negotiations to this effect failed utterly, disgraceful as they were, and are fully described in Coxe's "History of the Bourbon Kings of Spain" and Cumberland's narrative of the proceedings, which are carefully mystified, but, as Captain Sayer truly remarks, their general nature is not questionable.

Further annoyances were inflicted on the defenders of the Rock by means of light gunboats, which approached and fired at night with great effect and serious injury to the place. They were irrepressible and had to be endured only. In July preparations were made against a more serious naval attack, the governor having news of the arrival of Spanish ships of war at Cadiz. August passed as the preceding months had fled without great incidents. In September the besiegers had pushed their approaches within eight hundred yards of our lines and the blockade was stricter than ever; a graver attack was apprehended. In October a new piece of good fortune befel the garrison—a cargo of lemons was obtained by means which, to say the least, were irregular. A Dutch convoy was discerned passing the Straits and, as necessity has no law, the boats of the English singled out one of the craft, a Dane, and carried her in to discover, to their great joy, that she was loaded with the invaluable anti-scorbutic in question; the governor, having thus taken possession, bought the fruit, the effect of the juice of which on the failing sick men was next to miraculous. The stock lasted efficaciously until the end of the siege and was a true blessing. (*See* the memorandum of Mr. Cairncross, a surgeon serving at Gibraltar, to Drinkwater's " History of the late Siege," p. 114.) Our ships now retreated within the New Mole and were protected by a strong boom. In August (1780) the Emperor of Morocco, our ancient ally, declared in form that he would no longer prevent hostilities from either party at war upon the other, even in his own parts. This was a severe blow to the besieged, whose craft had been comparatively safe in the Moroccan harbours and often brought stores from those places. Minorca remained the sole source of supply to our garrison after this event, which had been brought about by Spanish influence which soon after was effectual in inducing the emperor to declare war against the English and rent the ports of Tangiers and Tituan to their antagonists. Intelligence and stores were thus alike cut off from that quarter and the latter became so costly that potatoes sold for £7 10s. 6d. *per cwt.* on the Rock. Gunboats attacked the town and shipping off the Old Mole Head and did some damage in November, 1780. The Spanish approaches, notwithstanding our fire, were brought nearer, towards the Mill Battery. The gardens of the Neutral Ground were taken possession of and supplies of vegetables thus still further decreased. In the winter months, however, the Rock itself furnished almost sufficient of these articles. The second branch of the Spanish approaches was completed on the 29th November and the return for the third branch towards the western beach begun. It was finished on the 2nd December and the next return towards the east commenced on the 14th December. A junction was made with the extremity of the eastern *place d'armes*, the fifth branch was next extended to the east flank of the Mill Battery and a mortar battery erected to command the sea on the north of Fort St. Philip. Thus the enemy crept on, closer and yet closer, to the Fortress; but their main hopes of success against it were based upon starving the garrison. In this undoubtedly they might have succeeded if their blockade had been perfect. Notwithstanding the rigour of the watchers, small craft frequently got in with many invaluable articles.

With all these modicums of help, the state of the besieged became gloomier as the spring of 1781 progressed. Relief was again at hand and on the 3rd of April in that year the Resolution, cutter, twenty-nine days from Plymouth, ran in, loaded with coal, rum and sugar and, better than these, brought the news of a fleet lying in Torbay with a relief for the Rock and under the command of Admiral Darby. It was time, for a farthing candle cost sixpence on the Rock. This news was confirmed by the motions of the Spaniards in drawing their forces together, so as to resist an external attack. Soon after arrived the Eagle, privateer, fourteen guns, with further news of Admiral Darby. Next came the Kite, cutter, Captain Trollop, who had seen the convoy at the entrance of the Straits.

At daybreak on the 12th of April the much-expected fleet

was in sight from our signal-house, but not discernible from below, because a thick fog lay on the water. As the sun arose and broke the veil of mist, "the garrison discovered one of the most beautiful scenes it is possible to conceive." So wrote the reasonably exultant Drinkwater, who, by this time, must have been more than half-starved. "The convoy, consisting of near a hundred vessels, were in a compact body, led by several men of war, their sails just enough filled for steerage, whilst the majority of line-of-battle ships lay-to under the Barbary shore, having orders not to enter the Bay lest the enemy should molest them with fire-ships." It was nearly a year since Rodney had presented a similarly hopeful sight to the people of the Rock. Their gladness rose to its extreme height and was manifested in every possible way. "They little dreamed of the tremendous blow which impended to annihilate their property and reduce many to beggary." Exasperated at the arrival of the second relief, the Spaniards, defeated in their hopes of famishing the English defenders, had recourse to this alternative, a dreadful and cruel one—so cruel that, even in the recent civil war in the United States, all but fanatics denounced the atrocity of bombarding cities in order to annoy forts which could not be reduced by any such savage measures. One hundred and seventy cannon and eighty mortars, widely distributed before Gibraltar, began to bombard the place about eleven o'clock on the 12th April and continued at the work for six weeks following, expending fifty-six thousand shot and twenty thousand shells. To what end was all this effectual, does the reader think? Seventy men of the garrison were killed! The fury of the fire was such that the besiegers' batteries were nearly as much injured by it as those of the Rock. "Within the fortress the city was almost entirely destroyed; scarce a house inhabitable, and such as were left standing were pierced by shot and shell. But, beyond this dilapidation, the effects of the fire were not remarkable, the batteries were still in serviceable condition, and the loss of life was singularly insignificant" (*Sayer*). The most painful result of this mode of attack was the temporary outbreak of many of the garrison, who, maddened by excitement and resentment, added to the joy induced by the arrival of the convoy, took to plundering the town and drinking the spirits which the horrified people could not remove from their houses. These excesses began on the evening of the third day and continued until Elliot shot the marauders who were taken in the act. Drinkwater not unreasonably apologises for the maddened troops and tells some odd tales of the conduct of individuals among them at this period.

Generally speaking, the Fortress answered not at all to this furious bombardment. The Rock Gun itself was struck and the flagstaff on the Grand Battery so far shot away that the remains of the flag had to be nailed to the mast. On the 19th, notwithstanding this infernal fire, the stores were landed, but many private ventures were carried away again for lack of customers who would venture to receive the goods. The fleet departed on its further errand in the West Indies and left the Rock to be pelted as the enemy vainly pleased to pelt it. The next turn of the wheel of war was on the side of the pelted. Nothing could have been more surprising to the assailants of Gibraltar. Meanwhile, a third and smaller, but very serviceable convoy came in "from aloft" as it is called, *i.e.* from Minorca, where Governor Elliot had secretly arranged the despatch of twenty victuallers under convoy, the effort of the land batteries was seconded most mischievously by the regular approach of gunboats which fired into the place in an afflicting but, for the grand end they had in view, ineffectual manner.

A tremendous explosion took effect in the enemy's camp near where the Catalonian troops, which were always quartered separately from those of other provinces, were placed, and under the Queen of Spain's Chair. This appeared to be in the laboratory for shells, &c. The besiegers turned out in force, but, so continual were the discharges, were compelled to keep at a distance until some time had passed, when men rushed in and carried away powder to prevent further mischief. A mortar was fired upon them at this time from Willis's Battery* and without harming them. More assailants were discovered encamped behind Barcelo's Battery, north of Algeciras, on the 20th June. The bombardment not appearing profitable now decreased in fierceness. On the 27th more troops were seen to arrive between the Palamones and Algeciras, the bombardment was for a few hours then revived by the gunboats and twelve or fourteen men of the 39th Regiment were killed or wounded, the most serious loss we had yet sustained. To check these attacks a mortar and twelve cannon were placed on the Old Mole Head and in the sand behind it and secured in timber frames; when fired the effect of these pieces was important in dispersing a battalion of Spanish guards and driving them from their posts. Another plan of the governor's was as serviceable as the last, it consisted in placing two razéed brigs as floating batteries between the New Mole and the Ragged Staff, east of South Port. More troops and more ships now appeared on the Spanish side. By July 12th the bombardment nearly ceased. Willis's Battery, which had suffered greatly, was repaired and increased in strength in

---

* This defence, so frequently mentioned here, may be seen in our map at a little t the north of a line drawn between the Rock Gun and the Moorish Castle. The black square which is nearest to the centre of that line, on its northern side, shows the 'p' in question.

the night of the 18th. On the 6th August an English sloop of war was seen becalmed off Cabrita Point and rowing towards the Rock; assistance was sent and, after sustaining the concentrated fire of fourteen gunboats and returning it with great gallantry, she got in by the aid of the western breeze and turned out to be the "Helena," Captain Roberts, fourteen small guns, fourteen days from home, with dispatches; her sails and rigging were greatly injured, but the loss of men very slight; this entrance was one of the most gallant actions of the siege.

Time sped thus with the relief of incidents which, terrible in themselves, had small effect on the end in view of the opposed nations; small craft came in, others were captured, some got out, others were taken in that act; the enemy continued to advance his formidable lines and strengthen his batteries, but it appeared to be true, as deserters informed the governor, that the Spanish troops in camp were chiefly militia, the greatest portion of the regulars having been sent to the attack of Fort Mahon, Minorca, under the Duke de Crillon, who had ten thousand men on that service and expected a powerful reinforcement of French from Toulon. Such troops as those which were reported to be in charge of the camp, are peculiarly liable to reverses of the kind which the next operation of the besieged inflicted upon the Spaniards in question.*

---

* An adequate idea of the fury of firing which at intervals broke the nearly torpid periods of the siege may be obtained on reflecting that when the enemy had constructed a threatening battery, twelve hundred yards from the Grand Battery and bearing on the Waterport and the town, the English attacked it with such vigour that in one day and night fifteen hundred and ninety-six shot, five hundred and thirty shells (mostly heavy), ten carcases and two light balls were poured in effectually upon this single spot. The return fire comprised one thousand and twelve shot and three hundred and two shells.

This operation was of the greatest importance and effected thus. The enemy had been chiefly occupied by engineering works during the many preceding months and constructed those threatening lines which, if anything at that period could serve their purpose, were likely to be successful. These works extended nearly to the foot of the Rock and all across the Neutral Ground. A keen eye had, however, detected an error in their construction which, under the anticipated circumstances, was far from being unpardonable; this in the end procured their temporary ruin and was of the gravest consequence to both parties at war. Captain Sayer notes the existence in the British Museum of an historical sketch of Gibraltar with MS. notes which are signed "W. Booth," and describe the writer as the original suggestor of the attack in question; he states " that he had discovered the approaches being without any works whatever to flank them; the batteries in the rear must, of course, strike the reverse of their (the enemy's) own works." The author does not say who this annotator was.

The last act on the part of the garrison, which the besiegers looked for, was that which Governor Elliot now determined to perform, although his troops did not exceed six thousand men and could not conveniently be recruited. Prompt, far-seeing and secretive, the governor took his own soldiers almost as completely by surprise as shortly afterwards the enemy, when, after the gates of the Fortress were shut at gun-firing, November 26th, 1781, an " evening garrison order" appeared, which Drinkwater gives in full, and commanded a considerable force to assemble on the Red Sands at midnight with devils, faggots and tools; the party thus ordered consisted of all the grenadiers and light infantry of the garrison, the 12th and Hardenberg regiments complete, one hundred artillery, engineers, one hundred and sixty workmen from the line and forty artificers, "each man to have thirty-six rounds of ammunition, with a good flint to his piece and another in his pocket. Brigadier Ross had the command. A reserve, under General Picton, paraded at the same hour on the Grand Parade; one hundred sailors were added to the former force and all went on silently and well.

"The moon had nearly finished her nightly course," when about a quarter before three o'clock the detachment began its march, by files, from the right of the rear line, for the attack. The advanced works of the enemy held, all told, about seven hundred men. "Although nothing could exceed the silence and attention of the troops, the enemies' advanced sentries discovered the right column, which was under the orders of Lieut.-Col. Hugo and consisted of about six hundred and fifty men, before they passed Forbes's Barrier (at the eastern angle of the Inundation) and gave the alarm. The column rushed forward and began to dismantle the works. Part of Hardenberg's regiment, having lost its way, found itself fronting the St. Carlos Battery, which stood a little to the south-east of the Old Windmill, and gallantly stormed them; the defenders ran away. Some companies of the 39th Regiment entered the battery, which is described as a stupendous work in the flank, and, not recognising the Hanoverians, fired at and killed several of them. This mischief was stopped by the use of the counter-sign "*Steady.*" The attacks of other parties were equally successful, the gun-batteries were carried and the enemy fled in all directions. While the destruction of this vast, long continued and enormously costly work went on, the attacking corps formed to protect the destroyers against the enemy who might attempt to stop the ruinous process. "The exertions of the artillery and workmen were wonderful. The batteries were soon in a state for the fire-faggots to operate, and the flames spread with astonishing rapidity in every part. The column of fire and smoke which rolled from the works beautifully illuminated the troops and neighbouring objects, forming altogether a *coup-d'œil* not possible to be described. In an hour the object of the sortie was fully effected; and trains being laid to the magazines, Brigadier Ross ordered the advanced corps to withdraw." "Just as the rear had got within the garrison the principal magazine blew up with a tremendous explosion, throwing up vast pieces of timber, which, falling into the flames, added to the general conflagration." Not the slightest effort was made by the Spaniards to save their works, or annoy the destroyers of the fruits of so many months' labour, and such vast expense. "Their artillery directed a ridiculous fire upon the town and our upper batteries," says Drinkwater. Our loss was two officers and sixteen privates taken prisoners and very few killed.

The result far surpassed the governor's expectations; well might he extol the courage of his soldiers. Thus audacity, speed and comparatively large numbers enabled them to perform one of the most remarkable feats in modern war; their success was due, in its extent at least, in no small degree to the panic which seized the Spaniards, not only as it would appear the soldiers of the lines and batteries, but the army which was assembled behind these and seems to have looked on without power to save or retaliate in any effective fashion.* They allowed the conflagration to continue all the

---

* When our troops entered the batteries the written report of the commanding officer was found in one of the splinter-proofs which, when the guard was relieved, was intended to have been sent to the Spanish general. The report expressed that

next day,* hanged several soldiers, probably those whose neglect permitted the surprise, and pelted the town with shot. We had destroyed two batteries of ten thirteen-inch mortars, three batteries of six guns each, exploded the magazines and wrecked the lines, traverses and approaches and returned to the Rock within three hours of setting out. The English did this nearly a mile from their garrison in the face of fourteen thousand Spanish troops. False alarms were more than once observed to affect the besiegers and preparations were made to meet new sorties which were not intended.

The stupor of these enemies of ours was profound. It lasted six days, when more than four thousand men were set to work to repair damages. About this time nearly seven hundred men of the garrison were sick. The losses of the garrison, between April 12 and December 31, were one hundred and twenty-one men, killed and died of wounds, forty-six disabled and four hundred wounded. The enemy continued to repair and strengthen the offensive works, adding *defensive* features to them. Such is a summary of events until the 25th of February, 1782, when the St. Anne ordnance ship came in with gunboats in frames, ready to be put together at the Rock. An external event happened on the 5th of February, which had great effect on the siege of Gibraltar, being the surrender of Minorca. This released great bodies of troops and permitted increased efforts against the Rock, for which General Elliot prepared; news came to him that great preparations were making at Cadiz.

" *Nothing extraordinary had happened!* " Drinkwater gives a very clear plan of this sortie, the offensive and defensive lines and batteries.

* Smoke proceeded from St. Paschal's Battery until the 18th December. This battery stood a short distance on the south-west of the Old Windmill, nearly in a line with and west of the St. Carlos Battery.

We need not enter into the details of the siege, from this time, until a new effort was made against the Rock. Adopting a plan of Chevalier D'Arcon's (a famous French engineer), which proposed combined land and sea attacks on an unprecedented scale, the Spaniards set to work to carry it out. They relied mainly upon a new form for battering-ships, obtained by cutting down large vessels, plating their sides with thick threefold beams of timber and placing in an interval between the latter and the ships a thick layer of wet sand, within which was a dense coat of cork. These materials were, by means of pumps, kept constantly wet in order to prevent the effects of red-hot shot. The cork was devised to obviate mischief from splinters. This fabric was strengthened still more by wooden bolts. To protect the crews while working the guns, a sloping roof was placed above them, with a netting of rope, over which, after the Roman mode, was a strong covering of hides.* Through the roofs the masts of the vessels penetrated and bore the rigging above all. These novelties were fondly expected to be impregnable and incombustible; to afford, accordingly, such complete security to their crews, that they were designed to be moored within half-gunshot of the English batteries, attended by large boats full of troops, who were to be landed promptly when the confidently-anticipated issue of their powers was visible in the ruin of our batteries. Besides these, forty thousand men were to be ready in camp to take the Rock by storm, *as soon as an opportunity offered.* They were protected and assisted by line-of-battle ships. The Count d'Artois, brother of the French king, with other great personages, was to be present at the final reduction of Gibraltar (for which twenty-four hours was the proposed period), and assist, by

---

* Drinkwater (page 295) gives views of both sides of these vessels.

means of the lustre of their ancestry, in the expulsion of the English. A French convoy of sixty sail, with troops on board, arrived, June 17, 1782, which, on 21st, disembarked and encamped immediately under the Queen of Spain's Chair. The Duke de Crillon took the command of the besieging armies. In one night (August 15th) the combined troops raised an epaulment, mainly of sand-bags, nearly five hundred yards in length, from their parallel to the eastern beach, ten or twelve feet in height and proportionately thick, and a communication was built of sand casks, one thousand three hundred yards long from the epaulment to the barrier of their lines. Produced by ten thousand men labouring at once, it was a wonderful labour, executed within eight hundred yards of the garrison and so silently as to have been unsuspected until day revealed it to the astonished English.

Meanwhile the governor, profiting by the absorption of his antagonists in their new scheme, continued to strengthen the Fortress. New batteries, bearing on Water Port, were opened in the Moorish Castle, at Upper Forbes's and elsewhere; galleries in the Rock were dug, extended and armed; a naval brigade was formed, practice with red-hot shot continued with noteworthy success; *chevaux de frise* were erected at the foot of Landport glacis to the causeway and large numbers of shells and carcases prepared for use against the battering ships. On the 15th July news came of Rodney's victory over the Count de Grasse in the West Indies, the capturing of that admiral and his flag-ship. The best spirit prevailed in the garrison; the men laboured with zeal; the 72nd Regiment, in particular, volunteered to assist, besides contributing its quota in forming the new covered-way from the Grand Parade to Orange Bastion. The services of one hundred men were accepted. Altogether, we kept about one thousand seven hundred men constantly labouring at this period (August, 1782), a trivial number compared with those of the enemy.

It was understood in the garrison that events were approaching a crisis, when, on the 1st of September, coal was distributed to the grates and furnaces for heating red-hot shot. On the 4th some of the battering ships came abreast of the Orange Grove and galleys with mantlets at their bows, to contain soldiers for the attack, anchored off the landing-place beyond Point Mala. On the 5th one hundred and fifty boats assembled in a line off Rocadillo Point, powder had been shipped to the floating batteries and their number was increased. The landworks were extended prodigiously by this time, but they were encumbered by enormous masses of unappropriated materials. The cannon and mortars in some places were removed or dismounted, to permit alterations. The judgment of Lieut.-General Boyd, Lieutenant-Governor of Gibraltar, detected the advantage thus offered to the besieged and he induced General Elliot to order the immediate use of red-hot shot against the works in question. On the 8th, at seven a.m., firing began from all the northern batteries, which bore upon the western part of the parallel, and continued during the day with prodigious effect. Much of the recently-constructed communication was destroyed and the St. Carlos and St. Martin batteries rendered useless; also Mahon Battery and its neighbour were burnt. Nor was this success all that resulted from the well-timed cannonade. Enraged by this *contretemps*, the Duke de Crillon retaliated in a furious fire from one hundred and seventy pieces of ordnance, mostly of large calibre, mounted, in many instances, on his unfinished batteries, which effectually exposed them to the knowledge of his antagonists. Although nine line-of-battle ships and fifteen gun and mortar boats aided in this business, no commensurate result was achieved. The ships repeated the attack on the morning of the 10th (September); but a red-hot shot on board one of them cooled the ardour of the crews and induced them to return out of harm's way. By seven a.m. of this day, five thousand five hundred and twenty-seven shot and two thousand three hundred and two shells, besides those from the mortar-boats and ships, had been hurled against the Fortress in this fit of fury. Our losses were trivial, the attack waste; yet it was continued from the sea on the 11th September. On the 12th appeared from the westward the combined fleets of France and Spain, consisting of seven three-deckers, thirty-one two-deckers, three frigates, besides bomb-ketches, xebeques and hospital ships. In the afternoon they were at anchor between the Orange Grove and Algeciras. In all there were now assembled before the Rock forty-seven sail of the line, ten battering-ships—carrying two hundred and twelve guns, besides three hundred frigates, bomb-ketches, gun and mortar boats and smaller craft for debarking men. On the land side was an army of forty thousand men and two hundred pieces of heavy ordnance, all commanded by an active and victorious general (*Drinkwater*).

The garrison comprised about seven thousand effective men, long-tried officers, a master in the art of defence, and NINETY-SIX GUNS. Such were the opposed forces. An omen which would have strengthened the hearts of a Roman army beyond mortal courage was observed by the sentry at the flag-staff—an eagle hovered over, alit upon, and spread its wings about the pole. The troops, seeing this at a distance, and mistaking the great bird for a flag displayed, which was the signal for an English admiral's (Lord Howe's) arrival, and, so they believed, in *chase* of the enemy, cheered loudly in joy. The mistake was not unnatural, considering the distance of the staff from the observers, and their expectations with regard to a great fleet which was believed to be on its way with reliefs.

The hour of the attack, the last potent stroke at Gibraltar, was now come. At seven a.m. on the 13th of September, 1782, ten formidable battering-ships were seen to get under way, and at a little past nine o'clock, took their places in fine order, their admiral about nine hundred yards off the King's Bastion, the other vessels north and south in a line. Anticipating the result they desired, the soldiers of the camp and, it is said, a large number of civilians, assembled on the hills which form a sort of amphitheatre on the north of the Rock, where they, as well as the shadowing smoke allowed, witnessed the final act of this great siege. At a quarter before ten o'clock our fire began and, with that of the enemy, soon became tremendous. The land batteries of the allies joined in the infernal work; four hundred pieces of cannon played at once. " Our heaviest shells often rebounded from the tops of the battering-ships and the 32-pound shot seemed to make no impression on their hulls." Whenever fire from our red-hot shot was kindled on board, it was promptly extinguished by the crews. Upon them our artillery was directed, without regard to the land batteries. They bore it for two hours, although two thousand shot were fired at them. " About noon the mortar-boats and ketches attempted to second the attack from the ships, but the wind changed to the south-west, and blowing a smart breeze with a heavy swell, they were prevented from joining in the action." Nevertheless, it is recorded that our artillerymen began to doubt the issue.* The wonderful construction of the ships seemed to defy the heaviest ordnance. In the afternoon, however, the aspect of events changed considerably, the smoke which

---

* The account of this attack is condensed from Drinkwater, II :

issued from the upper part of the flag-ship increased, despite the application of abundant water; the admiral's second (on board of which was the Chevalier D'Arcon) was in the same state, her magazines were drowned in fear of an explosion, so that she was already *hors de combat*; confusion was visible on board several other vessels and, by evening, the enemy's fire was reduced, except from one or two batteries which lay on the north and were, because of their remoteness, little injured. When the firing began to slacken, signals were made from the southernmost ships and, as the evening advanced, many rockets were thrown up to inform their friends of their extreme danger and distress, then several boats rowed towards them. Our artillery must, at this period, have produced dreadful havoc: an indistinct clamour, with lamentable cries and groans, arose from on board during the brief intervals of cessation. A little before midnight a wreck floated in, upon which were twelve men, who of sixty in a launch alone escaped. Our fire continued during the night but with less vivacity, because the governor, uncertain about the demands of a second day, sent the almost exhausted artillerymen to rest and replaced them from the Marine Brigade. About an hour after midnight the battering-ship which had suffered the greatest injury and was often on fire during the day, was helplessly endangered; by two o'clock she appeared one continued blaze from stem to stern, her neighbour on the south was likewise on fire, but did not burn so rapidly. The light from these masses and minor conflagrations illuminated the sea; the Rock and shores glowed dreadfully in the vast heaps of smoke which hung above and were seen so far as the eye could reach. It was a dismal illumination for those who stood about the Queen of Spain's Chair and on the hills: they came to see victory and saw ruin. The outcome of three years' combined attack and mighty labours; the expenditure of millions, the waste of thousands of lives, were testified by that glare, that livid smoke, those dreadful shrieks and doleful groans! Between three and four o'clock in the morning of the 14th, six others of the battering-ships showed signs of their approaching fate and day witnessed the utter destruction of all, one blew up about five o'clock a.m.; in the next quarter of an hour a second followed in that fate. The Marine Brigade of Gibraltar, under the command of Brigadier Curtis, put off to the rescue of the miserable crews and with great difficulty saved the lives of a large number among them. Six ships were soon in flames, three more blew up before eleven o'clock, the other three—their magazines having been swamped—burnt to the water's edge. With one of these the admiral's flag was burnt. Of the remaining two which the garrison hoped to have for trophies —to such a pass had the attack sunk— one was set on fire by the Spaniards and exploded, the other by the English in the afternoon. In the evening of the second day the enemy's whole armament of battering-ships was lost, with it the guns and stores, and two thousand men,* including prisoners. The expenditure of the enemy in shot, powder and shell is not known, but it may be guessed at by reflecting that three hundred and twenty pieces of artillery were employed with not less vigour than our own which consisted of eighty guns, seven mortars and nine howitzers— and discharged eight thousand three hundred rounds, more

---

* A Spanish return for the battering-ships alone admits a l of ve th— ! hundred and seventy-three men; five thousand one hundred a d y r n w board these ships, or about thirty-six men per gun besides the crew.

than half of which comprised red-hot shot, and seven hundred and sixteen barrels of powder. Our loss in killed and wounded was surprisingly small, consisting of one officer (Captain Reeves of the Royal Artillery) killed and three others wounded, two serjeants killed, thirteen men killed and sixty-three wounded. The damage done to our works was disproportionate to the violence of the attack and due largely to the land fire. Before night of the 15th the Fortress was ready to stand another assault.

Such an attack was anticipated at the time and intended by the enemy, but the judgment of the Duke de Crillon overruled the passion of some among his officers. If the opinion of the Chevalier D'Arcon is valuable in this particular and his information reliable, it appears that the batteries were mismanaged from the first and that the one shot which ruined the "Talla Piedra," the Spanish admiral's ship, commanded by the Prince of Nassau, remained unmastered for six hours, whereas it might readily have been extinguished by removing the ship for a while from the heat of our cannonade. "She did not become ungovernable until after midnight." (Account by the Engineer, quoted by *Sayer*, p. 393.) The duke was openly at variance with the engineers, he proposed a combined attack by the batteries and fleets, but his subordinates averred that the ships could not endure the fire of the Rock. It may be wondered why the powerful fleets floated inactive, while the batteries bore the brunt of the war, the reply is, that the wind prevented them from getting near enough to the Rock.

Such was truly the end of this great attack, which for the gallantry displayed by the besieged may be compared with the most splendid feats of modern patriotism.

During the remainder of September the Spaniards continued to fire on the garrison and proceeded with engineering works on the land. Many ships loosened their topsails and it was expected that the combined fleets were about to disperse; nevertheless they continued in the Bay and were determined, it appeared, to oppose the entrance of the English fleet under Howe. A dreadful hurricane, which began in the night of the 10th of October, cast the Spanish and French ships into great disorder, compelled the firing of signal guns for aid; at daybreak a Spanish two-decker was in a crippled state close to the shore of Orange Bastion, *i.e.* half-way between the Old Mole Head and the King's Bastion; she endeavoured to weather the Rock, but was fired at from the latter defence; she ultimately grounded near the Ragged Staff and surrendered. She was the San Miguel, seventy-two guns, six hundred and thirty-four men who became prisoners of war; the ship was got off, refitted, and armed for England. Other ships were seen on shore near the Grand Magazine, which stood about half way between Rocadillo and the Orange Grove; a French ship of the line lost her foremast and bowsprit; nothing but the cessation of the storm saved several others. Soon after the English fleet came in, landed its stores and relieved the regiments; after some fencing on the part of Cordova, the Spanish admiral, it sailed out again. On the 20th an indecisive action took place at sea. On the 16th October the army began to break up, although the winter camp was still to consist of twenty thousand men; no ships were left by the enemy in the Straits or to the eastward, few were at Cabrita Point. After this the siege seemed to be maintained more as a form during negotiations, than with hopes of success.

One of the most interesting facts of this period of the siege was the attempt of the enemy to *blow up the Rock* (¹) by means of a mine in its northern part; men had been repeatedly seen marching in that direction and some curiosity expressed as to the object of their approach, but no one seriously expected such an attempt. Something of this sort had been begun in the siege of 1727, and under Willis's Batteries, which mine was loaded but never fired. On the 15th of December the place of these new labours was discovered—it was a little to the west of south of the Devil's Tower; the party coming to work at it was permitted to approach within two hundred or three hundred yards before grape and hand-shells were discharged at them. They continued to work with surprising obstinacy and, later, the exploding of their charges in the mine could be distinctly heard. An attack on the St. Michael, which lay at anchor off Buena Vista, and partial execution of their wild plan with the mine below Willis's, were the last efforts of the besiegers, except smart sea attacks on Christmas Day, 1782, another on the 4th January, 1783, and a few less important cannonades.

On the 2nd of February news came that the preliminaries of peace were signed between Great Britain, France and Spain. The sea blockade was notified by the Spanish commander to be discontinued on the 5th. "About noon an elevated gun was wantonly (triumphantly) fired over their (the besiegers') works, which was the last shot of this great siege." It was March 10th before the Thetis, frigate, came in, with Sir Roger Curtis, the before-mentioned brigadier, on board and dispatches confirming the news which every other source had conveyed. On the 12th, General Elliot and the Duke de Crillon met on the Neutral Ground. The war was over. Gibraltar remained with us; but not (1782) until another attempt had been made by our English ministry to have it surrendered. Lord Shelburne and Mr. Banks were rash enough to propose the cession; but such was the temper of the House of Commons and the nation that, having due regard to their places, these officials promptly backed out of their opinions. Burke, Lord North and the Duke of Grafton attacked the worthies who had been unusually foolish in making such a proposition at such a time. It was impossible to avoid making General Elliot a peer, with a grant of fifteen hundred pounds per annum; but the reward was not bestowed until four years after he had been created a *Knight of the Bath* (!). The peerage was absolutely pumped out of the "fountain of honour" by sheer shame and the force of public opinion. As the defender of Gibraltar was no courtier, it is a pity that he consented to confer honour upon those whom the court delighted to honour.

Since this period the Rock has remained at peace, except in 1806, July 6th. Sir James Saumarez (Lord de Saumarez, Nelson's second in command at the Nile) began a tremendous conflict with a much superior French force, in the Bay of Algeciras, when he lost the Hannibal, seventy-four, which grounded on a reef. The admiral was compelled to enter Gibraltar to refit, with a loss of three hundred and sixty men, killed and wounded. With only half the number of his antagonists, who had been strengthened with nine vessels, he sallied out on the stormy night of the 12th July, and attacked the latter off Cabrita Point. The Real Carlos and Hermenegildo were assailed by Captain Keates, in the Superb, seventy-four. The former took fire, when the Superb directed her guns upon the San Antonio and captured her. In the darkness the Hermenegildo and Real Carlos fought with each other, until the latter blew up and so destroyed the Hermenegildo. Less than fifty men of the united crews, two thousand four hundred in all, survived the explosions. Thus were lost to the Spaniards two line-of-battle ships. The other ships of the enemy got away.

An event of great note at Gibraltar was the arrival of

the Victory, with the body of Nelson on board, October 28th, 1805, a week after the Battle of Trafalgar. Since then the chief matters in its military history have been the extension of its armament to seven hundred guns, *i.e.* seven times as many more than served at the Great Siege, and the construction of the vast series of galleries which penetrate the solid rock in tiers above tiers. The heaviest guns of the Great Siege are now the lightest of the service; in fact, almost superseded by far more powerful weapons.

www.ingramcontent.com/pod-product-compliance
Lightning Source LLC
Chambersburg PA
CBHW032102220426
43664CB00008B/1102